Civilizations in World Politics

A highly original and readily accessible examination of the cultural dimension of international politics: this book provides a sophisticated and nuanced account of the relevance of cultural categories for the analysis of world politics.

The book's analytical focus is on plural and pluralist civilizations. Civilizations exist in the plural within one civilization of modernity; and they are internally pluralist rather than unitary. The existence of plural and pluralist civilizations is reflected in transcivilizational engagements, intercivilizational encounters, and, only occasionally, in civilizational clashes. Drawing on the work of Eisenstadt, Collins, and Elias, Katzenstein's introduction provides a cogent and detailed alternative to Huntington's. This perspective is then developed and explored through six outstanding case studies written by leading experts in their fields. Combining contemporary and historical perspectives while addressing the civilizational politics of America, Europe, China, Japan, India, and Islam, the book draws these discussions together in Patrick Jackson's theoretically informed, thematic conclusion.

Featuring an exceptional line-up and representing a diversity of theoretical views within one integrative perspective, this work will be of interest to all scholars and students of international relations, sociology, and political science.

Peter J. Katzenstein is the Walter S. Carpenter, Jr. Professor of International Studies at Cornell University, USA. His research and teaching lie at the intersection of the fields of international relations and comparative politics. Katzenstein is widely published on questions of political economy, security, and culture in world politics. Katzenstein is President of the American Political Science Association (2008–09).

Contributors: Emanuel Adler, Patrick Thaddeus Jackson, David C. Kang, Peter J. Katzenstein, James Kurth, Bruce B. Lawrence, David Leheny, Susanne Hoeber Rudolph.

Civilizations in World Politics

Plural and pluralist perspectives

Edited by Peter J. Katzenstein

Routledge
Taylor & Francis Group

LONDON AND NEW YORK

First published 2010
by Routledge
2 Park Square, Milton Park, Abingdon, Oxon OX14 4RN

Simultaneously published in the USA and Canada
by Routledge
270 Madison Avenue, New York, NY 10016

Routledge is an imprint of the Taylor & Francis Group, an informa business

Typeset in Times New Roman by
Book Now Ltd, London
Printed and bound in Great Britain by
TJ International Ltd, Padstow, Cornwall

British Library Cataloguing in Publication Data
A catalogue record for this book is available from the British Library

Library of Congress Cataloging in Publication Data
Civilizations in world politics : plural and pluralist perspectives / edited
by Peter J. Katzenstein.
    p. cm.
Includes bibliographical references.
1. Cultural pluralism—Political aspects. 2. Civilization. I. Katzenstein,
Peter J.

HM1271.C577 2009
305.8009—dc22   2009006957

ISBN10: 0–415–77710–0 (hbk)
ISBN10: 0–415–77711–9 (pbk)
ISBN10: 0–203–87248–7 (ebk)

ISBN13: 978–0–415–77710–0 (hbk)
ISBN13: 978–0–415–77711–7 (pbk)
ISBN13: 978–0–203–87248–2 (ebk)

for Janou

Contents

Contributors

Emanuel Adler is the Andrea and Charles Bronfman Chair of Israeli Studies at the University of Toronto and co-editor of *International Organization*. He is best known for his contribution to the subjects of epistemic communities, security communities, and constructivism.

Patrick Thaddeus Jackson is Associate Professor in the School of International Service at American University, and the university's Director of General Education. He is presently completing a book on the philosophy of science and its implications for international relations research.

David C. Kang is Professor of International Relations and Business at the University of Southern California. He is currently working on a book about the international relations of historical East Asia.

Peter J. Katzenstein is the Walter S. Carpenter, Jr., Professor of International Studies at Cornell University. His work addresses issues of political economy, security, and culture in world politics.

James Kurth is Professor of Political Science and Senior Research Associate at Swarthmore College, where he teaches international politics and American foreign policy. He is the author of over 100 professional articles on these topics and also on cultural conflicts and the global economy.

Bruce B. Lawrence, Marcus Family Professor of the Humanities and Professor of Islamic Studies at Duke University, specializes in social movements and intellectual debates that define the Muslim world, from its inception until the present. He has authored or edited sixteen books and more than 150 refereed articles.

David Leheny is the Henry Wendt III '55 Professor of East Asian Studies at Princeton University. He is the author of two books about Japanese politics: *Think Global, Fear Local* and *The Rules of Play*, both published by Cornell University Press.

Susanne Hoeber Rudolph is the William Benton Distinguished Service Professor of Political Science, Emerita University of Chicago. Her most recent works (with Lloyd Rudolph) are *Explaining Indian Democracy: A Fifty-Year Perspective, 1956–2006* (2008) and *Making U.S. Policy for South Asia: Regional Imperatives and the Imperial Presidency* (2008).

Preface

The general idea for this book has been with me for many years. It crystallized as I developed a new lecture course on American foreign policy. Reluctant to embrace the concept of exceptionalism, I thought about how best to capture America's distinctiveness. Whatever their disagreements on specifics, students of American political development and foreign policy agree readily with Rogers Smith on the existence of multiple traditions in America's past. And so do students of civilizations, as I discovered while reading more broadly about the multiplicity of traditions and processes that characterize the civilizations analyzed in this book. Vital, energizing disagreements rather than stultifying, artificial coherence are the source of a civilization's attraction. America is part of a plural world of civilizations. And, like other civilizations, its multiple traditions make it pluralist.

This view differs sharply from the argument of clashes between unitary civilizations that Samuel Huntington advanced more than a decade ago. Huntington's argument deserves close attention not only because of its intellectual merits but also because it has been translated into thirty-nine languages. The opening chapter of this book offers a rebuttal of Huntington's central thesis. And it concedes readily that Huntington's primordial analysis offers important, though partial, insights into civilizational politics, insights that we should integrate eclectically, when necessary, with alternative perspectives.

Sam, I am sure, would have liked to engage and disagree with this book's argument. As many of his students wrote after his death, he loved vigorous intellectual debate and disagreement. And he was, as am I, fully aware of the tentativeness of all conclusions in the social sciences. As I am a great admirer of his scholarship, it is a source of great sadness for me that he was too ill to answer a letter I wrote to him about eighteen months before his death. That letter acknowledged my intellectual engagement with his work and expressed the hope that we might be able to talk about these ideas personally. Although this wish remained unfulfilled, I hope that conversation will now engage many of Sam's students, friends, and readers.

This book emerged from a roundtable and a panel held, respectively, at the 2007 and 2008 annual meetings of the American Political Science Association.

A lengthy background memo which I drafted for the 2007 meeting elicited spirited discussion and found the roundtable participants willing to move from talking points to fully developed papers. Subsequently, I recruited additional authors to broaden the empirical basis for the book's analytical perspective. I also began to look for a press interested in publishing this project. It was my particular good fortune that Craig Fowlie seized on the opportunity the moment I approached him. Craig was unflaggingly helpful and supportive in seeing this project through from the first round of reviews to the selection of the cover. Our last conversation was as brief as the first. I thought I had to explain to him how the central idea of "plural and pluralist" might be represented visually. Politely, Craig cut me off after the first sentence by simply saying "I get it." A few weeks later he suggested Kandinsky's strikingly beautiful and evocative *Accent en rose* (1926) for the book's cover. Nicola Parkin steered the manuscript through the production process with a deft touch. Sarah Tarrow, as always, kept control over me and the authors with grace and good humor. Without her editorial and administrative help I can no longer imagine how to prepare a manuscript for publication.

I dedicate this book to Janou, who will take great delight in turning its pages and who, soon, will produce her own crayoned roses.

Peter J. Katzenstein
Ithaca, NY
March 2009

1 A world of plural and pluralist civilizations

Multiple actors, traditions, and practices[1]

Peter J. Katzenstein

> Civilization may flourish on many stems. The Gods may be called by many
> names. . . . No one has the key. There are no chosen people.
> Fosco Maraini (quoted in Eisenstadt 1996: 5)

This book is about plural and pluralist civilizations.[2] Civilizations exist in the
plural. They coexist with each other within one civilization of modernity, or
what we often call today a global world. Civilizations are pluralist. Their
internal pluralism results from multiple traditions and vigorous debates and
disagreements. This is not to deny that, in specific political units existing
within civilizations – states, polities, or empires – pluralism can give way to
unity as political and discursive coalitions succeed in imposing a singular view
and set of core values over alternatives. Since civilizations are relatively loose
systems and encompassing across both space and time, however, such unity
tends to be the exception, not the rule. The existence of plural and pluralist
civilizations is reflected in transcivilizational engagements, intercivilizational
encounters, and civilizational clashes.

  This is not a book about civilization conceived in the singular, as a
coherent cultural program organized hierarchically around uncontested core
values. Historically, the concept of civilization, in the singular, was a
European invention of the eighteenth century. It provided the foundation for
an argument about a "standard of civilization" (Gong 1984a; Barth and
Osterhammel 2005), conceived of as condition not process, that was eventually enshrined in the law of civilized nations. Edward Keene (2002) has shown
that the toleration that characterized intra-European affairs in the nineteenth
century was absent in the relations between "civilized" European and "uncivilized" non-European states. The European standard of civilization was
grounded in race, ethnic affiliation, and religion, and the belief in the superiority of European civilization was often supported by doctrines of scientific
racism. Only white, European Christians were civilized. Others were uncivilized, not worthy of protection by the law, and thus exposed fully to the
collective violence that European imperialists meted out on a global scale.
The same distinction informed earlier instances of European expansion, for

example between Church and infidels and between the Old and the New World. Far from being restricted to Europe, the distinction between civilized and uncivilized people has occurred also in the relations among non-European civilizations (Osterhammel 2005: 376–81). Throughout the ages and in all corners of the world, "barbarians" have knocked on "civilized" doors.

In contemporary world affairs, arguments about the standard of civilization still resonate. They are commonly invoked, for example, in discussions of failing states, of how East Asian states should cope with the challenges posed by the West (Suzuki 2005, 2009), and of global standards of good governance, property rights, and transparent markets (Bowden and Seabrooke 2006). Indeed, adherents of the view of economic globalization as an unstoppable force tend to argue that a growing homogeneity is being dictated by market forces that, for better or for worse, have acquired an unstoppable logic. Although the merits of this argument are debatable, it points to an undeniable fact. A world of plural civilizations is embedded in a larger context no longer defined by a single standard expressing a firm moral hierarchy. Instead, that larger context characterizes a civilization of modernity stressing individualism, diversity, ecumenicism, and a loose sense of shared moral values.

The chapters in this book analyze America, Europe, China, Japan, India, and Islam and give powerful support to this plural and pluralist view of civilizations. Although the authors show their disagreements on a number of theoretical questions, their analyses overwhelmingly point to internal pluralism and the coexistence of plural civilizations. The analyses of James Kurth (Chapter 2) and Emanuel Adler (Chapter 3) show the rise and fall of alternative conceptions of Western, European, American, and global civilizations reflecting pluralism rather than coherence. Similarly, David Kang (Chapter 4) describes how, historically, a coherent set of Chinese practices was emulated by Korea and Vietnam and to a lesser extent by Japan. These three neighbors became part of Sinic civilization without losing many of their most cherished local practices. David Leheny (Chapter 5) details how contemporary Japan is resisting modes of civilizational analysis that do not start from the presumption and end with the affirmation of Japan's uniqueness and its infinite capacity to adapt to foreign cultural imports without ever sacrificing its essential core values. And yet, even that basic consensus does not stifle alternative voices looking to Asia or the West for alternative ways of conceptualizing Japan's civilizational role. Finally, in full agreement with existing scholarship (Arnason 2003b; Osterhammel 1998, 2001; Hobson 2004; Bowden 2007), Susanne Rudolph (Chapter 6) and Bruce Lawrence (Chapter 7) offer case studies of India and Islam as quintessential instances of plural and pluralist civilizations.

By their mere existence, civilizations undercut both the realist confidence in the superiority of military power and the liberal presumption that universalistic secular liberal norms are inherently superior to all others. "How many divisions has the pope?" Josef Stalin asked derisively, a few decades before a charismatic Polish leader of the Catholic Church pushed the Soviet Union into the dustbin of history. And if the values of secular liberalism were naturally overwhelmingly attractive, then there would be no need to cultivate that attraction (Bially Mattern 2005: 591). Attraction would be rooted in the unquestioned acceptance of the universal standard that secular liberalism provides. Civilizations thus deserve more attention than they have received.

In successive sections, this chapter reviews some of the relevant contemporary writings on civilizations; develops an analytical distinction between dispositional and discursive modes of analysis; presents three theoretical perspectives that view civilizations in terms of multiple modernities (Eisenstadt), multiple zones of prestige (Collins), and multiple processes and practices (Elias); explores multiple civilizational actors, traditions, and practices, building on the insights of the three theoretical perspectives and drawing on the arguments developed in the six case studies in this book; and ends with a brief conclusion.[3]

Pluralist and plural civilizations

In public discourse civilization is often used in the singular, in contrast to this book's insistence on pluralist and plural civilizations. In America and Europe, for example, civilization is often referred to as an all-embracing vision of the West, a universal, substantive form of perfectability that incorporates all parts of the world, based on the growth of Western reason. This view of civilization in the singular is not restricted to the West. It also characterizes the public discourse of many non-Western parts of the world. In Japan first, now China, and soon perhaps India, the voices proclaiming the dawn of Asia's civilizational primacy in world affairs are growing louder. Like Orientalism, Occidentalism suffers from characterizing "East" and "West" in the singular.

Civilizational analysis

American political science has largely neglected civilizational analysis (Akturk 2009). During the first ninety-nine years of its existence, between 1906 and 2005, the *American Political Science Review (APSR)* published only one article that contained "civilization" in its title; a second article mentioned the concept in its abstract. Between 1948 and 2005, *World Politics*, a leading journal of comparative and international politics, did not publish a single article on this subject. Unsurprisingly, Adda Bozeman's (1960) magisterial treatment of culture and international politics received a dismissive review in the pages of the *APSR* (Puchala 2003: 1). Samuel Huntington's (1993, 1996) work has created renewed interest among a small number of political scientists who have tried to test his core claim. But it has been engaged much more actively by public intellectuals and in the public domain than in scholarly circles. In general, for political scientists, civilizational analysis seems too broad, too nebulous, and too apolitical to warrant sustained scholarly attention.

Not so in sociology. Johann Arnason's (2003a) probing theoretical overview and two outstanding collections (Arjomand and Tiryakian 2004b; Hall and Jackson 2007b) explore the conceptual foundations of civilizational analysis and make a strong case for a relational style of analysis. Contemporary sociological writings speak of civilization in the plural. They do not recognize fixed entities but focus instead on intercivilizational encounters and transcivilizational engagements (Bowden 2009; Cox 2001: 109; Mazlish 2004a: xii, 294; Mozaffari 2002; Sternberg 2001; Holzner 1982). Within that common outlook, Gerard Delanty (2006: 45–6) argues that civilizational analysis has taken three different approaches since the 1970s, highlighting mastery, hybridity, and cross-contamination. Avoiding sharp binary distinctions, sociological analysis tends to rely on differentiated analyses of developments within and across civilizations. That perspective highlights the importance of an Afro-Eurasian ecumene, stretching from Morocco to China, as a transcivilizational bridge connecting East and West. This scholarly tradition objects to essentialist treatments of civilizational configurations, rejects binary models of civilizational analysis, and criticizes the overextension of Said's (1979) concept of Orientalism.

Definitional disagreements about the concept of civilization are formidable and legion (Bowden 2004a; Mozaffari 2002; Elias 1994; Cox 2000, 2001; Mazlish 2001, 2004a; Arnason 2003a; Nelson 1973; Swedberg 2008; Tehranian 2007; Braudel 1994). Many of the definitions appear to agree with Toynbee, Quigley, and Elias, for whom civilizations are social modalities that center on urban forms of life; are based on resources and divisions of labor that make urban life sustainable and free elites from the necessity of producing to secure their daily subsistence; and provide the social space for cultivating a life of refinement and reflection.[4] "City," "civil," and "civitas" are some of the concept's etymological roots (Bowden 2004a: 27–41). Language and literature are widely considered as the core of civilizational complexes. For William McNeill (1990: 8), "a shared literary canon, and expectations about human behavior framed by that canon, are probably central to what we mean by a civilization." In addition, religion is widely acknowledged as a central characteristic of civilizational complexes. In the eighteenth century, Mirabeau the elder was one of the earliest theorists of civilization. He argued that religion was a principal source of civilization because it contributed to the softening of manners (Mazlish 2004b: 14). It is thus hardly surprising that Freud saw in civilization a suppression of natural instincts and the elevation of institutionalized madness over individual sanity.

Civilizations are not enlarged nation-states – coherent cultural complexes. To be sure, as Clifford Geertz (1973: 17–18) argues, "cultural systems must have a minimal degree of coherence, else we would not call them systems; and by observation, they normally have a great deal more." But, Geertz continues, "the force of our interpretations cannot rest, as they are now so often made to do, on the tightness with which they hold together, or the assurance with which they are argued." And so it is with civilizations. They are loosely coupled, internally differentiated, elite-centered social systems that are integrated into a global context.

This is, broadly speaking, the intellectual stance that William McNeill (1990, 1992) came to in an article he wrote more than a quarter of a century after the publication of his landmark study *The Rise of the West: A History of the Human Community* (1963). A central deficiency of his earlier book, McNeill (1990: 4, 8–10, 13, 19) writes, was the assumption that "separate civilizations form real and important human groupings and that their inter-actions constitute the main theme of world history." Instead, influenced by the work of his colleague at the University of Chicago, Marshall Hodgson (1974, 1993), McNeill critiqued his own work for its neglect of what he vari-ously called "cosmopolitan" and "ecumenical" processes, historically in South Asia and the Middle East and, under the impact of modern communi-cations technologies, even more strongly in contemporary world affairs.

Such processes are open-ended. For McNeill (1990: 19), they provide a fundamentally important foundation for a world of plural civilizations. "Cultural pluralism and differentiation is a dominating feature of human history; yet beneath and behind that pluralism there is also an important commonality." Furthermore, as Sheldon Pollock (2006) argues, the common-ality of a global ecumene does not require a central power. In contrast to Romanization, for example, for many centuries Sanskrit transculturation coincided with the spread of vernacular languages. The reason is not obvious at first glance. James Scott (2003: 8, 23) offers us a clue. He quotes Edward Leach as observing that, in Southeast Asia, hill people followed a "Chinese model" and lowland people followed a Sanskritic model. The reason, Scott suggests, is that people climb hills in order to escape from the civilizational projects pursued in the valleys by coercive and exploitative arrangements of court or state. Hill populations in Southeast Asia proved relatively resistant not only to Sanskritization but also to Buddhism, to Islam, and, in the Philippines, to Christianity. Sanskritization was not directed by any political center and spread furtively, without the pomp and circumstance of military conquest. But it could not climb hills. Scott mentions that Fernand Braudel made the same observation in Europe. Civilizations are powerless "to move vertically when faced with an obstacle of several hundred meters" (Braudel 1972: 33). Politics in valleys and hills and across continents and oceans is producing a world of both sameness and difference.

I describe civilizations as configurations, constellations, or complexes. They are not fixed in space or time. They are both internally highly differenti-ated and culturally loosely integrated. Because they are differentiated, civil-izations transplant selectively, not wholesale. Because they are culturally loosely integrated, they generate debate and contestations. And, as social constructions of primordiality, civilizations can become political reifications, especially when encountering other civilizations. Civilizations constitute a world that is neither a Hobbesian anarchy nor a Habermasian public sphere, neither empire nor cosmopolis (Adamson 2005; Dallmayr 2005). Instead, they are weakly institutionalized social orders reflected in and shaped by a variety of practices and processes.

Civilizations evolve gradually in response to both their internal pluralism and their external encounters (Cox 2000: 217, 220). They express different modes of thought. They integrate disparate, co-mingling elements: different places; different senses of past, present, and future; different conceptions of the relations between individual and community; and differently understood cosmologies about the relations between humanity, nature, divinity, and cosmos.

Civilizations: disposition and discourse

Mustafa Emirbayer (1997) has distinguished between actor-oriented and process-oriented styles of analysis. Thinking in terms of static objects differs sharply from thinking in terms of unfolding relations. Typified by economic styles of analysis, rational-actor and variable-based analysis are examples of the former. They focus on the interaction between fixed entities. Sociological styles of analysis such as transactional and network analysis are examples of the latter. Their unit of analysis is the unfolding relationship placed in a spatial and temporal context. The two perspectives are not necessarily contradictory. Practice is an attribute of actors. And practice creates the shifting of the positions that actors occupy in one or several networks as well as the structure of networks as conceived in the relational perspective. Patrick Jackson (2007) makes a distinction analogous to that of Emirbayer: between dispositional (or actor) and discursive (or relational) styles of analysis. It is helpful for illuminating different approaches to civilizational analysis.

Dispositional analysis is exemplified by Samuel Huntington's (1993, 1996) thesis of civilizational clash. Huntington views civilizations as coherent, consensual, and able to act. Discursive analysis, as in Jackson's (2006, 2007) analysis of the idea of the West in the late 1940s, regards civilizations as contested, conflicted, and expressed as discourse. The contrast between dispositional and discursive analysis is unmistakable (Jackson 2007: 38–9). For one, civilizations are actors with dispositional characteristics. For the other, they are discursive practices. For one, civilizations exist objectively in the real world as coherent cultural complexes. For the other, they exist as intersubjective or collective beliefs that are mobilized politically to create, maintain, or shift socially significant boundaries. One focuses our attention on the interaction of entities with invariant dispositional properties. The other highlights the social transactions that create those entities in the first place and the practices that sustain or alter them over time. In one view, civilizations are like states and other political communities that exist by virtue of a preexisting consensus on core values. In the other, civilizations are marked by traditions, processes, and practices that are mobilized discursively to create socially significant boundaries. For one, civilizational actors derive from objective demarcations of sociocultural space. For the other, civilizational actors are the result of intersubjective understandings that are produced and reproduced discursively.

Dispositional analysis

Samuel Huntington's (1993, 1996) celebrated and controversial article and book about civilizations have undoubtedly become the most widely quoted and translated analyses of the post-Cold War international order. More than any other scholar, Huntington succeeded brilliantly in his primary objective, providing a new paradigm for looking at world politics after the end of the Cold War and the collapse of the Soviet Union. Furthermore, he insisted on the existence of plural civilizations and anticipated that other civilizations – Sinic, Hindu, or Islamic – might succeed that of the West. Huntington's reception was more avid and positive outside of the United States – the book was translated into thirty-nine languages – than inside. The success was rooted in the book's presentation of what appeared to be a new map of world politics. In fact, this new map basically replicated the old Cold War map. The political and economic clash between communist authoritarianism in the East and capitalist democracy in the West was replaced by the civilizational clash between a cultural West and an Islamic and Sinic East. In this basic sense Huntington did little more than update, rather than replace, established ways of thinking about the world.

This book agrees with Huntington on the existence of plural civilizations. Furthermore, it also agrees with Huntington that under specific conditions, discussed below, political coalitions and intellectual currents can create primordial civilizational categories that are believed to be unitary and may even be believed to have the capacity to act. But this book also disagrees with Huntington. First, civilizational configurations are most similar not in their cultural coherence and tendency toward clash but in their pluralist differences and in their intercivilizational encounters and transcivilizational engagements. Violent clashes occur for the most part within rather than between civilizations. Encounters and engagements, reflecting multiple traditions and practices, are typically peaceful forms of borrowing that run in one direction when the technological differences between civilizations is large, and in both directions when they are not.

Huntington's main thesis expressed one important political insight while missing a second. Huntington astutely recognized the growing importance of plural civilizations after the collapse of the Soviet Union and the end of the Cold War. This remains the book's most important and enduring contribution. Few if any observers of world politics were gauging its pulse as attentively as did Huntington. The significant insight he missed was the key importance of the internal pluralism of civilizational constellations. Since it required a heroic leap of abstractions away from evidence that was in plain sight, Huntington was wrong to press civilizational analysis into the familiar Cold War frame. Presuming, as he did, that sociocultural homogeneity was the defining marker of both the "West" and the "Rest," his generalization about the inevitability of clash anticipated 9/11 correctly. But his argument also predicted growing conflict between Sinic and American civilizations, which has failed to materialize. The relations between these two are better characterized as a combination of encounter and engagement than as clash.

Huntington was criticized from the realist right as well as the cultural left. Some of the harshest commentary on his writings came from realists who pointed out that most of the world's violent clashes occurred within rather than between different civilizations. Huntington was also criticized unsparingly from the cultural left. His assumption that civilizations were a kind of mega nation-state with a stipulated cultural homogeneity that could be summed into categories such as "West" and "Rest" was met by skepticism and disbelief. His conceptualization simply neglected a generation's worth of intellectual developments that had discarded essentialist styles of reasoning. Furthermore, it risked creating self-fulfilling prophecies about clashes that were manufactured not by facts on the ground but by the popularity of his own writings. While these criticisms were powerful, they overlooked important strengths in Huntington's argument. Realists typically failed to acknowledge that he had identified a very important cultural shift in world politics. And cultural critics overlooked the possibility that social categories of primordiality can reflect and create intersubjective realities of cultural coherence and unity. Indeed, the enthusiastic reception of Huntington's writings indicated how widely primordial categories of thought were accepted, not only in the United States but around the world.

Scholarly discussion of Huntington's work yielded two major conclusions. First, virtually all statistical and many qualitative analyses have shown that major clashes occur primarily within rather than between civilizations, and that civilizations are not the axis along which wars are fought. Huntington was not too bothered by such empirical criticisms. He wanted to provide a new mental map for our understanding of world politics after the end of the Cold War. And without fail he would challenge his empirically minded critics to do better than he had done in thinking paradigmatically. The lack of empirical support for Huntington's central claim, however, is so damaging that by now it must be considered to be factually wrong (Fox 2004: 155–225; Ben-Yehuda 2003; Chiozza 2002; Henderson and Tucker 2001; Russett, Oneal, and Cox 2000). A reformulated and less general claim might hold that, in situations where peaceful intercivilizational encounters and transcivilizational engagements are overwhelmed by conflict spirals that lead to war breaking out along civilizational fault lines, as some argued was true in Bosnia in the 1990s, such wars are particularly vicious and difficult to settle (Huntington 1996: 212, 246–98). This is an interesting proposition. But it eliminates Huntington's paradigmatic claim of providing a new mental map for world politics. And, despite its potential usefulness for policy-makers, to my knowledge we lack systematic studies that have tested this empirical hypothesis.

Second, like many others, Amartya Sen (2006: 45 and 10–12, 40–46) has criticized Huntington for succumbing to the "illusion of singularity," the view of collective identities as singular, unchanged, and unchanging traits of actors. Huntington's (2004a, 2004b, 1996: 305–8) analysis of the character of American identity develops an argument that is consistent with his essentialist view of civilizational identities.[5] In brief, Huntington argues that America is a country of settlers rather than of immigrants. All Americans have embraced the Anglo-Protestant creed as the core value of America. In this view Catholics, Jews, Muslims, agnostics, and atheists have all comfortably settled into one large Anglo-Protestant tent. And, if Latinos do not follow suit, then the America we know will be deeply challenged and perhaps be undone. That argument did not sit well with many reviewers, on either empirical or political grounds (Laitin 2008; Fraga and Segura 2006; Wolfe 2004; Aysha 2003).

In contrast to Huntington's exclusive focus on the "clash" of civilizations, the chapters in this book highlight the omnipresence and importance of many other forms of intercivilizational encounters and transcivilizational engagements. For example, Emmanuel Adler (Chapter 3) and David Kang (Chapter 4) highlight a variety of political practices that "normative power Europe" tries to export today to both America and Islam, and that China projected in the past to its neighbors. In addition, Susanne Rudolph (Chapter 6) and Bruce Lawrence (Chapter 7) point to the prevalence of the furtive spread, over long distances, of Indian and Islamic civilizational practices, without any central political direction, often as a byproduct of maritime trade. Lack of central direction proved to be a source of attraction and strength, not of repulsion and weakness. This generalization resonates with James Kurth's (Chapter 2) analysis of the victory of a multicultural, secular coalition in America that has hollowed out and globalized American civilization during the last two generations. Kurth sees in this a fundamental weakening of a unitary, realist-mercantilist conception of American civilizations that in earlier decades had been brutal in its assimilationist power over various groups of immigrants. In this analysis, America, once a unitary and cohesive civilization, had become a civilization marked by polyvalent values and multiple traditions.

Furthermore, in contrast to Huntington's (1996: 82, 207–45) analysis of the balance of power between civilizations conceived of as coherent and unified actors, this book emphasizes the balance of practices reflected in and aggregated into various processes of intercivilizational encounters and transcivilizational engagements. This is in line with Richard Rorty's (1993: 115, quoted in Crawford 2008: 29) observation that "there is a growing willingness to neglect the question 'What is our nature?' and to substitute the question 'What can we make of ourselves?'" Civilizations are malleable, reflecting protean human practices. Emanuel Adler (Chapter 3), for example, describes in considerable detail novel political practices invented in recent years in the interest of replicating in the European periphery the security community that has evolved during the last half century in Western Europe's center. Between the two extremes of an all-embracing cultural imperialism imposed by external forces and wholesale local appropriation shaped fully by internal forces, the normal pattern is hybridization – multiple encounters and engagements.

Finally, Huntington locates the clash of civilizations in an anarchical international system, evoking the realist tradition that so heavily influences his formulation. He argues that the belief in the existence of one modern and "universal civilization" is a misconception that is "misguided, arrogant, false and dangerous" (Huntington 1993: 41; 1996: 41, 56–78, 301–21). In contrast, this book embeds clashes, encounters, and engagements in one overarching civilization of modernity or ecumene that is infused by some common secular values and overlapping religious beliefs. Huntington's (1996: 95–101) civilizational thesis, however, is based exclusively on the revival of religious sentiments and denies the influence of any common secular values. Anarchy is not the broader context for the relations between different civilizations. John Meyer (1994) and his colleagues (Meyer *et al.* 1997), for example, refer to this broader context as a world polity. Although its global script is recognized by all actors as legitimate, it is often coupled only loosely to state behavior. Albert, Brock, and Wolf (2000) call this broader context a world society and community that is civilizing, however weakly, world politics beyond the system of states. And Bruce Lawrence (Chapter 7) shows that historians of Islam have written about this encompassing frame in which several civilizations coexist as a broader ecumene. Shmuel Eisenstadt (2001) characterizes this frame neither as a world polity, nor as a world society, nor as a global ecumene, but as a civilization of modernity – a secular, technological social order based on a normative commitment to the expansion of human rights and the improvement of human welfare. This civilization of modernity interacts with and is constituted by a plurality of civilizations.

Discursive analysis

From what he calls a post-essentialist stance, Patrick Jackson (2007) argues that we should think of civilizations as political, specifically rhetorical, practices that create both boundaries between and coherent narratives of civilizational destinies. Relying on public discourse, Jackson (2006) has offered a searching examination of the rhetoric of "Western civilization." Although after 1945 Americans asserted that it had existed for two millennia, dating back to ancient Greece, Western civilization has existed in public debate for only about two hundred years, following discussions among a group of conservative German academics in the early nineteenth century. Presumed to be unproblematic in its boundaries, Western civilization after the end of World War II came to contain Germany, one of its most ferocious enemies in the first half of the twentieth century. Jackson shows that the rhetorical reconstruction of a world in ruins after 1945 had an effect on Germany's integration into Western Europe and the North Atlantic community. Public rhetoric bound together a transnational coalition of liberal Americans and conservative West Germans. Western civilization was a discursive resource that delegitimated all policy options other than West Germany's incorporation into the American imperium.

Jackson provides a case study of the language of legitimation, of the drawing and redrawing of civilizational boundaries. At the origin of the Cold War a clash of civilizations, created and maintained by public rhetoric, helped create, reflect, and reinforce the division of the world. This civilizational dimension of Cold War politics has largely been lost in realist and liberal reconstructions that conceive of international politics as a game played by actors with given identities and fixed interests. Jackson's striking conclusion (2006: x) differs from and extends Huntington's. Public rhetoric on both sides of the Atlantic shows that, from its inception, the Cold War was a civilizational conflict. Public discourse and behavior drew sharp civilizational boundaries between East and West – before and after the Cold War.

The public invocation of civilizations has causal force and is politically consequential. Jackson (2004: 175) has shown, for example, how at three key points of American foreign policy – 1917, 1941, and 2001 – the rhetorical commonplaces of the time invoked "civilization" or "the civilized world," in the singular, as the protagonists in different wars. It remains an open question whether at other critical junctures of history such rhetorical commonplaces, with their appeal to universalist notions and a Manichean worldview, also inform political debates in other settings – or, alternatively, whether world politics is characterized by dialogues that are based on the assumption that both parties to the dialogue are open to changing their views (Dallmayr and Manoochehri 2007; Dallmayr 2004, 2005; Herzog 1999).[6] In any case, Jackson insists that we should not be sidetracked into seeking civilizations in the real world. They do not exist as coherent cultural complexes with dispositional essences. To argue otherwise, Jackson (2006: 8) insists, would be akin to inferring from the practices of a group of religious believers that the divinity they worship actually exists. What is true for communities of religious believers and the existence of divinity, Jackson argues, holds also for scholars of civilizations and the existence of civilizations.

Primordiality as disposition and discourse

Jackson's argument is persuasive – within limits. He writes in his concluding chapter to this volume that social relations "have the effect of reproducing the object from moment to moment" (p. 183). Jackson accords social relations a power to change actors, from one moment to the next, that is implausible in view of the reification of civilizational categories that his studies have revealed in the immediate post-World War II period on both sides of the Atlantic. According to his analysis, at the outset of the Cold War, the West existed with identifiable historical, religious, and political traits. The fact that it included Germany, only a few years earlier the West's most determined and powerful enemy, mattered less than that the category of "the West" was believed in. This fact can endow civilizational categories with actor-like dispositions that resist easy alteration from moment to moment. It is not the category but the act of reification or construction that is politically consequential and that requires political analysis. In convincing ourselves and others of a specific mental map, and aligning our identities and interests with that map, we rely on rhetorical constructions to impute meaning that otherwise eludes us. For empirically inclined scholars who prefer to work eclectically, primordiality offers a plausible addition to discursive and dispositional approaches.

Primordiality is a crystallization in social consciousness that is simplifying. It can focus on civilization as it does on gender, kinship, territory, language, or race. The specific collective identity invoked is defined either in terms of "civility" (drawing boundaries between "us" and "them" with a specific focus on rules of conduct and social routines) or in terms of sacredness (drawing boundaries between "us" and "them" with specific reference to the transcendental, defined as God or Reason) (Eisenstadt and Schluchter 1998: 14). A conceptual middle ground from which to deploy, as the evidence may require, either dispositional or discursive or both styles of analysis is more appealing for empirical analysis than favoring either of its two alternatives a priori (Markovits 2007: 663). We need to know both how civilizations become and what they are and do. For, as Yale Ferguson (2007a: 191, 195) points out, there appears to exist a sufficiently wide and deep consensus about the very term of civilization. Indeed, in primordial constructions of self and other, dispositional and discursive analysis are probably deeply entangled with one another rather than existing side by side.[7] Most of the chapters in this book adhere in their analysis to this eclectic position.

Civilizations are nesting or nested in other cultural entities and processes. Syncretism, for example, is one form of politics in which civilizational, religious, and national sentiments meet (Haas 2000). Deeply meaningful to many members of the cultural elite, as self-conscious and lived identities, civilizations do not rank at the top for most people and typically do not manifest themselves in an everyday sense of strong belonging. Making civilizations primordial is a political project that aims at creating a taken-for-granted sense of reality that helps in distinguishing between self and other and right and wrong. It requires elimination of the awareness that civilizations are multiple traditions of religious, philosophical, and scientific ideas, and that they are reflected in multiple processes and practices.

For example, David Kang's analysis (Chapter 4) of the historically very different relations between China and its nomadic neighbors to the north and its Sinicized neighbors to the east and south provides a good illustration of both processes co-occurring. Conflicts over relative gains between China and the nomads were augmented by the fact that nomads had no interest in adhering to China's civilizational standards. A chasm of identities and practices separated the two, generating an almost permanent state of war. In contrast, convergence in one civilizational standard shared by China and its neighbors to the south and east resulted in prolonged peace. Furthermore, as Xu Xin (2009: 51) argues, today the Chinese notion of all-embracing unity (*da-yitong*) is not contested by adherents of China's various intellectual traditions. It is "the profound and essential value deeply embedded in Chinese culture and history," with significant consequences for how the Chinese view the world and conduct their foreign policy. Occasional dissents from this view may point to the historical record, indicating that the time of division in Chinese history was longer than the time of unity. But they fall on deaf ears. Instead, a deep-rooted Sinocentric worldview, as Lien-sheng Yang (1968: 20) argues, "was a myth backed up at different times by realities of varying degree, sometimes approaching nil."

Civilizations come to exist in the conventional understanding of that term as "being believed to exist," as tightly or loosely coupled, and taken-for-granted or highly contested cultural complexes. Being named is an important aspect of the existence of civilizations, not just mere rhetoric or cheap talk.[8] Huntington's book and articles, after all, were translated into scores of languages, while the rejoinders of his critics were not. Huntington was very explicit in wishing to give his readers a compelling paradigm for a better understanding of world politics. He may have been wrong, as Jackson points out, in thinking that civilizational analysis was an innovation at the end of the Cold War when in fact it was only a repetition of what had happened at the Cold War's outset. And he may have been wrong in asserting that civilizations are tightly coupled and coherent actors. But the very success of his writings created a primordial category that naturalized the world and made it intelligible to many of his readers. Primordial civilizational discourse naturalizes particular institutional or practical arrangements. And thus it can create actorhood, validating dispositional theories of civilizations.

This primordial alternative to exclusively dispositional or discursive conceptualizations of civilizations requires political analysis of the causes and conditions of the success or failure of political efforts to eliminate the multiplicities that inhere in encompassing and loosely coupled civilizational complexes. David Leheny (Chapter 5), for example, offers a compelling analysis of Japanese discourse, less encompassing and more tightly coupled than any of the other civilizational configurations examined in this book. He is able to show how the Japanese are remarkably unreceptive to civilizational writings stressing multiple traditions. Instead, Japanese discourse validates cultural arguments about Japanese uniqueness, including its ability to absorb freely many components from other civilizations without losing Japan's essential spirit.

Summary

In this book dispositional and discursive modes of analysis are exemplified, respectively, by James Kurth's analysis of America in Chapter 2 and David Leheny's analysis of Japan in Chapter 6. Kurth relies primarily on dispositional arguments. But he also argues that within Western civilization over recent decades the gap between American discourse and European disposition widened, helping to bring about an epochal shift from a Western to a global civilization. Like Huntington, Kurth relies on dispositional analysis. But he breaks sharply with Huntington's core claim by insisting on the centrality of the clash within Western civilization and, for that matter, within America. Leheny's analysis is primarily discursive. Yet Leheny agrees with Kurth about the gap between discourse and disposition. While Japanese practices change, Japanese discourses do not. Specifically, Japanese historical narratives continue to occupy a liminal space that bridges binaries, such as modern and traditional, East and West. The two chapters share another theme. In Leheny's analysis, Japanese discourses center on essentialist civilizational notions of the kind that Kurth tends to take as a given as he develops his argument. Japan's unique essence, Leheny argues, lies in being an authentic counter to the construction of an imagined, modern, and inauthentic West, and thus the legitimator of Asian difference to the universal pretensions of the West. In highlighting Asian difference, Japan's civilizational discourses minimize possible differences between Japan and Asia.

Theories of civilizations: Eisenstadt, Collins, and Elias

As Durkheim and Mauss (1971: 809; Swedberg 2008) have pointed out, civilizations lack "well-defined limits; they pass the political frontiers and extend over less easily determinable spaces." Civilizations constitute a kind of social milieu that encompasses a number of different nations. Like the national sentiments that are lodged within them, the symbolic frontiers of civilizations demarcate similitude from alterity (Durkheim and Mauss 1971: 811). And they exist in time, normally over long periods. Open to contestations and dialogues, they express worldviews, particularly in the area of language and culture broadly understood, and in religion (Puchala 1997: 8, 10).

Shmuel Eisenstadt, Randall Collins, and Norbert Elias are three prominent scholars of civilizations who have grappled with the intermingling of different civilizational complexes in one global setting. For Eisenstadt, change in today's single and encompassing civilization of modernity activates the cultural repertoires of the different civilizations of the past. This combination of sameness and differences generates multiple modernities. For Collins, civilizations are marked by different knowledge domains, illustrated in his analysis by different schools of philosophy, which are set off into different zones of prestige marked by lively dialogue, debate, and competition, and organized around a small number of centers. Elias, finally, regards civilization not as a condition but as reversible processes that impose psychological and social restraints. These three theories provide the foundation for this book's analysis of civilizations in terms of multiple actors, traditions, and processes, as the next section, using the various case chapters, will illustrate.

Religion and multiple modernities (Eisenstadt)

In his voluminous writings on civilizations, Shmuel Eisenstadt starts with a key distinction between two types of civilizations. Axial Age civilizations emerged together with the major world religions around the sixth century BCE (Arnason, Eisenstadt, and Wittrock 2005).[9] The civilization of modernity (Eisenstadt 2001), by way of contrast, is a product of the very recent past, starting with the scientific and technological revolution brought about by the European Enlightenment and marked by an unprecedented openness to novelty and uncertainty.

Eisenstadt takes the concept of the Axial Age from Karl Jaspers (1953; Levine 2004, 1995). It denotes a formative period in world history when a number of powerful cultural developments occurred independently from one another in China, India, Iran, Palestine, and Greece. Humankind moved at that pivotal moment in world history from an instinctual disposition to a self-reflexive striving for transcendence and self-determination. For Jaspers and Eisenstadt, the sixth century is an axis that divides history, a transformative break brought about by the appearance of the world's great religions and the onset of humankind's spiritualization.

Jaspers's argument was anchored in eighteenth- and nineteenth-century German philosophy and social theory (Fichte, Schelling, and Hegel) and its preoccupation with autonomous human self-direction (Kant) and cultural creativity (Herder). In the twentieth century, Weber's sociology of world religions, Scheler's philosophical anthropology, and Simmel's argument of a transformative turn to the ideational in human life were all important precursors to Jaspers's insight. In each of these formulations, the autonomous role assigned to ideational factors is the same as in Jaspers (Levine 2004, 1995): a shift in religion from serving as a tool to satisfy human needs to a guide for following divine norms (Weber); a move from adaptive rationality and practical intelligence to the capacity for self-consciousness and self-reflexion that distinguishes between essence and existence (Scheler); and the elevation of the realm of human freedom above the realm of human purpose (Simmel).

Eisenstadt's comparative analyses of Axial Age civilizations is important for his central argument – the delayed impact that the different religions embodied in these civilizations had on the eventual emergence of one global civilization containing multiple modernities.[10] Following Max Weber, Eisenstadt argues that the different religious cores and cultural programs of Axial Age civilizations are historically grounded, continually reconstructed traditions. The religious cores of civilizations thus continue to have a strong impact on the unending restructuring of their chief states. Eisenstadt dissents from Weber's Eurocentrism by insisting that this reconstruction is shaped in all civilizations by specific antinomies: transcendental and mundane, universalistic and particularistic, totalistic and pluralistic, orthodox and heterodox. And these antinomies motivate political struggles that have a strong impact on political institutions, social and economic structures, and collective identities. All Axial Age civilizations have generated proto-fundamentalist movements. In the West, Jacobinism became an oppositional movement in European civilization that exploded in the twentieth century under the banners of communism and fascism. Modern fundamentalism in non-Western civilizations combines the impact of Western Jacobinism with indigenous fundamentalist movements. Jacobin impulses in modernity thus are not passing phenomena in the history of civilizations. They are permanent features. Fundamentalism is an engine of change in all civilizations and a core aspect of the civilization of modernity.

Early modernities (sixteenth to eighteenth century) provide a transition between Axial Age civilizations and modernity and thus exemplify and deepen the theme of multiple modernities (Eisenstadt and Schluchter 1998). Language offers a good explanation of this period of transition. The turn to vernacular languages occurred in both Europe and India. In Europe, but not in India, it was accompanied by the emergence of more clearly defined territorial boundaries. In India, but not in Europe, vernacular languages complemented rather than replaced the sacred languages of Sanskrit and Pali (Pollock 2006: 259–80). In China and Japan, classical languages and political orders survived those turbulent centuries. While China experienced a major break in the age of axial religion, as the only civilizational state Japan did not. Yet in both states a public sphere evolved in early modernity – although one that was not tied, as in Europe, to civil society. Instead, China's public sphere became the world of academies and literati, which was tied closely to the official sphere (Woodside 2006). In Tokugawa Japan, people and territory were united (*kokka*). But even in that holistic conception politically relevant distinctions emerged, between official and non-official and between social and non-social. As in China, the realm of the private was denigrated and widely regarded as undercutting the pursuit of the common good. In Islamic law, Sufi orders constituted a dynamic public sphere that operated quite independently from the political or official sphere. Charting such a multiplicity of early modernities undercuts the charge of Eurocentrism in Eisenstadt's civilizational analysis (Pasha 2007: 65, 70). Europe is, as Eisenstadt and Schluchter (1998: 6–7, 15) argue, an analytical ideal type, not a normative reference point. Reflecting primordial categories and human practices, concepts such as "Western" or "Eastern" are unavoidable in comparative analysis. Contextualization and differentiation make them flexible in the development of diverse perspectives.

The first modern civilization was West European. Based on the

Enlightenment and crystallized politically in the American and French revolutions, it developed in the specific context of European Christianity. Its cultural core was a bundle of cognitive and moral imperatives for more individual autonomy, fewer traditional constraints, and more control over nature. The first modernity was constructed and reconstructed in the specific context of Judeo–Greek–Christian cultural universalism and in the political pluralism of its various center–periphery relations and political protest movements. Subsequently, West European modernity spread to Central and Eastern Europe, North and South America, and also to other non-European civilizations. For Eisenstadt (2001), the civilization of modernity is defined not by being taken for granted, but by becoming a focal point of contestation, an object of uninterrupted conflict engaging both pre- and post-modern protest movements (Kocka 2001: 6).The civilization of modernity embodies a multiplicity of different cultural programs and institutions of modernity that derive from the interaction between West European modernity and the various civilizations of the Axial Age.

Modern societies are therefore not converging on a common path involving capitalist industrialism, political democracy, modern welfare regimes, and pluralizing secularisms. Instead, the different religious traditions act as cultural sources for the enactment of different programs of modernity. For example, West European modernity was transformed in the United States under the specific circumstances of a settler and immigrant society. James Kurth underlines in Chapter 2 the continued relevance of fundamentalist religious movements for the multiple traditions and various dimensions of social structure, political institutions, and collective identities of the American state. A second example is offered by Japan's reconstruction of modernity. Japan is the only civilization that did not experience a break in the Axial Age. It is based on specific patterns of emulation and selection that evolved a distinctive set of sociopolitical structures and collective identities. Since the Meiji revolution Japan's deeply anchored syncretism of religious belief systems has been highly eclectic in the values it has adopted and flexible in the interpretation of the dramatic shifts in political context it has confronted.

The legacies of different world religions thus create multiple modernities as sources of cultural innovation. In the evolution of the socioeconomic, political–legal and technical–scientific dimensions of the civilization of modernity, forces of convergence are always balanced against forces of divergence. Modernity is inescapably multiple and undergoing a constant process of reinvention in which all traditional elements that rebel against it have themselves a modern, Jacobin character. In sum, although the aspirations of the world's important civilizational states may be totalistic, they are pluralistic in their cumulative impact on the multiple traditions that, for Eisenstadt, constitute a single civilization of modernity (Arjomand and Tiryakian 2004a: 3; Sternberg 2001: 80–81).

Cultural competition and zones of prestige (Collins)

Randall Collins (2004, 2000, 1999, 1998) has provided an admirably pithy, highly plausible, complementary view of civilizations as zones of prestige organized around one or several cultural centers.[11] The attractiveness of these zones of prestige radiates outward with variable strengths. Distances are not only geographic but take the form of networks of attraction that carry prestige through various channels, passing over or penetrating other civilizational zones. This conceptualization focuses our attention on social activity and cultural variety. It avoids regarding civilizations as cultural codes, as patterns governing beliefs and institutions that are endowed with an enduring essence. Civilization is not an actor or an attribute of actors; it exists as a set of relationships and practices and also as a primordial construction of identity.

The power of a civilization depends on the practices that promote or diminish its magnetism. Such magnetism reflects creativity, typically shaped by rival positions and disagreements that command attention. Competing schools of thought that are in vigorous debate and disagreement thus are crucial to civilizational prestige. Civilizations are marked by dialogue, debate, and disagreement that generate intellectual and artistic tension. In their engagement of the world, both attraction and propagation characterize zones of civilizational prestige that are composed of multiple, competing networks and distant connections. Such zones attract students and visitors of different kinds, some from very far away. Conversely, zones of high prestige also send out teachers and missionaries, both to civilizational peripheries and to other civilizations. Zones of prestige are not free-standing and monolithic. Diversity and active debate among rival positions spur creativity and stymie uniformity of opinion.

Civilizational ruptures can occur for many reasons, as they did in the relations between China and Japan during the Tokugawa period. In that case, as well as with the earlier Chinese resistance to the import of Indian Buddhism, cultural resistance was not simply derivative of a broader struggle against geopolitical and economic hegemony. This contrasts with some of the anti- and post-colonial movements in the second half of the twentieth century. A slow shift away from European- and, at times, even American-centered domination was also a move away from metropoles that, together with their political preeminence, had lost some of their civilizational attraction. Conversely, struggles for political liberation, such as the Indian independence movement, and moves for economic advancement, such as Japan's rise after 1945, can occur without a simultaneous rejection of the cultural imports of existing zones of civilizational prestige. The dynamics of civilizational politics cannot be reduced simply to political or economic factors.

This fact is confirmed by those historical instances in which militarily weak or defeated parts of the world that were economically lagging remained zones of civilizational prestige with deep sources of attraction to many members of the military or economic centers of domination. Ancient Greece and twentieth-century France are good examples. Greece, despite its military conquest by Rome, far from losing its civilizational prestige, in some ways absorbed Rome culturally. It had institutionalized networks of opposing schools of thought and creativity in a system of higher education that fostered the kind of intellectual rivalries that created cultural attraction; Rome did not. Twentieth-century France offers another example of a zone of civilizational prestige that persisted as the country relinquished its central position in the global and European capitalist system. Despite this slide, Paris has remained an important center of intellectual creativity and fashion in literary theory, philosophy, and parts of the social sciences. In sharp contrast to the more professionally oriented and politically more isolated world-class universities that emerged in the United States, Paris nurtured intersecting networks of intellectuals who focused on academic subjects and connected them to broader issues in the worlds of high-culture entertainment, journalism, and politics. In the natural sciences and engineering, however, the links between university-based research, government, and the world of corporate or start-up capitalism were more vibrant in the United States. The infrastructure of military and economic primacy was thus much better served by the evolving American than by the French pattern of creativity.

Cultural prestige and military or economic primacy thus should not be equated unthinkingly. Robert Gilpin argues quite correctly that numerous factors such as respect and common interest underlie the prestige of a state as the everyday currency of international relations:

> Ultimately, however, the hierarchy of prestige in an international system rests on economic and military power . . . the fact that the existing distribution of power and the hierarchy of prestige can sometimes be in conflict with one another is an important factor in international political change.
>
> (Gilpin 1981: 30–31)

Even in such situations, however, it seems plausible to assume that struggles for military and economic catch-up will involve a good deal of emulation of the practices that characterize zones of civilizational prestige. And emulation and rejection are often deeply intertwined. The cultural dynamic in such processes often reflects the intellectual interests and career aspirations of elites no longer dependent on travel to or imports from zones of prestige, eager and able to exploit and build up further the creativity of a zone that is no longer a civilizational periphery. For this to happen, two conditions must be met. The material conditions for cultural production must have advanced to a threshold level. And rival schools of thought and creativity must have come into being to create vibrant debate within this emerging zone of prestige as well as between it and the former center from which it is beginning to break away.

Civilizing process (Elias)

Norbert Elias has written the foundational analysis of the civilizing process in Europe, spawning an innovative literature that extends well beyond his empirical European referent.[12] The civilizing process that Elias (1978a, 1982, 2000, 1997; Mennell 2007: 4–18; Goudsblom, Jones, and Mennell 1996; Mandalios 2003: 65–70; Duerr 1988, 1990, 1993, 1997; Mennell and Goudsblom 1997) analyzed was the result of a struggle between aristocracy and bourgeoisie. Such a process, Elias argued, was putting distance between the psychological and behavioral structure of an uncivilized or unmannered child and a civilized or well-behaved adult. The civilizing process has several dimensions. First, it refers to an evolving habitus of social manners marked by the increasing importance of internalized self-restraints and lower thresholds of embarrassment and repugnance over what is considered as uncivilized conduct. Second, with the expansion of the state's military and taxation power, the civilizing process describes the gradual internal pacification of European societies as well as a growing emotional identification among members of society. Public acts of violence that were common in the past have become more reviled; and the capacity for human empathy as a foundation for society-wide and cosmopolitan sentiments has increased. At the same time, the scale of interstate warfare has grown sharply. Finally, as the result of these developments, chains of social interdependencies have become longer and political rationalization has advanced. Put differently, changes in personality, sociopolitical structure, and habitus alter the way in which individuals and groups construct what is civilized and uncivilized, reasonable and unreasonable. In different societies, court and bourgeois rationality emerged in competition with one another. The sum total of such historical and spontaneous processes of interactions among individuals, society, and the state, Elias argued, produced the civilizing process and the eventual transformation of European society.

Against this historical background and theoretical explication, it is understandable why the very concept of civilization connotes to many a hierarchical view of the world that contrasts "advanced" with "backward" peoples and polities. Yet Elias was not a proponent of Eurocentrism. Modern European societies are not the only ones that undergo a civilizational process. Mennell (2007: 295–6), for example, shows that the development of American manners and habitus between the eighteenth and twentieth centuries was broadly similar to that of Europe between the late Middle Ages and the nineteenth century. This holds even though the absolute rates of certain kinds of violence on a per capita basis are much higher in the United States than in Europe. Although marked by specific institutional features, as was true of Europe, the origin and institutionalization of the American state was rooted in war, both international and civil, including the war between the white settlers and indigenous peoples who were either dispossessed or eradicated.

All societies must socialize their members (Linklater 2004: 8–9; Mennell

1996). And in all societies these processes yield contingent outcomes that are politically reversible, as illustrated by the Nazi regime (Elias 2000). Decivilizing processes always accompany civilizing ones. For example, social groups and individuals who advance the civilizing process often do so by drawing sharp distinctions between insiders and outsiders that tend to cement their own rule. Claiming civilizational superiority as a condition is a political tool that has little to do with civilizational processes. Elias (1994) argues that, when power ratios are very uneven between a favored in-group and a disfavored out-group, it is normal for people to believe that power differentials inhere in civilizational difference rather than in an evolving and changeable civilizing process. When power differentials shift, so do senses of civilizational superiority and inferiority. Elias is therefore not a defender of Europe's supposedly superior social or political achievements. Furthermore, although he recognizes some evidence (aristocratic norms of chivalry, bourgeois norms of morality, global norms of human rights) to support the argument that a civilizing process has attenuated the security dilemma in international politics, on most counts he subscribes to a Hobbesian view of international relations and recognizes a tendency toward violence in the engagement between different political communities or states (Linklater 2004: 14–17).

Although Elias studied the civilizing processes in Europe, his analysis is applicable elsewhere, yielding some contradictory insights. In an important book, Gerrit Gong (1984a; Barth and Osterhammel 2005), for example, argues that the European society of states provided a standard of civilization – conceived of as condition rather than process – that distinguished clearly between civilized and uncivilized peoples. The factual basis of that claim was contestable in many instances and was most problematic in the case of Greece, supposedly the very foundation of European civilization. Greece had been an Ottoman province for five centuries, and its political and social institutions revealed that historical experience (Stivachtis 1998). As the European states expanded their imperial missions, the conflict with non-European political communities and states was not only political, economic, or military, but also civilizational. Although other standards of civilization existed, the European one came to prevail throughout the world (Phillips 2008: 327–84). By the end of the nineteenth century, the international society of states was being transformed into a society of self-proclaimed civilized states. And, by that standard, most of the non-European world was uncivilized (Hemming 1999). This designation mattered, for it robbed those communities and states of the partial protection that the evolving law of nations might have provided. Mussolini, for example, enjoyed the full protection of international law when he decided to wage gas warfare on the Abyssinians in the 1930s.

The distinction between civilized and uncivilized peoples and states coincided largely with those of race, ethnic origin, and religion. White Europeans who were Christians were civilized. Those lacking these markers were not. In East Asia, for example, the European standard gradually superseded the Confucian order in the nineteenth century as China's standard of civilization concerning international trade, diplomacy, and law imitated the dominant European one, codified in treaty law and subsequently reflected in European writings on customary law (Gong 1984b: 172). In international law, the standard of civilization argument, in the making for several centuries, was buried by the victory of anti-colonial nationalist movements after World War II, before reasserting itself somewhat and in different form with a change in state identities that followed on the heels of the end of the Cold War (Mozaffari 2001).

Brett Bowden (2005: 2) has amended Gong's argument in three plausible ways. First, while Gong mentions the civilizational and cultural conflicts that attended European expansion, he did not give full weight to Europe's aggression, to the violence of its conquests, and to the brutality of its suppression of indigenous peoples, based on discourses of exclusion and the denial of sovereign rights (Keal 2003). Espousing a civilizational standard and engaging in collective violence were both integral parts of the European expansion. Second, the encounters between popes and infidels and the Old and the New World remind us of the fact that Europe's imperial expansion started much earlier than in the nineteenth century. Although it was less dynamic, that earlier expansion shared many of the same characteristics with the burst of imperialism in the nineteenth century. Finally and crucially, similar civilizational conflicts have also occurred among and between the non-European civilizations of the world.

Older versus newer theories of civilization

Older civilizational analysis (Farrenkopf 2000: 33–6; Ifversen 2002; Huntington 1996: 55) differs from these more recent approaches on the issue of modernity and civilizational competition. Does history reveal one or multiple modernities? For Arnold Toynbee, Asian and Islamic civilizations could modernize successfully but only at the cost of considerable Westernization, a euphemism for cultural standardization along Western lines. Against this view, the Muslim world and Asia have in recent decades provided alternative visions and practices. Note the plural. Anti-Western writings and political movements are neither a hodge-podge of anti-colonialism nor a conservative, religious reaction to global modernity. Anti-Westernism is shared by both religious revivalists in the Islamic world and secular politicians and writers in the Middle East and Asia who are working in the Enlightenment tradition (Aydin 2007: 1–2). And they are articulated as much today as they were during the heyday of Western colonialism in the Middle East, Asia, and Africa. Religious tradition and the legacy of colonialism are both relevant to anti-Western discourses and politics. Yet we should not reduce criticism of Western civilization to either or both of these factors. Pan-Islamic and pan-Asian movements are part of the global circulation of anti-Western ideas that have a Western origin. In Eisenstadt's formulation they are manifestations of multiple modernities that coexist in one global civilization of modernity.

New approaches to civilization stress flexibility and multiplicity and thus differ from Spengler's (1939) theory of civilizational cycles, which stipulates the existence of a pluralism of modernities stretching across different historical eras. For Spengler, the fate of modern civilization was tied unavoidably to the West. Other civilizations might succeed the West's universal empire through economic competition and political power, but not through civilizational succession. Steeped as they are in the notions of uniform and coherent cultural traditions as core elements of a civilization, neither Toynbee nor Spengler shares much with Eisenstadt's idea of multiple modernities, Collins's conception of civilization as based on vital disagreements, or Elias's analysis of a multiplicity of civilizational processes.

Multiple modernities coexist in and help shape one global civilization of modernity. Eisenstadt accounts for this outcome in terms of the plural and pluralist cultural programs continuously activated by the religious cores of the world's major civilizations. The fact that religion is the source on which opponents of Western modernity often draw is evidence that Eisenstadt cites prominently (Fox 2004: 158–9). Collins's idea of competition within and between zones of civilizational prestige also accommodates comfortably the notion of a modernity that is a common frame, shaped by competition within and between different zones of civilizational prestige. Such zones are connected by interlacing networks crossing long distances, marked by diversity and disagreement, and reflected in what people do and think rather than what civilizations are. And Elias's analysis of civilizing and decivilizing processes charts the ups and downs of civilizations that allow for many different kinds of outcomes. The reversibility in civilizing processes focuses our attention on dynamic social interactions rather than on static cultural essences. It creates space for diversity and pluralism rather than imposing homogeneity and unity.

Multiple actors, traditions, and practices

Civilizational constellations are shaped by multiple types of actors, traditions, and practices. Admittedly, the category of multiplicity is subject to objections from some quarters. Listing different types of actors will offend intellectual sensibilities attuned to the building of a deductive science of international politics. The analytical sparseness required by such an intellectual enterprise assumes the existence of only one type of actor, the state. Furthermore, in the interest of simplification, it is imperative that the state be thought of as an undifferentiated actor. In this perspective, all states are uniform and of one type. Building analysis on the assumption of the existence of different types of actors, and insisting that these actors are marked by internal differences, is, from this vantage point, deeply unsatisfactory.

Unfortunately, an overly developed sensibility for analytical sparseness is fatal to any attempt to understand civilizational politics.

Multiple actors

Civilizational constellations are not political entities in and of themselves (Puchala 1997: 12). Instead, they contain various types of political actors: states, polities, and empires (Huntington 1996: 44). Their international standing is determined by the perceived credibility of current power and prestige, the perceived salience of an active historical memory, and the prospect of an appealing, imagined future. If such appeals are acknowledged as politically authentic, civilizational actors are politically consequential.

The case chapters in this book show a broad array of different civilizational actors. First, in Japan's civilizational configuration, the familial state is the central actor. This is true also of America where, in sharp contrast to Japan, the liberal state is an integral part of a more encompassing imperium. In contemporary India the state matters; but, historically, Indian civilization has flowered and prevailed surreptitiously and over long periods and distances without taking any explicitly political, let alone statist, form. In China, historically the state was central and provided a template that Korea, Japan, and Vietnam adopted in organizing their own states. In contemporary China, the state remains central but does not control a far-flung diaspora which is indisputably part of China's civilizational configuration. An emerging European polity is composed of member states which both pool some parts of their sovereignty and jealously guard others. Finally, today the global reach of Islam's *umma* bypasses the world of states altogether. And Islam's diaspora points to a deterritorialized form of politics, as is true of Judaism, in which ethnic and religious borders are reinvented to re-create some semblance of lost civilizational coherence in the patchwork quilt of modern urban life, especially in Europe. Yet, at the same time, Muslim states continue to portray themselves as carriers of Islamic civilization.

States are centers of political authority with distinct identities and institutions, and are endowed with the capacity of collectively mobilizing resources in the achievement of political objectives. States are not the only such centers of authority. Far from being unitary, states take on very different forms. Their hallmark, centralized territorial rule, persists today in many parts of the world, not unchallenged, but as part of overlapping and intersecting networks of rules in which states, often but by no means always, hold a preeminent position. States are often nested in such broader structures of authority, both older ones such as historical empires and newer ones such as emerging polities or governance structures.

The degree of "stateness" is variable. Compared with continental Europe, for example, the United States is marked by relative statelessness (Nettl 1968). Its elected government is comparatively limited in its power. Individual rights, a litigious culture, a constitutionally mandated separation of powers, and the institution of judicial review all constrain the power of the state. The presidency, especially in times of national emergency, can acquire extraordinary powers, illustrated by the policies adopted after 9/11. But the overreaching of one branch of government should not be confused with the creation of an institutionally strong state. Other states such as Japan can draw on broader and deeper sources of state power than can the United States. State power is somewhat smaller in India and perhaps also in China, especially if we refer to China as the combination of both the territorial state of China and the networks that connect a large Chinese diaspora. Historically, the triumph of the European state over alternative forms of political organization was based on its superior record of keeping peace at home, securing property rights in markets, collecting taxes, organizing a common defense, and waging war. Today, at the European level, stateness remains low in the case of Europe's emerging multi-level polity. And it does not exist in the case of global Islam, which Mustapha Pasha (2007: 62) quite fittingly calls an Islamic Cultural Zone.

The sociocultural embeddedness of the state also varies. State policies and practices may be constituted by domestic norms; they may be guided by domestic rules; or they may be merely permissible under domestic rules (Andrews 1975). In the case of civilizations, the pull of domestic norms over the state or other types of actors tends to be particularly strong, complementing or reinforcing rather than substituting for national, regime, or group norms. Civilizational politics exhibit a thick context of sociocultural norms informing state purpose and strategy.

Polities form a second type of civilizational actor. They are broader centers of authority that are not exclusively territorially based. Michael Mann (1986, 1993) sees a world with complex changes that make states in some parts of the globe lose control over some political domains while gaining control over others as the need for increasing regulation of human affairs intensifies. In Mann's view, states are becoming more and more polymorphous and crystallize in multiple forms; they do not exist as singular actors. Ferguson and Mansbach (1996; Ferguson, Mansbach *et al.* 2000), in contrast, rely on the concept of polity to cover the manifold and increasing changes that have affected the role of the state historically and in contemporary world affairs. For them, states and polities are both parts of multiple, overlapping and intersecting networks.

John Meyer (1994; Meyer *et al.* 1997) and his colleagues and students have developed systematically the idea of one global polity which provides cognitive and normative models that help constitute contemporary states. Such models provide contemporary states with universal rules in which to ground their claims to legitimacy. As was true of nineteenth-century America, far from producing anarchy, political conformity is being generated by the reliance on common cultural material: law, science, civic associations, religious sects, and nationalism. Thinking of American analogues for the international system, Daniel Deudney (2007: 161–89) has referred to this as the

Philadelphia system. What was true of nineteenth-century America, Meyer (1994) argues, is also true of today's global polity. That polity acts like a consultant and for the most part produces talk that is addressed primarily to constituent states and influences the goals they set (social and economic development as well as welfare, justice, rights, and equality). Indeed, "it becomes rational rather than treasonous to propose copying policies and structures that appear to be successful in a virtuous or dominant competitor" (ibid.: 13). The usefulness of the concept of polity thus depends on the empirical phenomena to which it is applied. Political analysis of the European Union (EU), for example, refers to it as a multi-tiered polity rather than as an embryonic federal or confederal system of government. In the case of China, it may make sense to operate with the concept of polity if the inquiry extends beyond the territorial state of the People's Republic to incorporate the role of the overseas Chinese. And, in the case of Japan, the concept has proved productive since it circumvents the problem of having to make, as in Europe, a clear analytical separation between state and society.

Besides states and polities, *empires* form a third actor in world politics. European empires exported state institutions to other parts of the world, where they provided an overlay to indigenous political forms of organization and loyalty which eventually nested within the institutional import from Europe. Numerous social, economic, and cultural developments in world politics have empowered non-state actors and made citizens more critical consumers of the public goods that states and non-state actors continue to provide.

In contemporary world politics, the American imperium is the closest analogue to empire. It conjoins the powers of a territorial empire with those of a non-territorial empire (Katzenstein 2005: 2–6). Imperium combines traditional elements of old-fashioned European imperialism with elements of rule that are distinctively new. The system of far-flung military bases and the power of the American military illustrate the importance of the territorial–military aspects of America's imperium. At the same time, the United States is also a central actor and part of a system that is creating new forms of non-territorial rule, for example in the evolution of governing mechanisms in financial markets or in the standards that help define the evolution of consumer society and definitions of individual happiness and contentment.

Historically, territorially based empires, or universal states, have been closely associated with civilizations. An empire differs from states and polities in size, scope, salience, and sense of task. Interimperial relations are defined by the relationship of subordinate states to the dominant power (Liska 1967: 9, 11). Empires remind us that an important part of international politics is defined by hierarchical rather than egalitarian relations among states (Lake 2009; Craig 2004; Hobson and Sharman 2005). Empires are marked by direct or indirect rule and differential bargains between the imperial center and subordinate political communities. When empires assert the unilateral right to define the criteria for membership in the community of civilized states, as was true of European states in the nineteenth century and the United States after 9/11, they move beyond the bounds of realist international politics (Khanna 2008; Ferguson 2007b; Nexon 2007a; Nexon and Wright 2007; Münckler 2007; Motyl 2006, 2001, 1999; Osterhammel 1995; Doyle 1986). Civilizational empires typically have multi-ethnic populations, are continental in size, and have cosmopolitan or universal aspirations (Akturk 2009). They operate often indirectly through heterogeneous and asymmetric contracts with local elites who are recruited from core or periphery, or are operating as leaders in their own right (Nexon 2007b: 7; Nexon and Wright 2007). An imperial ideology often complements self-professed standards of civility and transcendental convictions.[13] And it is imperial behavior that in the past generated the most important intercivilizational encounters. The balance of capabilities between empires thus is often a highly salient factor shaping the manifold types of encounters and engagements that ensue. Donald Puchala (1997: 28) concludes his survey of intercivilizational encounters with the argument that the historical significance of states and empires "is not that they won or lost wars, made rational choices or irrational ones, or behaved realistically, neo-realistically, or unrealistically, but rather that they protected or extended the civilizations with which they were associated or failed at this." With the disintegration of the land-based Habsburg and Ottoman empires after World War I, the overseas European empires after World War II, and the Soviet empire at the end of the Cold War, the era of territorial empire has largely ended, as the United States learned in its unsuccessful wars in Vietnam in the 1960s and 1970s and in Iraq after 2003.

The non-territorial side to the American imperium has political and sociocultural features. The American imperium has considerable power to define the political norms and rules governing international politics (Richardson 1991). International regimes, a variety of global governance arrangements, soft law, and different methods of policy coordination are shaped to some extent by the norms and practices the United States has actively promoted during the last half century. In contrast to other empires, in the American imperium these norms cannot simply be broken with impunity by the strongest power, following the dictate of "might makes right." Instead, significant international decisions are now taken by majority rule, and international arbitration procedures have grown in importance. Both developments have undermined the unanimity principle and the principle of the sanctity of state sovereignty. Furthermore, some norms, such as those prohibiting unprovoked aggression or the waging of genocidal wars, have become widely accepted and, if violated, can result in international sanctions and the criminal prosecutions of individuals. On issues such as Guantánamo and Abu Ghraib, American policy since 2003 has clearly been affected by strong international condemnation. Indeed, American justification for the war against Iraq is based on both encompassing international norms and narrow American interests. The American imperium thus is not exempted from its own normative pressures (Zürn 2007: 690–93).

The sociocultural side of the American imperium goes well beyond the explicitly political aspects of authority and legitimacy. Technological advances and the shrinking of time and space have made available to more people and over longer distances the model of "the American way of life," in all its manifestations, admirable to some and appalling to others. The open-door policy that was a hallmark of US expansion in the second half of the twentieth century has created the conditions for the informal penetration of foreign societies into various manifestations of American social life and cultural experiences. The existence of social ties with pre-colonial elites that establishes the precondition for the successful exercise of informal imperial governance (MacDonald 2007) is less important than the unmediated seductive fascination with the energizing impulses of a liberal brand of democratic capitalism and an entrepreneurial culture that promises self-advancement. As an idea and as a dream, America has always had a non-territorial aspect to it, acting as a spur to both political imagination and fear. Both have grown with the shrinking of time and space, and so has America's political relevance in global politics.

This conception of imperium is different from Henry Luce's (1941; Hogan 1999) prescient celebration of the American century at the onset of the involvement of the United States in World War II. Luce had fastened on Toynbee's concept of the "universal state" as the ultimate stage of a civilization, and in a familiar Hegelian turn cast the US in the role of the new universal state for humankind. In contrast to Toynbee (and Eisenstadt), Luce downplayed the role of religion; and he emphasized civilization in the singular (Cox 2001: 108–9). His formulation resembled that of nineteenth-century European imperialists. But it differed from European formulations in the attention it paid to the non-territorial aspects of power rooted in American ideas, products, and technology. As Robert Cox (2000: 219, n. 6) observes, this presented a trap for American observers. Two decades after Luce, the American historian William H. McNeill (1963) wrote his widely acclaimed, read, and cited *The Rise of the West: A History of the Human Community.* At the end of the Cold War, McNeill (1990) self-critically observed that the title and subtitle of his book expressed an unconscious and unwarranted form of intellectual imperialism. The title assigned to the temporary role of the United States an altogether disproportionate influence in human history. What was true of McNeill in the 1960s has been true more recently for others who have consciously or unconsciously subscribed to a Western-centric view while celebrating or decrying America's imperium (Hobson 2004).

This categorization among states, polities, and empires is not iron-clad. Actors often inhabit overlapping spaces. This is true of the United States, which is both a state and an imperium. It is true of European states, which are pooling some of their sovereignty to Europe's emerging polity. But it is also arguably true of China which, following Lucian Pye (1990: 58), is not just another nation-state but "a civilization pretending to be a state." As Xu Xin

(2009) argues, China is in the midst of transforming a civilization into a nation-state.

Multiple traditions

Civilizational constellations lack the clear boundaries, internal coherence, tight integration, centralization, and enduring character that in public discourse, and Huntington's formulations, are typically associated with them (Hall and Jackson 2007a: 7–8). Civilizations are not static and consensual but dynamic and politically contested. If we think of them in terms of multiple modernities (as in Eisenstadt), or zones of prestige that embody intellectual disagreements (as in Collins), or multiple processes (as in Elias), it is only one additional, small step to think about them in terms of multiple traditions. Civilizational states are not unified carriers of coherent values – secular liberalism (America), Asian values (China and Japan), religious fundamentalism (Islam), the values of the Enlightenment (Europe), or political toleration for different religions, secularisms, liberalisms, and illiberalisms (India). Instead, each civilizational constellation is marked by political battles and contested truths, reflecting multiple modernities, shifting zones of prestige, and numerous civilizational processes. Furthermore, the multiplicity and pluralism that is observable today has marked civilizational constellations in the past (Senghaas 1998: 24–67). Although each of them will express different processes of contestations around different issues, all civilizations live under the emblem of "unity in diversity."

All of the case studies in this book point to the pluralism of civilizations as reflected in the vibrancy of their multiple traditions. James Kurth provides in Chapter 2 a genealogy of the transformation of Classical, Christian, and Western civilizations into a contemporary global one. America's religious foundation in Reform Protestantism (English Puritans and Scottish Presbyterians) and the British Enlightenment set it off from the European continent and made it an alternative to a Western civilization that receded during the twentieth century. Reform Protestantism rejected hierarchy and community and prepared the grounds for the American Creed and the rule of (hard) law – contract and constitution as defining institutions of free market capitalism and liberal democracy. This American Creed, Kurth argues, eventually became the core of Western civilization. This process involved a ruthless *Kulturkampf*, assimilation through Americanization of Catholic and Jewish immigrants who arrived in ever larger numbers during the nineteenth century. And it required the United States to fill the international leadership vacuum created by Europe's decline. The result was a united American nation-state and a cohesive Western alliance, which prevailed in a global struggle with fascism and communism in the twentieth century. Eventually, starting in the 1960s, a number of different developments coalesced to create a great clash within America that established the conditions for a multicultural society (Moreau 2003). The intellectual and business elites of that new society regarded the concept of Western civilization as outmoded, archaic, and oppressive, replacing it with a new global civilization celebrating individual and universal human rights and global markets. This is a civilization without God, Kurth argues, a civilization of pre-Axial Age neo-paganism that many Europeans distrust and that the remnants of other (Sinic, Indian, and Islamic) Axial Age civilizations resist.

Emanuel Adler's analysis in Chapter 3 makes an analogous case for Europe. Adler's analysis converges with Kurth on the argument of the emergence of a new global civilization; but he differs sharply from Kurth's view of contemporary America having experienced a historic victory of multiculturalism over militarism. Adler argues that, in the past four hundred years, modernity was lodged between the universalizing practices of European civilization, in the singular, and specific nationalist ideas. Since the middle of the twentieth century, European civilization has been in the process of undergoing a fundamental change. Provocatively, Adler argues, contemporary Europe is the only civilization that has reinvented itself as the first postmodern security community. Europe is not merely one instance of Eisenstadt's multiple modernities. It is post-modern. Normative Europe is developing novel practices that seek to detour American and Islamic civilizations with their traditional power politics approaches. If there is a clash between civilizations, Adler argues, it is occurring between Europe's postmodern civilization on the one hand and the civilization of modernity on the other. Although Adler insists that "normative power Europe" is novel and historically unique, it is worth pointing out that this post-modern civilization is grounded in the very self-restraint that Elias characterized as central to the civilizing process that had transformed Europe in its distant past.

The various meanings attached to China and the different ways in which the state practices of Chinese civilization were implemented in neighboring states, David Kang argues in Chapter 4, constitute one important source of the multiple traditions in the Sinocentric world. Another source was the numerous reinventions and reinterpretations of Confucianism which, in its various forms, grafted itself onto social and cultural patterns in neighboring states that never let go fully of their indigenous and Buddhist ideas and practices.

Japanese intellectuals, David Leheny argues in Chapter 5, have been curiously indifferent to civilizational analyses that stress the theme of internal pluralism and heterogeneity. They have instead been partial to a concept of culture that connotes the uniqueness of Japan conceived of as a coherent and unified complex. In contrast to Huntington's (1996) general analysis, Eisenstadt's (1996) and Arnason's (1997) detailed writings on Japanese civilization have fallen on deaf ears. Public discourse reveals a widespread agreement on Japan's national identity as being marked by both its rapid modernization in one global civilization and its indisputable uniqueness in a world of plural civilizations. Historical narratives about Japan's identity have in recent years been consumed by conservatives worrying that Japan might lose its accustomed position of agency in and leadership of East Asia, as China resumes its role as the traditional leader of Sinic civilization. But conservatism is only one among several intellectual traditions in Japan. Leheny also refers to important writings by rabid nationalists, pro-Asian progressives, and left-wing multiculturalists.

India, Susanne Rudolph argues in Chapter 6, is prototypical for a hetero-geneous and pluralist view of civilization. Classical Indian civilization had a capacity for peaceful diffusion. Rudolph identifies the existence of four vari-ants of Indian civilization since about 1750: an Indophilial Orientalism shaped by the officials of the East India Company that prevailed until the early nineteenth century; an Indophobic Anglicist view that arose in the first quarter of the nineteenth century, expressed by utilitarians and evangelical East India Company officials; an inclusionary liberal nationalist variant articulated by Indians who rejected the Orientalist European images of India; and, finally, an exclusionary Hindu civilizational variant seeking to displace its secular, nationalist rival. Rudolph adds an interesting twist to Kurth's concluding argument in Chapter 2 – the resistance of Axial Age civilizations of America as the center of a newfangled neo-paganism in world affairs. She ends her chapter with the tale of a Hindu leader adopting the language of multiculturalism while misappropriating Samuel Huntington's (2004a, 2004b) interpretation of America as a white Protestant settler rather than a multicultural, multi-religious immigrant society.

Finally, in Chapter 7 Bruce Lawrence provides abundant evidence for Islam's multiple traditions. He argues that civilizational discourse is neither an invention of nor a social construct limited to the West. The conceptual foundation of the analysis of world civilization was laid by one of the great Islamic intellectuals, Ibn Khaldun, who in the fifteenth century sought to adjudicate between Islam's many conflicting traditions. At the core of Khaldun's vision was the denial of East and West as irreducible opposites. Islam was neither enemy nor outlier of either East or West. Instead, as one of the great contemporary scholars of Islam, Marshall Hodgson, has argued, it was a bridge between them as well as between ancient and modern social systems. Islamic civilization originated in the desert before the subsequent emergence of urban civilization. Together, both sources became the basis for Islam's far-flung civilization, with its many connections to other civilizations. Referring to Hodgson, Lawrence characterizes Islam as a large geocultural grid featuring cross-regional filiations that link the Afro-Eurasian world and that include but go beyond loyalty to Islam, as creed, liturgy, and law. For Lawrence, it is the Indian Ocean more than the Middle East and North Africa that gave Islam its specific civilizational shape and made it a pan-Asian cultural force. And in South Asia, historically, Lawrence argues, Persian elements were more crucial in the evolution of Islamic civilization than were Turkish and Arabic ones. The Persian elements in South Asia centered on the principles of hierarchy and deference in pre-modern kingships. The Persian language and a splendid court culture created an expanding cultural elite that was allied with Persian values even when it was not supportive of Islamic norms.

Despite the commonality of their internal pluralism, these civilizational configurations differ in their degree of inclusiveness and exclusiveness. In Japan and Europe, actors are seeking to differentiate themselves clearly from suspected or feared "others." Both configurations show political coalitions and movements that reflect essentialist conceptions of a collective self in the case of Japan and of a universal ethos that is inflected by an enduring tradition of Eurocentrism (Delanty 1995: 12). Despite strong traditions of ethno-nationalism and racial thinking, the highly variegated traditions of Buddhism have provided Asian political actors with ample cultural material to incorporate others, although not always peacefully. Since the beginning of the American republic, a strong racial strain has led to a clear differentiation of settlers and immigrants from indigenous American-Indians and imported African- and Asian-Americans. Subsequently, in the second half of the twentieth century, the United States experimented, more or less successfully, with the incorporation of marginalized populations and the creation of a growing number of hyphenated identities. Contemporary India exhibits both inclusive tendencies in its secular and exclusive ones in its Hindu nationalism. Finally, in far-flung geographic settings, Islam as a truly global civilization also reveals great differences between exclusivist and incorporating political practices. Islam in Southeast Asia, for example, lacks the kind of dominating ideology, religious or otherwise, that marks China and India. Islam as a bridge civilization, akin to the category of semi-periphery in Wallerstein's world system analysis, as Bruce Lawrence argues in Chapter 7, was always attentive to and inclusive of local differentiation and particularities.

Multiple processes

Civilization is not a condition but a process. Those who think of themselves as civilized were, at an earlier time, uncivilized and are always at risk of becoming so in the future. Today's world of plural civilizations is marked by practices that Sheldon Pollock (2006: 10–11), writing about the pre-modern era, referred to as "cosmopolitan transculturization." Civilizational complexes do not show themselves as "stable entities that interact in thinglike ways, rather than . . . as constantly changing repertoires of practices." These practices sum, in the aggregate, to civilizational processes (Kavolis 1982) such as Americanization, Europeanization, Sinicization, Japanization, Indianization, and Islamicization.[14] They are producing and reproducing behavioral and symbolic boundaries. And they are more (as in the case of Japanization) or less (as in the case of Islamicization) territorially grounded and linked to political power.

The civilizing process (in the singular) that Elias analyzed domestically has a close affinity, in its global and international manifestations, with Max

Weber's analysis of the "rationalization" of the world. Resonating fully with Eisenstadt's concept of one civilization of modernity as the successor to the different Axial Age civilizations, Niels Petersson (2005) has pointed to the central role of the idea of functioning economic markets in the civilizational mission of nineteenth-century imperialism. Under the heading of the global standard of market civilization, Brett Bowden and Leonard Seabrooke (2006) extend the analysis to include its contemporary manifestation. Although today's terminology differs from that of the nineteenth century, "good governance" connotes many of the things once covered by the old civilizational terminology. Benchmarking and the diffusion of standards of correct economic conduct are closely linked to the functioning of markets which now, as then, are viewed as instruments for pacifying international relations. And, in politics, human rights and democracy round out a policy package promoting neo-liberal economic globalization, considered as appropriate for the twenty-first century as was carrying the white man's burden in the nineteenth.

As embodiments of multiple modernities and different zones of prestige, civilizational processes (in the plural) are not only integrative, as important contemporary theorists of globalization argue, but also differentiating (Arnason 2004: 104–5). Indeed, the standard of civilization legacy can be found in two contemporary arguments about modernity and rights (Bowden 2004b: 59–65). Insistence on a global convergence in one "standard of modernity" elicits often strong dissent. For example, in a world of competing notions of human rights, there is an ongoing debate about the relative importance of civil and political compared to economic and social rights.

We can trace transcivilizational engagements and intercivilizational encounters in a variety of different practices. In their internal and external relations, civilizations are marked by debate and disagreements. Contestation generates different processes and outcomes. One such outcome, cultural imperialism, describes the unilateral imposition of the norms and practices of one modernity or zone of prestige upon local norms and practices that it seeks to displace or destroy. A second outcome describes the wholesale adoption by local actors of the format but not the content of imported cultural products and practices (Otmazgin 2007: 8–9). Finally, a third outcome describes a world of hybridization in which local norms and practices are altered by selectively appropriating imported practices and thus reshaping civilizational processes.

A focus on such processes shifts our attention away from coherent actors with identifiable attributes to contexts that embed such actors. Civilizational processes are produced, sustained, and altered by human practice. World systems theory and the *Annales* school have adopted this perspective and focused on material exchanges. A processual analysis of civilizations does the same for cultural material – information, ideas, values, norms, and identities. It highlights shifting balances of practices within and between different civilizational complexes (Adler and Crawford 2006: 7; Jackson 2006: 9–12).

Emanuel Adler offers in Chapter 3 a rich discussion of Europe's contemporary practices that affirm its evolving normative power. Europe mobilizes policy instruments in a deliberate attempt to bring about the convergence of norms that improve domestic conditions and enhance regional stability. Especially in the process of enlargement, Europe seeks to extend the security community it has become since the end of World War II. A new border control regime, the Schengen area, is a clear example. European borders are no longer the sites of clashes, as Huntington would have it, but sites of exchange. The great and unanswered question is whether European practices of redrawing borders can, in the Balkans, transform a civilizational fault line and deal with Turkey's ambiguous relationship to Europe. After a decade of political engagement, it looks as if Europe's scorecard is cautiously optimistic for the Balkans, while it remains pessimistic on the issue of Turkish accession. Civilizational encounters with Muslim minorities within Europe's urban areas illustrate the unfolding of a potentially transformational local politics that leads political observers to both cautiously optimistic and guardedly pessimistic appraisals. These instances reveal a variegated set of political practices that simply do not lend themselves to any simple summary such as the "clash" of civilizations. Institutionalized practices of region building – for example, in the Euro-Mediterranean partnership (EMP), the "Barcelona Process," the "European Neighborhood Policy" (ENP), and the "Mediterranean Union" – also aim at the convergence of civilizations (Adler and Crawford 2006). The salient issue is not the success or failure of these initiatives; most of them have made, at best, modest advances. It is instead the fact that the EU is seeking to export political practices and habits that have created dependable expectations of peaceful change (Mitzen 2006). This explains the strength of Europe's commitment to and constant invocation of human rights as enshrined in various European and international treaties, as well as its commitment to the principles of social rights and solidarity enshrined in the institution of the European welfare state. Strong support of the Kyoto treaty and legally binding emission standards, the International Criminal Court (ICC), and the EU's post-national citizenship rooted in rights rather than substantive notions of peoplehood affirm Europe's status as a normative power that seeks to transform its relations with other actors in international politics.

David Kang's discussion of Sinicization in Chapter 4 offers a wealth of historical examples of Chinese civilizational practices. In contrast to Europe, China was not greatly invested in exporting its practices to its neighbors to create a stable and peaceful regional realm. Instead, Korea, Vietnam, and Japan chose to emulate Chinese state practices because they were an effective means for exercising domestic control and managing foreign relations, especially with China. Central bureaucracies were modeled after those of China, including the calendar, writing system, education system, and civil service exams that emphasized knowledge of Confucianism and Chinese culture. Korea was most directly exposed to Chinese influences. But China did not dominate Korea. Instead, Korean neo-Confucians chose to impose Chinese ideology and practices on Korea. In the case of Vietnam, the emulation of Chinese practices was an attempt to avoid Chinese occupation and to demonstrate a high level of civilization through self-Confucianization. In Japan, Chinese influences, though always present, were less powerful than they were in Korea and Vietnam. Yet Japan, too, imported Tang dynasty institutions, norms, and practices. China also remained a highly salient model for the shoguns of Tokugawa Japan.

Civilizations have an inherent dynamism that can take many different forms. For purpose of illustration, and with no claim to offer a full inventory, the chapters in this book suggest the following four: silent spread, social emulation, self-affirmation, and explicit export. Rudolph in Chapter 6 and Lawrence in Chapter 7 offer intriguing analyses of the first dynamic. With the Indian Ocean acting like a turntable, classical India and Islam in South and Southeast Asia as well as the Middle East spread silently across vast distances, overcoming all resistance. And Islam showed an enormous capacity to self-replicate across the Afro-Eurasian ecumene, with the Persian language and Islamic religion providing two important vehicles. Second, Kang shows in Chapter 4 that pragmatism and self-restraint can provide encouragement to the emulation of practices that are instrumentally effective or intrinsically admirable. Sinicization worked in just that way. Historically, China's dynasties lacked all missionary zeal in exporting their characteristic practices. Third, Leheny's discussion in Chapter 5 shows civilizational actors with a reservoir of soft power that was as important in helping to articulate a specific identity as in providing a roadmap for the exercise of a specific form of civilizational power. Finally, Kurth in Chapter 2 and Adler in Chapter 3 show expansion by military and normative means that often take the form of the explicit export of institutions and practices. This export can be traced by dispositions and discourses that, through coercion, persuasion, or their combination, help shape international processes of bargaining and coalition formation (Deitelhoff 2009; Krebs and Jackson 2007).

The expansive dynamics inhering in different civilizational configurations are probably related to the degree of internal group cohesion. Among the contemporary cases included in this book, Japanese civilization is probably the most cohesive, which may well explain both its limited reach and the infatuation of the Japanese with the concept of soft power, as Leheny argues in Chapter 5. The overwhelming power of the Han Chinese in China and the recent discovery of soft power by Chinese intellectuals and politicians quite possibly point to a similar limitation. For better and for worse, Islamic and American civilization have global relevance. With their internal heterogeneity and their polyvalence, they engage and address the concerns of many different kinds of groups all over the world. James Kurth shows in Chapter 2 how immigration, since the mid-1960s, is changing America. The election of Barack Obama in 2008 signals an end to an America that had ruthlessly Americanized immigrants before the 1960s. The construction of a new multicultural society is not only altering the American state but also, I would argue, enhancing the appeal of American civilization on a global scale, thus adding power to the American imperium.

Civilizational processes of engagement, as this discussion of the export and emulation of practices illustrates, are open-ended. The menu of choices and the political repertoires of action of those engaging them are not. Both need to be brought together in one conceptual universe and coherent set of empirical observations, as Patrick Jackson correctly insists in the book's concluding Chapter 8. There, he discusses the identification of civilizational features as expressed by the practices and ideas of participants within a civilization rather than by scholars imposing their categories from without. It remains an important future task to combine the analysis of two issues in a single framework: inquiries into relatively open-ended processes of transcivilizational engagements and intercivilizational encounters and investigations and of the circumscribed repertoires of individual actions and group practices.

Conclusion

Pluralism and plurality are the concepts that best encapsulate contemporary civilizational politics. Civilizations are not what they are often thought to be – internally coherent arrays of values. They acquire such coherence only when established discursively as primordial constructions with dispositional capacity. In their transcivilizational engagements and intercivilizational encounters civilizations are marked, as Eisenstadt argues, by multiple modernities. Within civilizational constellations, pluralism refers to differentiation and contestation which, as Collins shows, are important ingredients for civilization's magnetism. Between civilizations, as Elias reminds us, processes create conditions for differentiation that runs the full gamut from peace to war. Don Puchala's (2003: 134–42) historical inventory of civilizational encounters suggests that clashes are rare.

This is not to deny the history of states, polities, or empires, with mature civilizations and convinced of their inherent superiority, which have closed themselves off from one another. When they encountered other actors from another mature civilization they may have attempted, and in the long term failed, colonization; they may have tried, and in the long term failed, isolation; or they may have chosen genocide. In the nineteenth and twentieth centuries, modernization generated such violent civilizational competition. Inside Europe, for example, the catastrophic first half of the twentieth century ended in two world wars and the Holocaust. Outside Europe, modernization fostered imperialism and colonial oppression on a global scale.

Typically, however, the relations within and between civilizations are embedded in a more encompassing ecumene, today's global world. Most civilizational encounters are peaceful and are defined by processes of cultural borrowing. Donald Puchala (2003: 138–9) argues that the global civilization of modernity is most readily encountered in the cosmopolis rather than in the hinterlands of different civilizations. New York, Beijing, Hong Kong, Tokyo, Paris, and Nairobi are the "brewing kettles" for the civilizational processes that Elias has analyzed within the specific historical context of Europe. They are now occurring on a global scale under the labels of Americanization, Europeanization, Sinicization, Japanization, Indianization, and Islamicization. Such processes become unidirectional only when the level of development between different civilizational configurations is highly asymmetric. The profiles between highly modern and less modern societies within one civilization typically diverge more than the profiles of different societies at similar stages of development in different civilizations. Contra Huntington, the clash, if indeed there is one, is thus occurring within rather than between civilizations (Senghaas 1998: 6).

In the future, we may well be heading toward a clash and potential violence of a different sort. It would implicate Toynbee's capital C civilization – in the singular. All of humankind and many other species and ecosystems sharing planet Earth are confronting a variety of threats to Civilization's ongoing physical viability. In this formulation, the essentialism of Civilizational identity is physical rather than primordial, discursive, or dispositional. It may act as a spur to social and political movements for a common Civilizational community of fate, somewhat analogously to earlier national communities of fate. But, even in this formulation of a different kind of Civilizational clash, politics (of science, social movement, education, and many other domains) will continue to be central. It remains an open question whether plural and pluralist civilizations harbor sufficient innovative potential and learning capacities to generate successful coping strategies for defending Civilization.

The following chapters (2–7) focus on six civilizational complexes – America, Europe, China, Japan, India, and Islam. They are illustrative, not exhaustive, and do not advance a specific viewpoint. These chapters provide instead preliminary evidence for an approach that stresses pluralism and plurality and proceeds eclectically by exploring dispositional, discursive, and primordial approaches. Patrick Jackson concludes the book in Chapter 8 with a theoretically inclined analysis that picks up some of the threads of this chapter.

Some will object that the civilizations discussed in this book are all part of one global world. And it is surely true that all six are embedded in one global civilization of modernity. But this does not free us from understanding plural and pluralist civilizations as shapers of multiple modernities. Others may object that America and Europe, on the one hand, and China and Japan (and perhaps even India), on the other, are not really distinct civilizations. Instead they should be grouped, as they often are by common language, into the broader categories of "West" and "East." Such binary distinction is misleading, this book argues, when applied, specifically, to Islam and, more generally, to the analysis of multiple actors, traditions, and processes that are characteristic of civilizations.

The opening line of Rudyard Kipling's 1899 poem "The Ballad of East and

West" suggests that the two shall never meet. This book disagrees. Civilizations are most similar not in their cultural coherence and isolation or tendency toward clash but in their pluralist differences, in their plurality, and in their encounters and engagements. We should resist the temptation toward excessive simplification, focusing only on clashes, encounters, or engagements. Instead, we should be ready to acknowledge the possibility of the co-occurrence of these outcomes and, in the future, perform the empirical analysis that permits us to distinguish among the conditions leading to one or several of these different outcomes. Encounters and engagements generate what Kwame Anthony Appiah (2006: 101) has called a "contaminated cosmopolitanism." This concept captures nicely the messy co-occurrence of sameness and difference that civilizational analysis illuminates as *the* defining trait of a world of plural and pluralist civilizations.

Notes

1 For their helpful comments and critical suggestions on earlier drafts of this chapter, I would like to thank my fellow authors in this book, who have been enormously generous in helping me along. I also thank all the members of the Cornell International Relations Faculty Seminar who gave an earlier draft a close reading and searching discussion. I have also benefited greatly from the critical comments and suggestions of Michael Barnett, Peter Gourevitch, Mary Katzenstein, Robert Keohane, Stephen Krasner, David Laitin, John Meyer, Daniel Nexon, Joseph Nye, Andrew Phillips, Leonard Seabrooke, Richard Swedberg, Bassam Tibi, and Ike Wilson. Two anonymous readers for Routledge offered detailed comments, informed by insightful theoretical and shrewd editorial judgments. In addition, I have received very helpful general reactions and specific comments on early empirical fragments of this paper from Durba Ghosh, Victor Koschmann, Mary Katzenstein, Shawkat Toorawa, and Robert Travers.
2 The openings of Chapters 6 and 7 by Susanne Rudolph and Bruce Lawrence have greatly influenced my thinking about the opening paragraph of this chapter. See also Arnason (2003a: 1).
3 I do not engage here the important and voluminous research program of David Wilkinson (1994, 1995, 1996, 1999, 2004; and Wilkinson and Tsirel 2006). Adhering to a network conceptualization of civilizations, Wilkinson is interested in measuring over millennia the power concentrations of different world and regional systems. This makes him less interested in the cultural aspects of civilizations, which he regards as politically ephemeral and analytically unworkable. His important work thus differs on two central points from the focus of this chapter: he is interested neither in how material capabilities are socially embedded nor in the relational aspects of power complexes (see also Puchala 2003: 121–3). By the same token, I share McNeill's (1990: 8) later skepticism concerning the definition of the concept of civilization on which he himself had relied in his *The Rise of the West* published in 1963, and which also informs Wilkinson's work: as societies in which occupational specialization has allowed the emergence of high skills in different domains of life. This definition may be useful to distinguish between Neolithic village societies and early civilizations; but it fails to make meaningful differentiations between the subsequent rise of a plurality of internally pluralist civilizations.

4 The concept of civilization is closely linked to the concept of culture, although in distinctly different ways in France, Germany, and Britain. Culture is variously defined as a "way of life" (Bagby), a "web of significance" (Geertz), a "set of public meaningful forms" (Hannerz), and as having its "own mentality" (Sorokin) (Puchala 1997: 7–8).

5 Lawrence Harrison (2006; Harrison and Huntington 2000) shares with Huntington's civilizational thesis and Huntington's analysis of America the view that national cultures are organized around core values; in the terms of this analysis, they are dispositional. To the extent that Harrison covers religion, his analysis overlaps with Huntington's. But, in contrast to Huntington, Harrison is much more attuned to and interested in the political conditions that affect cultural change.

6 The argument about intercivilizational dialogue is open to question. When the study of Truth is believed to be at stake, rather than intellectual engagements over rival truths, insistence on dialogue can also be viewed as a form of intellectual oppression and, in any case, is beside the point. See Jenco (2005).

7 In this view, actors are constituted by both their social relations and their corporate identities, intrinsic qualities that constitute actor individuality (Wendt 1996: 50–51). Furthermore, Hayward Alker (2007: 54–6) rightly insists that, even if we acknowledge the importance of the discursive turn, it would be a bit unsettling not to take account of the fact that we are living through a scientific revolution that is giving us dramatic new insights into the intrinsic characteristics and dispositions of individuals. Why would we want to eliminate altogether from political analysis a category, just as it is being remapped by exciting advances in the life sciences? The extent to which we privilege dispositional, discursive, or eclectic conceptualizations should be judged pragmatically, as a matter of empirical research strategy. It should be noted that elsewhere Jackson and Nexon (1999: 307–9) have made a similar intellectual move. They introduce the category of "project" as a special kind of civilizational constellation with agent properties. For them, a project is a social entity that makes choices and has causal power. All projects are constellations, but not all constellations are projects. The existence of civilizational projects, how they form and how they change, must be a subject of inquiry and cannot simply be taken for granted, reduced to more fundamental units, or explained in terms of external shocks. We should analyze the processes that make civilizational projects what they are, without precluding a focus on what they do. Common rhetorical tropes about civilizational boundaries typically refer to broad and diffuse actors which can accommodate other actors, such as states or nations, that are nested within them. In contrast to state and nation, appeals to civilizational boundaries are open to virtually anyone and in any political site (Jackson 2007: 46–7).

8 Huntington's analysis offers a good illustration of this point when he writes:

> civilizations have no clear-cut boundaries and no precise beginnings and endings. People can and do redefine their identities and, as a result, the composition and shapes of civilizations change over time. The cultures of peoples interact and overlap. The extent to which the cultures of civilizations resemble or differ from each other also varies considerably. Civilizations are nonetheless meaningful entities, and while the lines between them are seldom sharp, they are real.
>
> (Huntington 1996: 43)

With this brief paragraph, Huntington elegantly circumvents the many difficulties raised by discursive and dispositional styles of analysis. Even though he concedes (ibid.: 44) that civilizations are not political entities that negotiate treaties, fight wars, or do any of the other things that governments do; simply postulating the reality of civilizations and thus reifying his basic unit of analysis makes it possible for him to treat civilizations as if they were actors that clash, balance, and behave like governments.

9   Nelson (1973: 96–7) locates a different kind of "axial shift" in the twelfth and thirteenth centuries, which witnessed an intermingling between Western Christianity and Islam, Byzantine Christianity, the Mongols, China, Africa, and the Jews. Nelson's dating is important theoretically because it highlights the decisive role of intercivilizational and transcivilizational encounters in Afro-Eurasia, a first instance of what today we call globalization (Arnason 2003a: 228). See also McNeill (1990) and Pollock (2006).

10 My summary of Eisenstadt's encompassing thought and voluminous writings (2004b, 2003, 2001, 2000a, 2000b, 2000c, 2000d, 1999a, 1999b, 1998a, 1998b, 1996, 1992a, 1992b, 1987, 1986, 1982, 1963; Arnason 2003a) is indebted to Spohn's (2001) and Mandalios's (2003: 73–6) discussions. Eisenstadt's scholarship on this topic is a partial revision of his own writings on modernization dating back to the 1950s and 1960s, and a forceful dissent from contemporary globalization theory and the philosophical discourse on modernity and post-modernity.

11 The following discussion draws heavily on Collins (2004).

12 Benjamin Nelson's (1973) work has important similarities to that of Elias (Holzner 1982; Mandalios 2003: 70–73). Ribeiro (1968) also writes about the civilizational process, although from a perspective and with empirical material that differs substantially from Elias.

13 Whether or not the Mongol empire, the largest in history, was in fact a civilization remains an issue of debate among historians. The case is relevant since Chua (2007: xxxi, 124–5, 328–33) interestingly asks whether the Mongol rather than the Roman empire (James 2006) offers the more relevant historical comparison for the United States today. But if what Ping-ti Ho (1998: 139) argues for Mongol China were to be true more generally – Mongol cosmopolitanism as a one-way street of reception – then neither the Mongols nor Rome offers an adequate historical analogy for the US civilizational imperium. Its greatest strength is to be aligned with a global ecumene and two-way processes of intercivilizational exchanges, resting on the provision of political leadership overseeing weak rules of intercivilizational engagement rather than on putting military boots on the ground. The attack of the Bush administration on Iraq illustrates how quickly political disaster follows from adhering to policies that contradict this inner logic of imperium.

14 Terminologically, an Islamicist is a specialization in Islam and an Islamist is a believer; Islamicization describes various processes involving Islamic civilization, Islamization the spread only of sharia law. Since its analysis goes well beyond religion, throughout this chapter I refer to Islamicist and Islamicization.

2 The United States as a civilizational leader

James Kurth

For much of the twentieth century, the United States claimed to be the leader and defender of Western civilization. More recently, it has claimed to be the leader and defender of globalization, or of a new global civilization. This chapter discusses the American conceptions of these two successive civilizations and of the US role within them. In doing so, we will examine different kinds of civilization, particularly between what Shmuel Eisenstadt and others have termed "Axial Age" civilizations versus "modern" civilizations. Our particular focus will be upon (1) the successive development and transformation of the Classical, Christian, Western, and contemporary global civilizations; and (2) the ascendancy of the United States to the role of the leading state of the two civilizations of the modern age, first the Western civilization and now the global one.

We will discuss the distinctive conception of Western civilization that developed within the United States, one that was derived from the original American religion, Reform Protestantism, and its secular descendant, the American Creed. After World War II and under US hegemony, this American conception replaced earlier European ones, which had undergone a sort of decline and fall. In turn, since the 1960s, this American conception of Western civilization has undergone its own decline and fall, both within Europe and within the United States itself, as the American conception has been reinvented – this time as globalization or global civilization – in a great civilizational contest within America itself. The resulting conception of global civilization has made America the principal adversary and target of particular repositories and remnants of the old Axial Age civilizations. These include China, India, Iran and Shiite Islam, and Sunni Islam and its transnational networks.

Introduction and overview

Conventional interpretations of Western civilization often described it as having three main sources: Classical culture, the Christian religion, and the modern Enlightenment (Kurth 2003). The US conception and definition of Western civilization did draw upon these sources. However, the American version of Christianity was very much a Protestant, and particularly a Reform Protestant (e.g. Calvinist) one rather than a Roman Catholic one. And its version of the Enlightenment was very much a British or Anglo-American one rather than a French or continental one.

Then, after a period during which it was the leading power of Western civilization, the United States, by a complex process which we shall discuss, left behind this role and became instead the leading power of a successor civilization, which was global civilization, and which included regions beyond any earlier definition of the West. Indeed, global civilization now seemed to incorporate many older civilizations in addition to the Western one, or at least incorporate the business elites of these civilizations. But, in large measure, the US conception still derived from its original Reform Protestant and British Enlightenment origins.

Social interpreters sometimes distinguish between the *dispositional* and the *discursive* features of a society. The former refers more or less to the actual institutions, processes and practices of the society, and the latter to its public ideologies, discourse, and rhetoric.

The American notions of what Western civilization was did indeed correspond to many of the actual institutions, processes, and practices in various regions – that is, to their dispositional features. But the fit between the American notions and the actual realities was less than perfect with respect to the countries of Western Europe which had a Roman Catholic tradition and a continental Enlightenment tradition. It was even less perfect with respect to Latin America and, obviously, Japan.

Nevertheless, American elites developed their particular notions of what Western civilization was into an elaborate ideology, discourse, and rhetoric – that is, discursive features. Consequently, the gap between American ideology and regional realities, between the discursive and the dispositional, widened as that ideology was projected further and further away from the Reform Protestant and British Enlightenment core, into countries with Roman Catholic and continental Enlightenment traditions.

When the United States was overwhelmingly the greatest military power and the largest economic power in the West, its ideology of Western civilization was more or less accepted by the various countries within the West. However, a decline in that power would inevitably lead to changes in that acceptance. Similarly, when the American elite was overwhelmingly composed of people who were Protestant and British in their origins and traditions (that is, White Anglo-Saxon Protestants, or WASPs), their ideology of Western civilization was more or less accepted by various ethnic groups within the United States. However, a decline in their power would inevitably lead to changes in that acceptance.

As it happened, in the 1960s there were great changes in regard to both the international and the domestic nature of American power. The revival of the Western European economies and the rise of the Japanese one reduced the attractiveness of American ideas about the economy. And the rise of non-

WASP groups into the American elite, as well as the rise of ethnic and racial groups of non-Western origin (first African-Americans and then Latino-Americans and Asian-Americans), reduced the attractiveness of elite ideas about culture and indeed of any ideas about Western civilization. Thus, by the end of the 1960s, there was little constituency left within the countries of the West, even within the United States itself, for an identity and ideology of Western civilization. As we shall see, this laid the foundation for a whole new civilizational discourse within the American elite. The ideology of *Western* civilization was replaced by an ideology of *global* civilization (Kurth 2001a).

In a pattern similar to the earlier one, these later American notions of what global civilization was did indeed correspond to many of the new actual realities, particularly those of the new business elites, in older civilizations around the globe – that is, it did correspond to their dispositional features. This was especially the case with the business elites of Europe. But the fit between the American ideology of global civilization – which was usually called "globalization" – and the actual realities was less than perfect with respect to those regions (and civilizations) which were beyond what, by any definition, had been part of the West – for example, China, India, and various Muslim countries. Consequently, the gap between American ideology and regional realities, between the discursive and the dispositional, widened as that ideology was projected further and further away from its American core, which was still largely a product of its original Reform Protestant and British Enlightenment origins. Thus, by the middle of the first decade of the twenty-first century, there was already increasing evidence that many people in other civilizations were rejecting many elements of the American ideology of globalization, of global civilization. There was even increasing evidence that this was true of business elites in these other civilizations, especially after the debacle of the US financial system in 2008 and the ensuing global economic crisis.

The United States was thus the leading power for about two decades (from the 1940s to the late 1960s) of something that it called Western civilization, and its leadership was more or less accepted by the other countries within that civilization. There then followed another period of about two decades (from the late 1960s to the late 1980s) when the United States was still the leading power of the countries in the West, but there was no longer much discourse about Western civilization. Then the United States was the leading power, once more for about two decades (from the late 1980s to the late 2000s), of something that it called globalization, of a global civilization, and its leadership was again more or less accepted by the business elites of the older civilizations which were now operating within this new global civilization. And so the obvious question today, on the eve of a new decade and perhaps of a new era, is in what sense will the United States be the leader of a civilization in the future and what will that civilization be? And perhaps another question is in what sense will this be a civilization at all?

Any contemporary discussion of civilizations will be shaped by the paradigm which Samuel Huntington presented in his epic *The Clash of Civilizations and the Remaking of World Order* (1996). Most of the other authors in the present volume differ from Huntington in important ways, and so it will be appropriate for me to describe my own position toward his paradigm.

Huntington's important and controversial arguments include the following: it is a particular religion which serves as the basic foundation and central essence of a civilization. Since religions reach deep into a society and into the identities of the people within it, and since they also endure for a long time, this means that civilizations have certain consistencies and continuities that are deeply rooted and long-lasting. Since different religions often conflict and clash with each other, this also means that different civilizations will do so.

For the most part, I agree with Huntington's controversial arguments about the centrality of religions and the consequences that they have for civilizations. However, I amend and even differ from his argument in certain ways. I will argue that, in the civilization which was formed by Western Christianity, a particular religion – Protestantism – developed and that this religion was very different from all previous religions. There also developed a particular secular worldview – the Enlightenment – which was very different from the previous religions. Together, Protestantism and the Enlightenment generated a dynamism which utterly transformed the Western Christian civilization and brought about the creation of the modern secular civilizations, first the Western one and then the contemporary global one. In other words, one of the greatest conflicts and clashes of civilizations has occurred within the West itself, between traditional Christian civilization and modern secular ones.

Moreover, this clash between a traditional religious civilization and modern secular ones has occurred and is still occurring within the other civilizations, particularly those that are the heirs to the Axial Age religions. It is not only within the West, but also within the rest, where some of the most intense clashes of civilization can be found. Since Shmuel Eisenstadt has written illuminatingly about the conflicts between the civilizations of the Axial Age and the civilizations of modernity, my own analysis will draw much from his. Overall, then, my approach represents a particular combination of both Huntington and Eisenstadt.

From the Axial Age to Christian civilization

The Axial Age civilizations: The great religious transformations

Shmuel Eisenstadt (and before him Karl Jaspers) proposed an important and fundamental way of thinking about civilizations. Eisenstadt argues that the origins of most of the great civilizations of today lie in a particular period, the "Axial Age," which occurred two and a half millennia ago – that is, around the sixth century BCE. It was at this time that several regions of the world (for example, China, India, Persia, Judea, and Greece) underwent a great religious transformation. The new religions became the basis for new civilizations. The legacies of these religions and civilizations persist even today, and they continue to shape the great conflicts (and also the modes of cooperation which often are parallel and interacting with these conflicts) of our own time (Eisenstadt 1986).

These several religious transformations were of course different from each other in many important ways. But they generally shared several characteristics which set them apart from the worldviews and ways of life that existed before the Axial Age, which continued to exist for millennia in other regions of the world (for example, Africa, pre-Columbian America, and, in an anomalous way, even Japan) and which, as we shall controversially argue, have reappeared in much of the modern and global civilization of our own time.

Recapitulating Eisenstadt (and Peter Katzenstein's overview essay in this project), we observe that the great religious transformations of the Axial Age comprised three component transformations or shifts of societal focus: (1) from human needs to divine norms; (2) from adaptive rationality to introspective self-reflection; and (3) from human or societal purpose to human, including personal, freedom. Together, these shifts of societal focus in effect amounted to raising a society up and realigning it on an entirely new axis – a great transformation indeed.

It is, however, natural (in several senses of the word) that after a time a society, or at least important elements within it, will be drawn back to the old ways of looking at the world and of doing things – that is, to become less focused upon the transcendent and more upon the immanent, to become less reflective and more instrumental, and to become less personal or individual and more collective or societal. In other words, it is common for many elements of a society to "fall away," to become "worldly" again, and, indeed, to revert to "the natural man." However, other elements of the society will resist and contest this natural (and naturalizing) process and will seek to recall the society to the grand transcendent vision of their earlier great religious transformation.

Thus, all Axial Age civilizations have developed fundamentalist movements within their core religions and, therefore, in their core states. These movements continually resurrect religious traditions, and, in doing so, they continually restructure their core states (Eisenstadt 1999a).

This process of continual resurrection and restructuring is shaped by the creative tensions between four contrasting polarities or priorities: (1) the transcendental versus the mundane; (2) the universal versus the particular; (3) the totalist versus the pluralist; and (4) the orthodox versus the heterodox. These creative tensions are not just expressed in contrasting intellectual (and theological and ideological) conceptions; they are embodied in contesting elements or groups within the civilization and its core state.

Adding to Eisenstadt and Katzenstein, we can observe that most of the Axial Age religions had the following features:

(1) texts, usually sacred scriptures ("In the beginning was the Word"). The learning of these *texts* was sometimes enhanced by *tests* (producing a sort of literary "TNT"), most famously in traditional China, beginning with the Tang dynasty.

(2) interpretation of the texts by a literate, learned group – for example, a rabbinate (Judea), scholar-gentry (China), or priesthood (as would later develop in Christianity). This resulted in a perpetual tension between the sacred *word* and the actual *world* – that is, between the transcendental and the mundane. This in turn resulted in further institutionalized tensions between the following: (a) the priests and the princes (who claimed to be the rulers of worldly life); (b) the priests and the prophets (who claimed that they had more direct revelation of the divine than did the priests); (c) the priests and the people (whose conditions of life were very different from the priestly elite and who naturally developed very different perspectives).

In short, in almost all of the Axial Age civilizations, there were institutionalized tensions between different centers of power. (However, an important exception to these particular kinds of institutionalized tensions, each of which involved priests, was classical Greece and Rome, where priests were not very central to the society.)

The Classical civilization: Greece and Rome

From the perspective of most interpreters of the Western civilization, its principal origins lay in one of the earlier Axial Age civilizations: the civilization formed by ancient Greece and Rome which has often been termed the Classical civilization. Classical civilization has been seen as the first of several sources of Western civilization and of several of its characteristic concepts and practices. In politics, for example, Greece contributed the idea of a republic, while Rome contributed that of an empire. Similarly, Greece contributed the idea of liberty, and Rome that of law. When combined, these ideas gave rise to the important concept of liberty under law, which many interpreters hold to be a distinctive, or at least an especially pronounced, feature of Western civilization when compared with most other civilizations.

As for a core state, it was not Greece that provided this role for Classical civilization, although Athens aspired to it during the Peloponnesian War and Macedonia sought it under Alexander the Great. Instead, it was of course Rome that eventually became the core state for Classical civilization. Indeed, the Roman achievement in this role was so successful and impressive that Rome and its empire set the standard for what a core state and empire should be, especially in the minds of its successor states in both Western Europe (or the lands of Roman Catholicism) and Eastern Europe (the lands of Eastern Orthodoxy) and for a millennium and a half after the final fall of Rome (the Western Roman Empire) in the fifth century.

The Christian civilization: the union of the Classical and the Jewish civilizations

This core state of the Classical civilization, Rome, famously and utterly destroyed the core state of the Jewish civilization, Judea, in 70 CE. However, there soon came about a union of the two civilizations (in other words, the union of Athens/Rome and Jerusalem) in the remarkable form of Christianity. This new religion eventually formed the Christian civilization, which until the nineteenth century was often termed Christendom. As a union of two civilizations, Christendom was in many ways unique among the great civilizations (although this uniqueness is now a disputed point among scholars). In any event, the union of elements of the Classical and Jewish civilizations certainly incorporated yet another creative and distinct tension within the new Christian civilization.

In contrast to the *union* of the Classical and the Jewish civilizations within the Christian civilization, there eventually came yet another new religion which represented the *supersession* of both major portions of the Christian civilization and surviving remnants of the Jewish civilization, as well as of earlier pagan (that is, pre-Axial Age) societies within the region of Arabia. This supersessionist religion was Islam, and it soon conquered not only the southern peripheries of the Christian civilization but also the core of the Persian civilization.

The Western or Latin half of the Christian civilization became the second source of what would eventually become Western civilization. (Similarly, the Eastern or Greek half, centered upon the Byzantine empire, became the second source of what many interpreters have seen as the Eastern Orthodox civilization.) Western Christianity contributed several central concepts and practices to Western civilization. Christian theology established the sanctity of the individual believer and called for obedience to an authority (Christ) higher than any secular ruler (Caesar), ideas that further refined and supported the concept of liberty under law. Christian institutions, particularly the papacy of the Roman Catholic Church and its ongoing struggle with the Holy Roman emperor and local monarchs, bequeathed the idea of a separation, and therefore a limitation, of powers. Many interpreters hold these ideas of the sanctity of the individual and the limitation of powers also to be distinctive, or at least especially pronounced, features of Western civilization.

After the fall of the Western Roman empire, Western or Latin Christendom never had a real core state. The Holy Roman empire, as its name proclaimed, aspired to be this, but its repeated failures over many centuries simply added another creative tension to the Western Christian civilization, this one being between priests and princes (at the highest level between the Holy Roman empire and the Roman Catholic papacy), which would eventually mature into the distinctively Western tension between church and state.

The splitting of the Christian civilization

Then, after a millennium of widely and deeply dispersed power centers and of the myriad of tensions (both creative and destructive) which attended this dispersal, Western Christendom during the Reformation split into two religions – Catholicism and Protestantism – with the latter in turn splitting into many denominations. This splitting into different religions had several consequences which were so fundamental and so powerful that they would eventually bring about the transformation of Western Christendom into the two new and different civilizations of the modern era, first the Western civilization and then the contemporary global civilization.

First, the splitting of Western Christendom into different religions accelerated and accentuated the splitting of the civilization into many states and eventually – after the Wars of Religion, which culminated in the Thirty Years' War (1618–48) – the development of the concept of a balance of power between these states. This concept of a balance between competing states, whose behavior was motivated far more by power calculations than by religious convictions, was especially pronounced in Europe, and it would greatly contribute to the secularization of European political and social elites.

Second, the Protestant religion turned out to be such a peculiar religion that it challenged not only the traditional Christian religion but many principles and practices of other religions as well, including those of the Axial Age. Thus it would also greatly contribute to the secularization of European political and social elites. However, in addition, this peculiar religion of Protestantism greatly shaped the distinctive national identity of what would eventually become the core state of the Western civilization and, indeed, the core state of the contemporary global civilization, the United States. And, as we shall see, the tensions between the Protestant religion and previous religions, on the one hand, and between the Protestant religion and succeeding secular worldviews, on the other, have generated a good deal of the dynamism and conflicts characteristic of the modern age, right down to the present time.

From the Protestant Reformation to the American Creed

Protestantism versus all other religions

Protestantism was a protest, a protest against the form that the Christian religion had taken in the Roman Catholicism of the late Middle Ages and the Renaissance. The Protestant Reformation was an effort to restore the Christian religion to the original faith expressed in the New Covenant or New Testament of the Bible (Kurth 1998) (the word testament means covenant). It was very much one of those fundamentalist movements that are so characteristic of Axial Age civilizations.

The Protestant reformers protested against numerous features of the Roman Catholic Church, including such familiar ones as the authority of the pope, the role of the Virgin Mary, and the selling of indulgences. But the really central and fundamental issues involved the way in which the Christian believer reached a state of salvation and the roles that the priestly hierarchy and the parish community played in the process. The Roman Catholic Church taught that the Christian believer reached salvation through the mediation of the priestly hierarchy and through participation in the parish community. The hierarchy and the community in combination yielded the surest path to salvation, which was participation in communal sacraments and rituals that were administered by the hierarchy.

The Protestant reformers protested against the idea that the believer *achieves* salvation through a hierarchy or a community, or even the two in combination. Although many of the reformers accepted hierarchy and community for certain purposes, such as church governance and collective undertakings, they rejected them for the most important of purposes, reaching the state of salvation. Rather, the believer *receives* salvation through an act of grace by God. This grace produces in its recipient the faith in God and in salvation that converts him into a believer.

The believer can achieve greater knowledge of God, however, through his reading of the holy scriptures. Like many Axial Age religions, but even more so, Protestantism placed great emphasis on the Word, as evidenced in the writings of the Bible. But this reading did not necessarily require the interpretations of a hierarchy or a community. Indeed, these might actually impede the right interpretation of the Bible by the individual believer.

All religions are unique, but Protestantism is more unique than all the others. No other religion is so critical of hierarchy and community, or of the traditions and customs that go with them (and therefore critical of much of what makes up a civilization). Indeed, most other religions are based upon hierarchy or community (in addition to Roman Catholicism, also Eastern Orthodoxy, Judaism, Islam, Hinduism, Confucianism, and even, to a degree, Buddhism). At its doctrinal base, however, Protestantism is anti-hierarchy and anti-community. The Protestant reformers therefore sought to remove hierarchy and community so that the individual Christian believer could have a direct relationship with God. (More accurately and subtly, so that the individual believer could have a relationship with God directly through the second person of the Holy Trinity, Jesus Christ, and so that he could receive salvation from God directly from the third person of the Holy Trinity, the Holy Spirit.)

The removal of hierarchy and community, traditions and customs – of any earthly intermediaries between the individual and God – strips away, at least for the most important purposes, any local, parochial, cultural, or national characteristics of the believer. In principle, grace, faith, and salvation can be received by anyone in the world; they are truly universal or catholic, in the original sense of the latter term. The Protestant reformers saw the vast variety of other religions, cultures, and civilizations (including all the other Axial Age civilizations) through a universal perspective, one that was even more universal than that of the Roman Catholic Church. This put them on a collision course with most of the other religions and therefore with the civilizations which these religions had produced.

The Protestant churches and church governance

Despite their doctrinal rejection of hierarchy and community for the purpose of salvation, many Protestant churches maintained some kind of hierarchy for purposes of church governance. The most hierarchical were those ruled by bishops and archbishops – the Lutherans (Germany and the Scandinavian countries), Anglicans (England), Episcopalians (the United States), and Methodists (England and the United States). (The word "episcopal" is derived from the Greek work for bishop.) Indeed, the organization of some of the churches in Europe, particularly the Anglican and Lutheran state churches, resembled closely that of the Roman Catholic Church, but with the pope removed and replaced by a "defender of the faith" in the form of the ruler of the state. The secular and political counterpart of this form of church governance, for both Roman Catholicism and this version of Protestantism, was of course monarchy.

Less hierarchical were those Protestant churches ruled by elders – the Calvinists (the Netherlands) and the Presbyterians (Scotland and the United States). (The word "presbyterian" is derived from the Greek word for elder.) Indeed, this form of organization looked rather like that of Judaism, around councils of rabbis. Here, the secular and political counterpart of church governance was aristocracy or oligarchy.

Least hierarchical were those Protestant churches ruled by the congregation themselves. Many of these were in the United States – the Congregationalists, the Baptists, and a vast variety of American denominational and especially non-denominational churches. Here, of course, the secular and political counterpart of church governance was democracy.

Despite their differences in regard to church governance and also similar differences in regard to community emphasis, however, all Protestant churches reject hierarchy and community as the means to salvation. At the level of fundamental theology and doctrine, Protestantism denies that hierarchy and community are of fundamental importance. Indeed, Protestants often assert that hierarchy and community, along with the traditions and customs that go with them, are obstacles to what is of fundamental importance – the way that the individual Christian believer reaches the state of salvation.

This Protestant rejection of hierarchy and community in regard to salvation eventually spread to their rejection in regard to other domains of life as well. First, some Protestant churches came to reject hierarchy and community in regard to church governance and collective undertakings. This was especially the case in the new United States, where the conjunction of the open frontier and the disestablishment of state churches enabled the flourishing of new unstructured and unconstraining denominations.

By the beginning of the nineteenth century, the Protestant rejection of hierarchy and community had spread to important arenas of temporal or secular life. Again, this was especially the case in the new United States. In the economic arena, the elimination of hierarchy (monopoly or oligopoly) and community (guilds or trade restrictions) meant the establishment of the free market. In the political arena, the elimination of hierarchy (monarchy or aristocracy) and community (traditions and customs) meant the establishment of liberal democracy (Mead 2007).

However, the free market could not be so free, nor the liberal democracy so liberal, that the result became anarchy. Although they could no longer be ordered by hierarchy and community, by tradition and custom, they had to be ordered by something. That something reflected the Protestant emphasis on written words and was a version of the written covenant between individual Protestant believers. In the economic arena, this was the written contract; in the political arena, it was the written constitution. Together, this meant that Protestant countries were especially inclined to value the centrality, the clarity, and the certainty of the rule of law rather than the decrees of rulers, and that their conceptions of that law were "hard" rather than soft.

Reform Protestantism and American national identity

Clearly, the Protestant religion was playing a pronounced role, a sort of archetypal one, on the westernmost frontier of Western Christianity, in that new and rising nation, the United States. But it was a distinctive version of Protestantism that largely performed this role and which did so much to shape the distinctive American national identity. This version was termed (somewhat confusingly) Reform Protestantism.

Reform Protestantism began, of course, with the Protestant Reformation, but specifically with the teachings of Jean Calvin. Calvinism began in Geneva and then spread to France, the Netherlands, and Britain. In England, Calvinism became Puritanism, which brought about the Civil War of the 1640s; in Scotland, it became Presbyterianism, which established a state church, the Church of Scotland. English Puritans and Scottish Presbyterians brought their versions of Reform Protestantism to America in the seventeenth century, and it became the dominant religion in New England and a prominent one in the other British colonies in North America (Hart and Muether 2007).

During the eighteenth century, and in both Britain and America, Reform Protestantism underwent a number of transformations (indeed, reformations) and divisions. Some of the new versions were called "dissenting" churches, and they included Methodists and Baptists, which by the early nineteenth century had become very large and popular denominations in

America. By the late nineteenth century, strict (for example, believers in biblical inerrancy) Reform Protestants were often called fundamentalists, and by the late twentieth century they were often called evangelicals. The diverse and widespread evangelical churches in America today, therefore, are the latest manifestation of a particular kind of the Christian religion, whose genealogy dates back to the Europe of almost half a millennium ago.

The division of American Protestantism into many dissenting churches and denominations was greatly facilitated by the existence of the western frontier. People dissatisfied for any reason with an existing, even established, church could in the end simply get up and go west (the "exit" option famously presented by Albert Hirschman in his book *Exit, Voice, and Loyalty* (1970)). The resulting multiplicity of dissenting churches readily became, with secularization, a multiplicity or pluralism of political factions. This, in turn, became the basis for several of the distinctive features of the Constitution of the United States (famously discussed by James Madison in *The Federalist*, number 10). These included the separation of powers in the Constitution itself and the non-establishment and free-exercise clauses of the First Amendment in the Bill of Rights.

By the early nineteenth century, therefore, religion in the United States had become characterized by a plurality of voluntary churches (for example, denominations or sects) that were not confined to any particular political unit or territory but instead were often spread throughout the wide area of the United States or even beyond. This enhanced a universalist sense of religious identity within these denominations, rather than a particularist one. And, in any one particular territory, the plurality of voluntary churches meant that there was a sort of marketplace of religions.

Whatever the versions, variations, and mutations of Reform Protestantism in the United States, however, they all shared in a thorough rejection of hierarchy and establishment in religious matters and, by extension, in political matters also; that is, they rejected the clam of religious authorities that the believer had an obligation *upward*. Moreover, they all shared in some degree a rejection of collectivity and community in religious matters and in political matters; that is, they rejected the claim of religious authorities that the believer had an obligation *outward*. Finally, they all shared in a thorough rejection of custom and tradition in religious and political matters; that is, they rejected the claim of religious authorities that the believer had an obligation *backward*. This triple rejection of binding ties upward, outward, and backward was a powerful impetus to what would become by the mid-nineteenth century the distinctive, widespread, and well-known phenomenon of American individualism.

The Civil Religion and the American Creed

The condition of Protestant pluralism had important implications for public life in the United States. Any public pronouncements on religious themes that honored citizens situated in one church were just as likely to offend those situated in another. This steadily drove public officials to a religious rhetoric of the least common and least offensive denominator, sometimes sounding more like Unitarianism than traditional Reform (and Trinitarian) Protestantism. This logic of religious pluralism was greatly reinforced by the substantial numbers of Roman Catholics and even Jews immigrating to the United States in the 1840s and after, driving public officials even further toward the rhetoric of the least common and least offensive denominator. This would be a public rhetoric that, while it would use conceptions that were congruent and congenial to the Reform Protestant ones, would make almost no references to religion at all. In regard to economic matters, the central conception was the free market; and in regard to political matters, it was liberal democracy. By the early nineteenth century, most Americans had come to believe that the only legitimate form of economics was the free market, ordered by written constructs, and that the only legitimate form of politics was liberal democracy, ordered by a written constitution. Americans had thus adopted a very pronounced belief and practice in the rule of law, and hard law at that. This was the mentality, really ideology, that was described so brilliantly and so beautifully by that young Frenchman who was both an aristocrat and a liberal, Alexis de Tocqueville, in his *Democracy in America* (1834).

Reform Protestant concepts thus provided a solid foundation for analogous and isomorphic secular ones, particularly economic enterprise, political liberty, and social equality. The religious and the political notions came together to form what became the American civil religion, which ever since the early nineteenth century has been a sort of least common denominator shared by large numbers, probably a large majority, of Americans.

Reform Protestantism had thus given birth to what by the early twentieth century would become the American Creed. The fundamental elements of that secular creed – free markets, liberal democracy, constitutionalism, the rule of law, and, at the core, individualism – were already fully in place in the United States by the early nineteenth century. For many Americans, the various old Protestant creeds would be replaced by the American Creed, which reached its fullest articulation in the first half of the twentieth century (Huntington 2004b). This American Creed definitely did not include as its elements hierarchy, community, tradition, and custom. Although it was not itself Protestant, it was clearly the product of a Reform Protestant culture and was a sort of secularized version of Reform Protestantism. The American Creed was the core of what Louis Hartz and others have since called the liberal tradition in America, but this liberal tradition was also very much a sort of secularized Reform Protestantism (Hartz 1955).

Beginning in the 1880s, there were new and massive waves of Roman Catholics and Jews immigrating to the United States, now coming from Southern and Eastern Europe. The American elites of the time were still largely Anglo-American and nominally Protestant in some sense, but for the most part they did not seek to convert the new immigrants to the Protestant religion. Rather they sought to assimilate them into the common ideology, the least common denominator, of the American Creed. These elites therefore undertook a massive and systematic program of Americanization, imposing on the new immigrants and on their children the English language, Anglo-American history, and American civics (Schlesinger 1998). The Anglo-American and Protestant elite was aided in its grand project of Americanization during this period by the booming US economy, which gave immigrants ample economic reasons to assimilate, and by the restrictive Immigration Act of 1924, which essentially halted immigration from Southern and Eastern Europe and allowed the Americanization project to operate upon and shape a settled mass.

This grand project of Americanization was relentless and even ruthless. It can be interpreted as a sort of American *Kulturkampf*, as a clash of contesting and authentic conceptions of what Western civilization and its institutions and practices should be. Many individuals were oppressed and victimized by it, and many rich and meaningful islands of different European cultures were swept away. These islands were the embodiments of authentic civilizational institutions and practices, which served as alternatives to the American ones. However, the achievements of the Americanization project were awesome, as well as awful. In particular, when the United States entered into its greatest struggles of the twentieth century, first World War II and then the Cold War, it did so more as a unified national state than as a divided multi-ethnic society. (Hitler consistently underestimated the United States because he thought it was the latter rather than the former; he was thinking that the US was still what it was at the time of World War I.) It was because of the Americanization project, therefore, that the United States had achieved enough unity and confidence that it could claim to be the leader and defender of Western civilization, first against the Nazis and then against the Soviets.

Indeed, one of the consequences of this grand project of Americanization was the spread within the American academic elite of the concept of the Western civilization. The political elite remained comfortable with the Americanization of the mass population. The academic elite (particularly at Harvard, Yale, Columbia, and Princeton), however, was in the business of teaching the elite of the future. For this purpose, simple Americanization was too rough and primitive. Rather than imposing Americanization unilaterally on people who were in some sense both European and American, it would be better to find a new common denominator for both Europeans and Americans. This became "Western civilization," at least as the Americans understood it – that is, with that civilization's core elements being the elements of the American Creed.

Much later, in the 1970s, the American Creed (and the liberal tradition) would themselves be replaced by a particular conception of universal human rights, or, more accurately, the elements of the American Creed would be generalized in universal norms. As we shall see, under the hegemony or leadership of the United States, first the American Creed became the core ideals of the modern Western civilization, and then universal human rights became the core ideals of the modern and contemporary global civilization.

From the Enlightenment to Western Civilization

The Enlightenment and the modern civilizations

While a new part of Western Christian civilization, the United States, was becoming a rising nation, one shaped very much by Reform Protestantism and its secular descendant, the American Creed, the original part of Western Christian civilization, Europe, was undergoing its own dramatic change, one shaped very much by a self-consciously secular worldview, the Enlightenment. Together, the changes in America and in Europe would produce two successive civilizations of the modern age, first the Western civilization and then the contemporary global civilization. Moreover, these changes amounted to a new great transformation, one that would eventually prove as fundamental as the great transformations of the Axial Age (Eisenstadt 2003). Indeed, as we shall argue, the great transformation of the modern age has gone far to reverse the epic achievements of the Axial Age.

The first of the modern civilizations was what came to be known as Western civilization, a civilization that existed more or less from the Enlightenment down to recent decades, over a period of about two centuries. The Western civilization in turn comprised two successive eras – the European one, which corresponded largely to the nineteenth century, and the American one, which corresponded to much of the twentieth century. The second modern civilization is the civilization in which we now live – that is, the global civilization. It is a civilization which represents the extension of the Western civilization to the furthest regions of the globe, far beyond its original core in Western Europe and its later core in North America. But, because of this vast extension, the global civilization is also a civilization which represents a new set of central ideas and creative tensions, which have displaced some of the earlier ideas and tensions that characterized the Western civilization. The most important of these new tensions are probably those between modern ideas and Axial Age ideas.

Many historians have seen the modern age beginning with the scientific and technological revolutions of the sixteenth and seventeenth centuries (for example, Galileo, Bacon, Descartes, and Newton) and the Enlightenment of the eighteenth century. Some interpreters even see the Enlightenment as the third great source of the Western civilization, following the first or Classical source and the second or Christian source. In particular, the Enlightenment provided Western civilization with the concepts and practices of liberal democracy, the free market, and the use of reason and science for making sense of the world. More particularly still, Britain's Glorious Revolution of 1688 emphasized liberty and constitutionalism, while the French Revolution of 1789 emphasized democracy and rationalism. The differences between the

British Enlightenment and the French or continental would give rise to important divisions within Western civilization during much of the nineteenth and twentieth centuries. This was the case in regard to the Industrial Revolution and the different responses to it; both state guidance of the economy and Marxist ideology played a much greater role on the continent than in Britain or the United States.

More negatively, the Enlightenment removed the Christian priesthood from what had been the Western Christian civilization. In doing so, it removed one of the pillars of that civilization and therefore the basis for one of its previous creative tensions. Moreover, the Enlightenment removed the sacred texts or the Word from the civilization, progressively replacing it with many diverse words (until now, in the Information Age, we are flooded by and immersed in an ocean of words.)

More radically, we believe, the Enlightenment (which in many ways lives on today, in the United States and Europe) consciously sought, and still seeks, to reverse the major innovations and great transformations of the Axial Age – that is, it seeks a shift of societal focus in at least three fundamental respects: (1) from divine norms back to human needs; (2) from introspective self-reflection back to adaptive rationality and practical intelligence; and, in the Marxist and nationalist versions of the Enlightenment, (3) from human or personal freedom back to human or societal purpose. For example, out of the Enlightenment there issued the Jacobinism of the French Revolution. And out of Jacobinism there eventually issued both communism and fascism, each of which certainly sought to subordinate human freedom to human purpose. (This is one example, however, of the important and consequential differences between the French and continental version of the Enlightenment and the British and Anglo-American version.)

Even more radically, the Enlightenment also represented a sort of return to the pre-Axial Age. It is not surprising, therefore, that the remaining remnants of the Axial Age civilizations – China, India, Iran (Persia) and Shiite Islamists, Sunni Islamists, and even Orthodox Jews and fundamentalist Christians – have rejected and reacted against the modern civilizations which have been so much shaped by the Enlightenment. Indeed, some Axial Age remnants – especially Shiite and Sunni Islamists and fundamentalist Christians – see the Enlightenment as a return to the ideas and beliefs which existed before the great religious achievements of the Axial Age and after, and thus as a return to a kind of paganism. They therefore see modern civilizations as actually being new pagan civilizations. Now, however, pagan civilization is on a giant, global scale (as with the contemporary global civilization).

These Axial Age remnants are thus now engaging in new versions of the continually recurring fundamentalist movements that have characterized the Axial Age civilizations – that is, movements against the continually recurring tendencies to "fall away," to become "worldly," and to revert to "the natural man." However, these new versions of fundamentalist movements can now also use Jacobin or oppositional-style methods – that is, modern-style methods – to achieve their aims (Eisenstadt 1999a). That is, they can combine the fundamentalist religious ideals and ends of the Axial Age civilizations with the modern means of the modern civilizations.

Western Civilization in its European era: from the Enlightenment to the decline of the European core

After the Enlightenment, the Western Christian civilization essentially became what would eventually be called Western civilization. The Enlightenment brought about the secularization of much of the intellectual class, the idea-bearing class, of what hitherto had been called Christendom. The remaining civilization was no longer a Christendom, in the sense of a Christian dominion, even though much of its ordinary population remained Christian. The French Revolution and the Industrial Revolution spread Enlightenment ideas and secularization to important parts of this population, although the Christian churches continued to be a vital force. But ever since the Enlightenment, it has not been accurate to refer to this civilization as Christendom.

Of course, the new civilization brought about by the Enlightenment had to call itself something. For a time in the late eighteenth and early nineteenth century, "Europe" became the preferred term for the civilization. But this was also the very time that saw the rise of European settlements in the New World to the status of independent nations. The most obvious and the most prominent of these new independent nations was, of course, the United States. This soon made impossible the term "European civilization."

For a brief and exuberant time in the nineteenth century, when this civilization seemed to be the only dynamic and growing one – indeed the only one around – and with all the others in manifest decline and decay, the preferred term was just "Civilization" itself. But this term, too, could not be sustained.

It was only at the beginning of the twentieth century that the term "Western civilization" was invented. The term registered the awareness that this civilization, unlike most others, no longer placed religion at its core. But it also registered awareness that this civilization was only one among many. It was a civilization past the enthusiasms of faith and also past the exuberance of being so blessed that it was in a class by itself. In short, the very term Western civilization was the product of a high degree of intellectualism, perhaps even a sickly self-consciousness. The term was itself an early sign of the decline of the civilization. It is no accident that, almost as soon as it was invented, it began to be used in this pessimistic context, as in Oswald Spengler's *The Decline of the West* (1918). Had the term Western civilization been left in the hands, or rather the minds, of Europeans alone, it probably would have had only a short and unhappy life. But, as we shall see, it was the New World that would be called in to redress the pessimism of the Old. In particular, the revival and reinvention of Western civilization would be a great project of the United States.

However, during the first century of this European or Western civilization (more or less corresponding to the nineteenth century), much was going on to deprive it of a coherent identity even within its original European core. At the same time that Christendom was becoming European or Western civilization, that civilization itself was actually becoming a series and collection of European nationalisms. These, as the historian Michael Burleigh has demonstrated, were really a series of secular religions or neo-paganisms (Burleigh 2007, 2005; Kurth 2001b).

Several of these European nationalisms aspired to become the hegemonic power in Europe, and therefore the core state of Western civilization. These "bids for hegemony," engaged in successively by Napoleonic France, imperial Germany, and National Socialist Germany, have been much discussed by historians of international politics. Each of these bids for European hegemony failed, but only during the course and at the cost of terrible world wars (the Napoleonic Wars, World War I, and World War II).

At the same time, Britain was establishing a different kind of hegemony, or at least leadership, in the world beyond Europe (Ferguson 2002). Karl Polanyi and others have argued that this hegemony (1) was based upon naval forces and financial power, rather than upon land forces, and (2) was often exercised through spheres of influence or indirect rule, rather than through military occupation or direct rule (Polanyi 1957). This was largely true with respect to Britain's role in Latin America and in much of Africa. However, the British role (and the British Raj) in India performed very much like a traditional land power, using the British-commanded Indian Army to control South Asia and to project British influence into much of the Middle East.

Later, in the twentieth century, the United States would take up the kind of British hegemony which was based upon naval forces and financial power and was exercised through spheres of influence and indirect rule. Some strategic analysts saw this as establishing a distinctively Anglo-American way of hegemony and therefore Anglo-American tradition in international and world politics (Mead 2007). This Anglo-American tradition would turn out to be the perfect preparation for the eventual American project of globalization at the end of the twentieth century.

Finally, in 1945 (which the utterly defeated Germans have referred to as "Year 0"), after the European core of the Western civilization had been greatly and gravely damaged, the civilization at last received a core state, which was the United States. The United States now claimed that it best represented the ideals and values of Western civilization, and therefore that it was not only the core state but also the civilizational state of Western civilization. But, as we saw above, the Americans had their own distinctive conceptions about what Western civilization was, conceptions which were based upon Reform Protestantism and the American Creed.

Western civilization in its American era: from World War I to the end of the Cold War

At the beginning of the twentieth century, the rising power of the United States had begun to make its economic influence felt in Europe. Then, in World War I, the US extended its actual military power there. At the same time, Americans breathed a new meaning into the term Western civilization, first as they dealt with European immigrants in America and then as they dealt with European nations in Europe itself. For Americans in the first decades of the twentieth century, Western civilization was the ideas of "individualism, liberalism, constitutionalism, human rights, equality, liberty, the rule of law, democracy, free markets, the separation of church and state" (Huntington 1996). As we have seen, this particular set of ideas was often called the "American Creed," which was very much a product of secularized Reform Protestantism.

With the Americans, the new *content* of Western civilization thus became the American Creed. But this content really represented only the most western part of Western civilization – for example, the British or Anglo-American Enlightenment, rather than the French or continental Enlightenment which characterized other parts of Western Europe or, a fortiori, the anti-Enlightenment (and earlier, the Counter-Reformation) which characterized Central Europe, especially the Habsburg empire.

Conversely, the new *context* for the American Creed became Western civilization. The growing influence of the United States, followed in the two world wars by its growing power, spread the ideas of the American Creed eastward, first to Western Europe and then to much of Central Europe.

When the United States came to Europe during the first half of the twentieth century, the combination of the new American energy and the old European imagery gave the American conception of Western civilization both power and legitimacy, in America as well as Europe. This power helped the United States win both World War II against National Socialist Germany and the Cold War against the Soviet Union, and this legitimacy helped it to order the long peace within Western Europe that was so much intertwined with that Cold War.

Of course, there were very substantial groups in Europe who contested this American conception of Western civilization, which they saw as being very particular and narrow and even flat and superficial. This was true even during the Cold War, when the Soviet Union seemed to be an obvious and proximate threat to Western civilization. The opponents of the American conception could be found on both the right and the left. They included traditional Catholics (heirs to the Counter-Reformation) and cultural conservatives, as well as radical Marxists (heirs to the continental Enlightenment) and cultural leftists. However, the United States made a grand coalition in Europe with the center-right (for example, Christian Democrats) and the center-left (for example, Social Democrats), and with these allies it largely succeeded in marginalizing and containing its opponents (Judt 2005).

Under the United States, therefore, the conception of Western civilization experienced a sort of heroic age in the mid-twentieth century. This was, however, long after the actual civilization itself (which then more often called itself European civilization) had experienced a more obvious and robust heroic age in the nineteenth century. The first heroic age had been exemplified in the expansion of European or Western civilization until some version of it ruled in all the regions of the world. The second heroic age was exemplified by the expansion of America into Europe, which turned out to be at the same time as the retreat of Europe from much of the rest of the world.

In the couple of decades after 1945, many historically minded commentators suggested that the way in which the United States became the first core and civilizational state for Western civilization – previously divided into a plurality of warring national states – was a recapitulation of the way in which Rome had become the first core and civilizational state for Classical civilization – previously divided into a plurality of warring city states – that is, that America now was to Europe as Rome had been to Greece.

In any event, for the first time since the Roman empire, the West (or, successively, Western Christian civilization and Western civilization) had a core civilizational state. At last united – appropriately under a state called the United States – the greatly and gravely damaged Western civilization underwent a sort of revival. Or, seen from the perspective of the 2000s, half a century later, perhaps this was only a sort of Indian summer, after which the winter of Western civilization would definitively descend.

During this American era, Western Europe was reconstructed within the North Atlantic Treaty Organization (NATO) and the European Economic Community (EEC). This period of the reconstruction of Europe (approximately 1948 to 1973) has been called – somewhat imprecisely – the "thirty glorious years." It took place very much under – and as a result of – the hegemony of the United States. Also during this time, Western civilization was taught to the youth of the West by the American definition and in the American way, as with the famous courses in Western civilization taught in the universities and colleges of the West during the 1940s–1950s.

However, the second, the American, heroic age of Western civilization soon came to an end, beginning with the student movements of the late 1960s, which rejected notions of Western civilization, and certainly with the end of the Cold War in the early 1990s (Judt 2005). It came to an end in part because the American conception of Western civilization no longer provided the United States with much legitimacy among Europeans. However, the main reason why it came to an end was because this conception no longer provided any energy within the United States itself, and this was because it no longer had any legitimacy among most Americans.

The decline of Western civilization in the American way

The decline of Western civilization is a tale that scholars have been telling ever since the end of the nineteenth century. As I have suggested, the rise of the term Western civilization was itself a sign of the first stage in that civilization's actual decline. However, at the end of the twentieth century, the decay of the conception and term was a sign of a much more advanced decline. The tale of the decline of Western civilization as a conception and term is part of the longer tale of the decline of Western civilization as a reality. At any rate, by now there is almost no one in the entire West who is still an advocate or defender of something explicitly called "Western civilization."

And so, now almost thirty years after the end of the thirty glorious years, we can see that the American era of Western civilization really was just an Indian summer for that civilization. Indeed, it was during this very era, when the United States claimed to be its core and civilizational state, that there were occurring several transformations which would bring an end to some of the remaining distinctive features of the Western civilization and would replace it with a new global civilization. Most of these transformations originated in and were promoted by that core and civilizational state, the United States itself.

From global civilization to the Axial Age

The rise of multicultural ideology

First, there was an American transformation from an ideology of Western civilization to an ideology of multicultural society (Schlesinger 1998). By the 1990s, if not earlier, the elites of the United States – particularly those in politics, business, academia, and the media – had ceased to think of America as a leader, or even as a member, of Western civilization. For the most part, Western civilization now meant nothing to them. Indeed, in the academic world, Western civilization was seen as an oppressive hegemony that should be overturned.

Instead, these American elites had come to think of America as a multicultural society, one which obviously included substantial communities of African-Americans, Latino-Americans, and Asian-Americans. The large majority of the latter two communities were recent immigrants or their descendants, a result of the new openness provided by the Immigration Act of 1965 (Huntington 2004b; Kurth 2004). The cultures of these communities were derived from the African, Latin-American, Chinese, Indian, and Islamic civilizations, rather than from the Western one, and any elite emphasis upon *Western* civilization would be alienating to them. If civilization was to be discussed at all, it had to be an *inclusive* civilization, one which clearly included the non-Western cultures now within the United States. These cultures had come from all around the globe, and so the most obvious civilizational candidate was a *global* civilization.

However, it was not inevitable that the reality of an American population which included many new immigrants from many old cultures – that is, a multicultural reality – would actually issue in a multicultural mentality and policy among the American elites. The 1960s–1990s was not the first time that the United States had experienced large numbers of immigrants from different cultures, with prospects for their acceptance of the dominant culture seemingly problematic. As we have seen, a similar condition had existed a century before, particularly from the 1880s to the 1920s, when the culture formed within the US by Western Europeans (principally by those of British descent) had to confront large numbers of immigrants from Eastern and Southern Europe (principally Poles, Jews, and Italians). These immigrants were all from Western civilization, but this had been no consolation to the Americans who were already here. Most of these "old-stock" Americans did not even know that they were part of Western civilization (the concept had hardly been invented yet), but rather many thought of themselves in terms of religious, national, or (spurious) racial identities. The American elites of that era solved the problem of a multi-ethnic society with a vigorous assimilation policy based upon the Americanization project and the American Creed.

During the 1960s–1990s, however, the second coming of a multicultural reality in America issued not in an Americanization project imposed by the American elites, but instead in a multicultural project. The reasons for this difference were many, and they included the legacy of the civil rights movement and the rise of the feminist movement. Both of these movements were analogous to the multicultural movement. However, a principal reason for the elites' choice of multiculturalism was the development, in their minds and at the same time, of another ideological construct, one which went beyond the ideological construct that was Western civilization. This was the ideology of universal human rights. This ideology represented another American transformation, and it would provide fundamental elements for a new global civilization.

The rise of universal human rights

It was a conjunction of several factors that caused American political and intellectual elites to embrace universal human rights in the 1970s. First, those elites who had condemned the US intervention in the Vietnam War needed to develop a new doctrine for American foreign policy to replace the doctrine of containment, which in their eyes was now discredited. Second, the surge in US trade and investment in newly industrializing countries beyond Europe and Japan caused some elites to see a need to develop a new doctrine for American foreign policy that could be applied to a wide variety of different (and often difficult) countries and cultures. This doctrine had to be much wider in geographic and cultural scope than the rather limited idea of Western civilization. Indeed, it would be best if the new doctrine were truly global and universal in scope – that is, that it would fit the emerging global economy and society. Third, there were changes within the American people themselves. America was transforming from an industrial to a post-industrial economy and thus from a producer to a consumer mentality. It was also changing from an ideology of "possessive individualism" to one of "expressive individualism." In this new post-industrial, consumer, expressive-individualist America, the rights (and definitely not the responsibilities) of the individual (and definitely not of the community) were the highest good.

In the new ideology, human rights are thus seen as the rights of individuals. The individual's rights are independent of any hierarchy or community, traditions or customs, in which that individual might be situated. This means that human rights are applicable to any individual anywhere in the world – that is, they are universal, and not merely communal, national, or civilizational. There is thus a close logical connection between the rights of the individual and the universality of those rights. Individual rights are universal rights, and universal rights are individual rights.

The ideology of individualism thus reaches into all aspects of society; it is a total philosophy. Like the original totalitarianism of the state and other Jacobin-descended movements, individualism is relentless in breaking down intermediate bodies and mediating institutions that stand between the individual and the highest powers or the widest forces. With the totalitarianism of the state, the highest powers are the authorities of the nation-state; with the ideology of individualism, the widest forces are the agencies of the global economy.

Individualism – with its contempt for and protest against all hierarchies, communities, traditions, and customs – represents the logical conclusion and the ultimate extreme of the secularization of Reform Protestantism and the Protestant Reformation. But this secularized Protestantism is a Protestantism without God, a reformation against all forms. It represents a rejection of all of the Axial Age religions and their civilizations. Indeed, with its pursuit of immediate and mundane objectives, it is rather like the pre-Axial Age worship of immediate and mundane idols and is, in effect, a new kind of paganism.

The ultimate goal of this secularized Protestantism is the advancement of its particular conception of universal human rights. But, during the Cold War, there were constraints on the full pursuit of this project. As long as the United States was engaged in its great bipolar struggle with the Soviet Union and with communist ideology, it had to show some respect for and make some concessions to the particularities of hierarchy, community, traditions, and customs in the countries that it needed as allies. These concessions were often departures from the normal US promotion of free markets and liberal democracy. However, the collapse of the Soviet Union in 1991 and the discrediting of communist ideology removed much of the necessity for such compromises and concessions. At the same time, the spread of the global economy and the competition among national governments to liberalize their economies in order to attract foreign capital legitimized the idea of free markets (Fukuyama 2006; Mandelbaum 2002). Now the United States could be unrestrained and uncontained in pursuing its grand project but particular conception of universal human rights. And this is what it did in many ways during the administrations of both Bill Clinton and George W. Bush (Kurth 2005).

The American construction of the modern global civilization

America has always been a leader of modernity and therefore of the civilization of modernity. Indeed, Samuel Huntington long ago declared that "America was born modern" (Huntington 1968).

Beginning in the 1960s, the United States began to spread this civilization of modernity beyond the West itself to the rest of the globe. In doing so, it became the principal creator of the modern global civilization. In the 1960s, a principal vehicle of this spread was American multinational corporations. In the 1970s, the Carter administration added the ideology of universal human rights. As we have seen, the particular definition of these supposedly universal human rights corresponded largely to an updated version of the American Creed. It was soon advanced by both Democratic and Republican administrations. In the 1980s came both the ideology and the reality of the Information Age, which quickly and easily promulgated the ideas of modernity throughout the globe. And, in the 1990s, all of these elements were gathered up and integrated into the grand American ideology and project of globalization.

As we have seen, during this period the American business, intellectual, academic, and media elites ceased to be Western in their self-identification, but instead became global and universal in their ideas and ideals. Their worldview became truly worldwide in its breadth (and also worldly in its depth, or rather in its lack of spiritual depth). By the 1990s, therefore, the United States had become the core state, the civilizational state, for the new global civilization, the latest form of the modern civilization. This global civilization had a particular (and, from the perspective of the Axial Age civilizations or its remaining remnants, a peculiar) core of beliefs, which in effect served as its "religion." This religion, of course, was no longer Christianity, but was instead the Enlightenment, which, as we have seen, was actually an anti-Christian religion.

In some respects, the Enlightenment worldview of the global civilization was still like the Anglo-American Enlightenment, which had included an emphasis on free markets and the limited state. In other respects, however, it was similar to the French and continental Enlightenment, which had included an emphasis on universalist ideology, military interventions, and Jacobin methods. Even more, however, it was analogous to the French post-Enlightenment, that is, to post-modernism, with its emphasis on deconstructing all traditional (and therefore all Axial Age) ideas and ideals and on promoting the equal validity of an immerse multitude of words. This post-modern ideology was of course reinforced by the great communication advances brought about by the technologies of the Internet and the Information Age.

The Axial Age resistance to the modern global civilization

Of course, it should not be surprising that the remnants of the Axial Age civilizations have reacted against and rejected this American-led modern global civilization. These remnants are found principally in China, especially among many state officials; in India, especially in the Hindu parties; in Iran and Shiite Islam, especially in the clerical regime and among the working class population; and in Sunni Islam (which, unlike the others, has no core state). These Axial Age remnants are of course contested by other groups within their respective societies who have benefited from and identified with many of the elements of modernity and the global civilization. Nevertheless, the remnants of the Axial Age civilizations are obviously rather large and substantial. Indeed, they are large and substantial enough for each to be able to claim convincingly that it can now offer an alternative vision of what a civilization should be, a vision that is different from the American one.

Thus, in the view of some (especially the business, intellectual, academic, and media elites of America), the United States is the civilizational state of a new and universal civilization – the modern global civilization. However, in the view of others (especially the political and religious elites of the Axial Age civilizations), the United States is indeed a great *state*, but it is not a *civilizational* state. Rather, many of them see it as an *anti-civilizational* state, a state without a true civilization, one which is sort of monster, pagan state and which is the adversary of true civilizations, such as themselves.

The elites of the Chinese and the Indian civilizations each have an obvious civilizational state, and they are greatly pleased that their states have been rapidly growing in wealth, power, and prestige. Even the elites of the Persian civilization have a civilizational state (Iran) which has been standing up to the United States.

But what of the religious elites of the Sunni branch of the Islamic civilizations? They clearly have no core civilizational state. They also see themselves and their civilization as being the very opposite of the United States in several important respects: (1) Sunni Islam is a civilization, even a great civilization, but one without a state, whereas the United States is a great state, but one without a civilization; (2) Sunni Islam represents an ideal waiting to become real, a spirit waiting to become flesh (in particular, the restoration of the caliphate), whereas the United States represents a mere material and mundane reality, from which the ideal and spiritual have departed; and, as a consequence of (1) and (2), (3), Sunni Islam is today in a condition of great vulnerability but great promise, whereas the United States is today in a condition of great power but little promise.

The Sunni Islamists or fundamentalists seek to bring about the realization of their religious ideal with the use of modern means (for example, terrorism using modern weapons), by bringing down what they see as their opponent, the anti-civilizational state that is the United States. For them, there is a great calling to fulfill, which is to create a great state, the caliphate, for a great civilization, Islam. We should not be surprised that they judge it permissible, even imperative, to use any means possible against a state that they see as a monster, pagan, anti-civilizational state. That state is our own.

3 Europe as a civilizational community of practice[1]

Emanuel Adler

Introduction

I identify civilizations with communities of practice and associate a major turning point in the history of civilizations with the development of a new kind of civilizational community of practice and the polities in which it becomes embedded. This community of practice is constituted by security-community practices (Deutsch *et al.* 1957; Adler and Barnett 1998b), in particular by novel self-restraint civilizing practices (Elias 2000, 1978b) that stand in contrast to power-politics practices of the modern era. Were this transformation to occur, at least from the perspective of the quality of power relations, it would transcend Shmuel Eisenstadt's (1987, 2000a, 2000b, 2003, 2004a) notion of "multiple modernities," and would de facto negate Samuel Huntington's concept of the "clash of civilizations" (1993). My hypothesis is that contemporary Europe or, as I will refer to it following Ian Manners (Manners 2002, 2006a, 2006b; Diez and Manners 2007), "normative power Europe" may be reinventing itself as a civilizational security community of practice, which could change the practice of international politics. Whether this succeeds depends on a competition between Europe, trying to change the world in its own mostly secular normative-power image, and the good old anarchical world, trying to shape and shove Europe in its own image.

I describe and explain the idea of civilizations as communities of practice and raise the hypothesis that, when it comes to resolving international conflicts, Europe may be de facto entering a post-modern phase. Next I depict two phases of European civilization, before and after Europe's reinvention as normative power Europe, and briefly describe its first civilizational phase. The next sections describe normative power Europe not only as a concept but also as practical reality and the practices on which Europe's post-modern civilizational polity cum community of practice now rests. I also briefly refer to Europe's interactions with Muslim civilization and the US to illustrate the competition between post-power politics Europe and the modern anarchical world.[2] The conclusion speculates about whether and how normative power Europe might stimulate the construction of a "cultural roundabout" (Toynbee 1988; Puchala 1997), or cross-fertilizing meeting point between civilizations, in the Mediterranean Sea.

Civilizations as communities of practice

Sociological analysis has portrayed civilizations as macro-formations, which, rooted in cultural and often religious frameworks, may become highly institutionalized and politically, socially, and economically differentiated (Eisenstadt 2000a). However, I depart from a civilizational analysis that focuses either exclusively on sociopolitical organization (Hobson 2004), or on a normative agenda (Gong 1984a), especially one that reifies culture (Huntington 1993).[3] I also distance myself from a post-colonial perspective (Ashcroft, Griffiths, and Tiffin 1998; see also Bhabha 1983) that takes civilizational analysis as a culturally and politically "tainted" project which, in the very act of constructing oneself as civilized, constructs "the other" in inferior terms. While I join a recent generation of studies that take civilizations as socially constructed entities (Hall and Jackson 2007a: 4, 6–10; Katzenstein in this volume), I also suggest that one should judge civilizations not for what they "are" but for what they "do." That is, we should conceive of civilizations as dynamic, loosely integrated, pluralistic, and heterogenic *communities of practice* whose boundaries extend as far as their practices. Communities of practice are a domain of knowledge that constitutes like-mindedness, a community of people that creates the social fabric of learning, and shared practices that embody the knowledge the community develops, shares, and maintains (Wenger, McDermott, and Snyder 2002: 28–9). While the concept has been used primarily to describe domestic and international/transnational communities (Wenger 1998a, 1998b; Adler 2005, 2008), it makes sense of macro-cultural communities, such as civilizations.[4]

Defining civilizations as communities of practice locates the concept of culture, to which civilizations are usually related (Puchala 1997: 7), neither exclusively in the minds of individuals or in the discourse they invoke, nor only in the sphere of intersubjective understandings arrived at interactively, such as a shared identity or "we-feeling" (Reckwitz 2002). Rather, the concept of communities of practice identifies culture with "we doing" or practices – socially meaningful competent routine performances (Adler and Pouliot 2008) – with which civilizations are uniquely identified and which differ from one other.

Defining civilizations as communities of practice also allows us to locate agency both in the political entities, such as states, empires, and transnational polities that share common practices, and in the communities of practitioners which, embodying the knowledge the community develops, shares, and maintains, carry the dynamic and novel features of a civilization (Collins 2004). A civilization, therefore, combines or requires an overlap between a political entity, such as a state, an empire, or a religious community – in Europe's case the political entity is a *transnational polity* – and a community of practice, which is how I interpret culture in action. On the one hand, communities of practice confer on the political entities the dispositions to *act* on behalf of the community of practice's knowledge, identity, discourse, and normative makeup in distinctive ways. On the other hand, through means of practice, political entities legitimize, empower, and institutionalize the community of practice's knowledge and discourse.

Communities of practice are real, both ontologically and epistemologically, because they encompass "not only the conscious and discursive dimensions and the actual doing of social change, but also the social space where *structure* and *agency* overlap and where knowledge, power, and community intersect" (Adler 2008; see also Adler and Pouliot 2008; Pouliot 2008). However, because people's practices determine the boundaries of communities of practice, and the knowledge and discourse on which they rest are not necessarily "congruent with the reified structures of institutional affiliations, divisions and boundaries" (Wenger 1998b: 118–19), such as states, they coexist and overlap with international actors.

Defining civilization as community of practice adds value to using civilization as unit of analysis. For example, equating Europe as civilization with a set of distinctive practices adds something palpable and valuable to studying Europe as a transnational polity. It also helps clearly to distinguish Europe's community of practice from other civilizational communities of practice, for example the US, the Muslim world, China, and India (Eisenstadt 2000a), and also from its own past community of practice.

Identifying civilizations as communities of practice requires attention to both the sources of civilizational practices and the magnetic pull civilizations exert *because* of their practices. Building on Collins (2004) and Katzenstein (this volume), therefore, I argue that civilizations can be taken as "zones of prestige" or "networks of attraction" (Collins 2004: 132–3) which, possessing a center or multiple centers – a core of power in Deutsch's sense (1957) – develop a material and cultural magnetic pull and thus attract other civilizations. According to Collins (2004), civilizational magnetism refers to a civilization's capacity to attract members of other civilizations with their "culturally impressive activities." I contend, however, that civilizations are emulated not only because of their high culture (such as the Louvre Museum in Paris), but also because of the material, organizational, and discursive advantages embodied in novel political, economic, security, and social practices (such as post-sovereign citizenship practices). A turn from high culture to practices helps elucidate how different civilizations interact, converge, share experiences, and learn from each other. It also helps clarify how practice diffusion promotes civilization expansion.

One of the reasons that civilizations are "zones of prestige" and possess a magnetic pull is that the knowledge on which some of their practices are based may be pregnant with ideas of progress. This does not mean that civilizational communities of practice *are* necessarily progressive. Rather, as representations of *an* (rather than *the*) idea of progress, new and novel practices, because they may be perceived as better, or less bad, than others, may help civilizations attract political entities of other civilizations.

It follows from this characterization of civilizations as communities of practice that they cannot "clash" in the traditional physical sense. Political entities, however, such as states, empires, religious and other transnational communities, can and do clash, sometimes violently, or, alternatively, they may cooperate, and even become integrated. Whether political entities across civilizations violently clash depends on the background knowledge that constitutes communities of practice. For example, political entities that have jointly learned to practice self-restraint are likely to cooperate, or at least peacefully coexist.

I will now make two additional consecutive theoretical moves. First, multiple modernities (Eisenstadt 2000b, 2003) – the notion that all civilizations have a dynamic cultural core with basic tensions and contradictions within it, such as the universalistic-utopian and pluralistic-pragmatic,[5] yet develop differing programs and expressions of modernity (for example, European civilization and the Muslim world) – express themselves not only as a set of values and norms, or even as social and political institutions or material outcomes, but mainly as a set of practices.

More important, a specific civilizational community of practice, which constitutes itself by dependable expectations of peaceful change (that is, security community-like practices), is expected to alter the nature and behavior not only of the polity, which carries the community of practice in its midst, but perhaps also of the surrounding civilizations with which it enters into contact. Were this to happen, we would then enter the realm of post-modernity, not in the general sense that Eisenstadt (2000b: 1) thought about when criticizing modernization theory, but rather in terms of relational practices, in particular, self-restraint civilizing practices (Elias 2000, 1978b), that civilizations use internally and externally to deal with conflict. This move would partly transcend modern power-politics practices, such as the balance of power, and would also necessitate the existence of a "post-modern" leading agent or civilizational carriers (Collins 2004) that can take us from here to there. More important, however, it would at least partly help transcend Eisenstadt's notion of "multiple modernities" and negate Huntington's "clash of civilizations."

Europe's civilizational reinvention

European civilization has gone through two phases that are based both on the "idea of Europe" – which, as Gerard Delanty argued, evolved throughout the last millennium and kept changing across time and space – and on the *civilizational practices of Europe*. These practices evolved partly as a consequence of European peoples trying to solve "the age-old problem of the universal versus the particular" (Delanty 1995: 85). Out of the dialectical relationship between the universal and the particular grew communities of practice that left an indelible mark on European civilization. In spite of their differences, the two phases of European civilization share some very important common characteristics, in particular, a high degree of multiplicity and cross-cutting of cultural orientations and a multiplicity of religions and traditions (Eisenstadt 1987: 47), and therefore "a constant negotiation process of difference, the existence of borderlands, the reinvention of the past," and the struggle, seldom successful, to imagine oneself as other, and other as self (Delanty 2002: 354).

European civilization's first phase

The first phase of European civilization developed from the encounter of Latin Christendom with Greek Christianity, the Muslim world, and Jewish culture. The very "idea of Europe" actually developed through the encounters between Europe and the Muslim world (Delanty 2003; Katzenstein in this volume; Hobson 2004). Although some of these encounters were more or less peaceful, European civilization also developed through the often violent encounter between European Christians and the Muslim infidels, the Spanish Moros, and the Ottoman empire.

From the sixteenth century, these political struggles drew lines in the sand between West and East and, together with the Reformation and the Wars of Religion in the seventeenth century, weakened the equation of Europe with Christendom. The Enlightenment and the English, American, and French revolutions helped reconstruct European identity around secular ideas and reason, accompanied by scientific revolutions about the understanding of nature and the place of humans in it (Eisenstadt 1987). Growing autonomy of the political, cultural, and societal centers; acceptance of innovation and an orientation toward the future; shifts in the conception of human agency and autonomy; and intense reflexivity (Eisenstadt 2000b: 3–7) gave rise to ideas of progress, which became embodied in universalistic practices, including private religion, parliamentary democracy, universal citizenship and suffrage, science, market economy and trade, and human rights. The modern sovereign state developed hand in hand with nationalism. Combined, they gave us *international* warfare, the balance of power, the modern system of alliances, and colonialist and imperialist practices. Other civilizations were magnetically attracted to and selectively adopted many of these European institutions and practices. Muslim states, for example, borrowed state sovereignty from Europe, but have been reluctant so far to borrow democracy and human rights.

Thus, while "the special characteristics of European modernity were initially focused on the attempts at the formation of a 'rational' culture, efficient economy, civil (class) society and nation-states, where these tendencies of 'rational' expansion could become fully articulated, and which would also create a social and political order based on freedom" (Eisenstadt 1987: 58), so too "did the Enlightenment find its expression in a distorted modernity that sought re-enchantment in nationalism" (Delanty 1995: 66). European modernity, therefore, developed two features, one embedded in universalizing practices based on background ideas of progress and reason, and the other embedded in particularizing practices based on nationalist ideas and practices. Sometimes it was not easy to draw the line between the two features. The "universalizing" conviction that European civilization was superior to Oriental civilizations, and that therefore it was the "white man's burden" (Rudyard Kipling) to civilize other peoples, rationalized the particularizing colonization of other peoples, not only by violent but also by cultural means (Hobson 2004: 240). Because Europe's particularizing forces easily overrode universalizing forces, the unity of a European civilization remained a utopian dream.

The religious differences between Latin Christians, Orthodox Christians, and Muslims, the variety of vernacular national languages, the past discontinuities in European history, and particularizing institutions and practices (such as the nation-state, the balance of power, the system of alliances, colonialism, and imperialist struggles for Africa and beyond) weakened universalizing practices. Thus, as Europe entered the twentieth century practicing balance-of-power and alliance politics, it expectedly ended up in an "unexpected" Great War which, together with the subsequent collapse of European empires, the Versailles peace conference, and the beginning of the decolonization process, shifted the center of gravity to the other side of the Atlantic. Fascism, Nazism, World War II and the Holocaust did the rest and effectively finished off the first phase of European civilization.

European civilization's second phase

After the collapse of Europe's first civilizational phase, and the US taking over the leadership of the West, the "choice" arose between decay (Toynbee 1988) or starting a new round of creative practice development which would make Europe the pole of attraction it once was. Pushed by disappointment and pulled by learning (Haas 1997), Europe chose to reinvent itself as a new political and economic "zone of prestige" and "network of attraction" that might once again magnetically attract the world. Europe's power to change the world thus lies not only in what it was, but what the world may now become with the help of its refurbished normative political practices.

Europe is now attempting to change the nature of the intercivilizational game, much the same as it did hundreds of years ago when it stumbled upon modernity and replaced former civilizational communities of practice with their modern counterparts.[6] Perhaps for the first time in history, "normative power Europe" (Manners 2002, 2006a) – a transnational polity with a security community of practice in its midst – may be reinventing itself as a civilizational *security community* of practice. Namely, it expands outwards, tries to attract other political actors, and takes the lead of transforming international politics with practices of peaceful change (Adler 2008). Contemporary Europe, rather than being a variant of "multiple modernities," may turn into a post-modern agent of security community relations within and among civilizations. This transformation would probably mark the first time in modern history that, at least from the narrow perspective of international practices, a civilization qua civilization may be crossing the threshold of post-modernity (Rifkin 2004; Ruggie 1993).

What makes "normative power Europe" different from past "civilizing" practices (Gong 1984a) is that it expresses Norbert Elias's view of the civilizing process, including *self-restraint* as a critical element of the background knowledge and competent performances of Europe's community of practice and transnational polity (Elias 2000, 1978b).[7] Elias ties the long-term civilizing process to the development of social standards of self-restraint over resorting to violence. According to Stephen Mennell (1992: 80), Elias's social mechanism of self-restraint evolved as a consequence of dynamic social interdependencies – people were "forced more often to pay more attention to other people." In the process, self-restraint came to depend on external constraints, but it was also internalized, thus becoming more automatic and all-embracing in public and private forums.

Few progressive thoughts may be as powerful as international relations' institutionalization of dependable expectations of peaceful change. Elias's move to self-restraint as a civilizational process is thus intrinsically related to security community and "power to." According to Eric Ringmar (2007), "power over" is the kind of power politics through which the modern world is governed, whereas "power to" means changing others in one's image via practice. Europe's agency requires, and even relies mainly, although not exclusively, on "power to" – the magnetic attraction of its practices, which the community of practice considers progressive, and active efforts to extend normative power Europe outward and thus broaden the boundaries of post-modern civilization.

Whether civilizations can bring "power to" into play without using violence and without eliciting a violent response is, as Elias reminded us (Elias 1997: 358–9), a relevant question. It is, therefore, equally relevant to ask whether, under certain conditions, communities of practice that rely on self-restraint may become, as Karl Deutsch used to say, the "core of strength" around which security communities are constituted.[8] Because people do what they do partly because of the communities of practice they form and sustain, when communities of practice expand across functional and geographical boundaries their background knowledge structures an ever larger share of people's identities and intentional acts (Adler 2008: 201). It is thus the diffusion of reflexively constituted practices by means of the agential power of communities of practice and the legitimating power of political entities to change the world in their own image that may mark how civilizations represent themselves in the political world. And the nature of practices that diffuse and become institutionalized may help determine whether civilizational encounters are peaceful, and thus whether security communities may expand across civilizational divides.

It follows, then, that the so-called clash of civilizations is a confrontation neither between the West and Islam (Huntington 1993) nor within Islam itself

(Lewis 2002), but between Europe and the rest of the world. This "clash" is between post-modernity, represented by Europe, which is only vaguely beginning to make inroads, and modernity, represented by the international system as a whole, which Europe would like to transcend. The enormous stakes of this "clash" pit Europe, which is trying to change the international system's structure – its rules and practices – toward intercivilizational politics based on security communities, and the international system – including civilizational entities, such as the Muslim world, the US, China, and Russia – for whom war is still imaginable and doable.

Can Europe, in its encounter with other civilizations, challenge these polities' frames of reference and thus peacefully pull them toward its practices? Probably not: while Europe tries to change the world in its own normative-power image, the old anarchical world is also trying to impose its own image. This competition is also a race between agency – as in Europe's efforts to transform power politics – and structure – a power-politics culture that lures Europe to its past. Moreover, Europe's capacity to attract will also depend on laying to rest pressures arising from inside Europe to move "forward to the past" – to become a great power in the modernist power-politics tradition.

To sum up, many "stories" can be told about the European Union (EU) – about economic integration, political integration, supranational governance, democratic deficits, overcoming nationalism, and neo-colonialism. But it is only when, from a civilizational perspective, we look at normative power Europe as a community of practice that we may begin to realize how, after European civilization "crashed" in the first half of the twentieth century, Europe reinvented itself as a civilization on the basis of practices that break ground with the concept of modernity from a power-politics perspective. Not unlike Ernst Haas's approach in *Nationalism, Liberalism, and Progress* (1997), a civilizational perspective places the EU and European integration in a long-term historical context, which therefore has less to do with particular trade policies or political models adopted after World War II than with hundreds of years of cultural and political evolution, some of the practical effects of which (for example, self-restraint) may progressively affect the "big structures and large processes" (Tilly 1989) of modernity and international relations.

Normative Power Europe

Normative power Europe resulted from a process that simultaneously made Europe more united (on account of pluralistic integration) and more diverse (as a result of EU enlargement), which started in the late 1940s when Jean Monnet and Maurice Schumann laid the foundations of the European Economic Community. It began to acquire its contemporary meaning, however, with the EU's program in cultural, political, and economic engineering, which rests on a moral political community (Delanty 1995: 128), and the evolution of a supranational community of practice – now expanding eastwards and southeastwards to "neighboring" cultures with which it has historical ties, and therefore also to Europe's own past (Delanty 2003).

Normative power Europe refers to Europe's capacity "to shape conceptions of 'normal' in international relations" (Manners 2002: 240); it rests on material resources and primarily on an entirely new set of governance practices relying on self-restraint and the ability to change something in the world, as well as to influence others, and in ways that appear legitimate. According to David Miliband, normative power Europe has become a "model power" that uses "the power of shared institutions and activities [practices] to help overcome religious, regional, and cultural divides" (Miliband 2007).

The concept of normative power Europe builds on and inherited its self-restraint attributes from what François Duchêne called "civilian power": "Long on economic power and relatively short on armed force," Europe as a civilian power would help "domesticate relations between states, including those of its own members and those with states outside its frontiers" (Duchêne 1973: 19). Moreover, it "is an attempt to suggest that not only is the EU constructed on a normative basis, but importantly that this predisposes it to act in a normative way in world politics" (Manners 2002: 252). There is thus a major difference between "soft power," conceived as a culturally based foreign policy tool to be used on behalf of the national interest (Nye 1990b), and normative power, which relies on the ability to attract states to become members or partners of a political community, access to which depends on the adoption of a set of norms, practices, and institutions.

A quick glance at the EU today shows that, while there are Europeans who still want Europe to become a "normal" superpower (Kupchan 2002), from the perspective of normative power "Europeans already wield effective power over peace and war . . . but they do so quietly . . . [without] battalions or bombers, but rather in the quiet promotion of democracy and development through trade, foreign aid and peacemaking" (Moravcsik 2002). Moreover, the EU as normative power obtains security by instilling expectations and dispositions in near-abroad states that adoption of its norms will gain them inclusion into the ranks of the Union. Normative power thus wields influence via EU accession (Moravcsik 2003) and by the spread of its new civilizational practices – in effect, its community of practice – to Europe's near abroad, sometimes via development practices and assistance, building global trust needed to manage crises, and working through multilateral means and world public opinion (ibid.; see also Whitman n.d.).

Depicting Europe as normative power Europe has expectedly drawn critiques. Robert Kagan (2003), for example, argues that Europe's "Venus-like" qualities are related to its lack of material power, and Guy Verhofstadt (2006) says that European power needs a European army to be credible. Helene Sjursen (2006) contends that, to become a normative power, Europe requires strengthening cosmopolitan law. Thomas Diez (2005) argues that other civilizations, such as the US, may also be normative powers, and Diez and Michelle Pace (2007) claim that Europe will become a normative power only when other political entities accept it as such. Moreover, Federica Bicchi (2006) argues that Europe should be more reflexive of the transmission of its practices and allow partners to play a meaningful role in collective decision-making, while Kalypso Nicolaïdis and Dimitri Nicolaïdis (2006) say that, to prevent constructing "others" as inferior, normative power Europe should adopt a post-colonial ethos.

These are powerful critiques. But contrary to those who would like to move Europe forward to the past, as Jan Zielonka (2008: 75) says, China and Brazil will not "change their course because the EU threatens them with coercion. They are more likely to follow EU's example if they see that the European way of handling productivity . . . may be good for them as well." The EU became a normative power not because it is weak – rather it is weak militarily because it has adopted innovative practices of self-restraint and peaceful change (Nicolaïdis 2003). In fact, it is precisely Europe's post-modern, self-restraint practices that distinguish it from the US. While it is true that normative power Europe's practices need to be more reflexive and inclusive (Bicchi 2006) and that Europe must overcome its colonial history, we should take normative power Europe as a work in process, a "EUtopia," or "'laboratory' where options for politics [and governance] beyond the states are generated" (Nicolaïdis and Howse 2002: 771). So conceived, in Ringmar's words: "the EU has next to no 'power over' anything at all – not even, in fact, proper power over its own constituent units – yet it evidently has a considerable amount of 'power to'" (Ringmar 2007: 202).

The practices of normative power Europe

Europe's security community of practice involves the knowledge that constitutes normative power like-mindedness; the community of practitioners, including both practice producers and users; and practices embodying knowledge the community develops, shares, and maintains. Also binding the community together is a sense of shared enterprise and mutual engagement, together with national and supranational physical, institutional, and cultural resources invested in normative power (Wenger, McDermott, and Snyder 2002: 28–9). Finally, the glue that bundles normative power Europe practices into a community of practice is its novel civilizational attributes that break ground with Europe's past.

Although the EU has been a prominent practice innovator, much of what Europe does these days, especially in its external policy, is conventional, such as providing development assistance and humanitarian aid, using political forums of dialogue and mediation, and deploying peacekeeping missions. The innovation, however, consists in its "mobilization of instruments to affect the convergence of norms determining domestic conditions that ought in turn to be more propitious to stability in the region" (Nicolaïdis and Nicolaïdis 2006: 348) and around the world. In other words, the internal system of governance the EU devised and its spread of its security community of practice are one and the same. EU practices, therefore, spread the message that the development of a security community of practice, working for Europe's partial abandonment of power politics, can also work for the international order as a whole. What makes normative power practices different, then, is that they are bent on transcending modern power politics.

Elimination of borders

In recent years, Europe created the "Schengen area," a trans-state territory without internal borders, which in 1999 was incorporated into the EU. A very intricate set of practices was developed to abolish common borders, create uniform procedures, harmonize policy (for example, on visas), and introduce cross-border surveillance rights (Zaiotti 2008). The civilizational angle of this major post-sovereign innovation could be overlooked if not for the fact that borders have

> long marked the rise of modernity and the geopolitical system of nation-states that it brought into existence . . . Borders are no longer dividing lines akin to the traditional frontier in the sense of a line demarcating one state from another . . . they have become . . . often sites of overlapping communities and regions.
>
> (Delanty 2007b)

Thus, if we extrapolate the Schengen practices to the interaction between civilizations, borders may be less the modern site where civilizations clash (Huntington 1993), or exclusively where they negotiate peaceful civilizational encounters, but the liminal area where self and other experiment with new and perhaps enlarged identities and shared practices. The spread of security-community border practices eastwards and southeastwards therefore holds the potential for the civilizational interaction of post-power politics.

Practices of EU enlargement, association, and partnership

EU enlargement not only means getting bigger but is "a matter of cultural transformation . . . in effect that the EU will expand . . . into societies which have experienced quite different routes to modernity." Consequently, as the civilizational community of practice moves eastwards and southeastwards – in the process offering membership or partnership to nations along the way – the resulting European polity "will have to face . . . the historical legacy of its multiple histories" and "learn to cooperate with Eurasia, including the largely Islamic societies, such as the countries of the Caucasus and the near East" (Delanty 2003: 10–12, 21). Thus, a combination of post-modern border and enlargement practices holds the potential for a major change in the interaction between civilizations and for changing "Europe" itself.

For enlargement's sake, via membership or partnership, the EU has devised (or borrowed) practices that enable European contemporary civilization to spread. For example,

> the EU's active role in the transformation of border conflicts is... constructed through providing association as a way forward for conflict parties to emulate the cooperation model on which the EU is founded. Through association, EU actors thereby endeavor to create a discursive framework that generates similar dynamics as integration, but falls short of sharing the EU institutions and involvement in decision making.
>
> (Diez and Pace 2007: 5)

However, as associate or partner countries achieve political and economic reforms stipulated in association agreements, they inch closer to their eventual membership of the Union. For example, in 2001, the EU signed agreements with Croatia and the Republic of Macedonia, which applied for EU membership.

The EU has also opened a second track of pluralistic integration that creates a sense of togetherness or regional "we feeling" and "we doing" without the need to offer EU membership. It has adopted and adapted a set of practices, first developed by the Conference on Security Cooperation in Europe (CSCE) a generation ago, intended to shape new transnational identities based on liberal values among states that belong to the EU's sphere of influence, such as Ukraine and Middle East states. Consonant with region-building practice, the EU invites prospective regional partners to join in constructing common regions – such as a Euro-Mediterranean Partnership (EMP), the so-called Barcelona Process, a "European Neighborhood Policy" (ENP), and, more recently, a "Mediterranean Union" – for the benefit of both European and partner states, and their respective peoples.

Launched in 1995, the EMP is a multilateral cooperative framework for the political, economic, and cultural relations of twenty-six European, Middle Eastern, and North African countries and the Palestinian Authority, aimed at achieving stability and security in the Mediterranean. It builds on the understanding that stability and security depend on cooperative partnership with non-liberal states and on the EU's expectations that the southward diffusion of its norms can help stabilize the region. To achieve this, the EMP envisioned a loose process of pluralistic integration, structured, like the CSCE Helsinki Process, into three "baskets," based on economic cooperation, partnership-building security measures, and a web of regional civil-society networks to promote a common culture (Euro-Mediterranean Partnership 2005).

"European Neighborhood Policy" refers to a 2003 initiative of the EU to create

> a "ring of friends" with whom the EU enjoys close, peaceful and co-operative relations... In return for concrete progress demonstrating

shared values and effective implementation of political, economic and institutional reforms, all the neighboring countries should be offered the prospect of a stake in the EU's internal market. This should be accompanied by further integration and liberalization to promote the free movement of persons, goods, services and capital.

(Patten 2003)[9]

Neither the EMP nor the ENP have really succeeded. This is perhaps why French President Nicolas Sarkozy has launched the "Union of the Mediterranean," a new initiative with emphasis on regional projects, to advance EU normative power goals while also perhaps slowing down the process of EU enlargement to Turkey and serving French and Sarkozy's narrower interests. The EU side of the bargain induces partners to accept liberal values of democracy, the rule of law, human rights, and peaceful change, with the expectation that these normative changes will lead to peace and stability. There is, however, nothing naïve and idealistic in the steps and practices the EU uses to build partnerships, neighborhoods, and unions. Rather, these steps and practices help translate normative power into real material influence and, sometimes, political control, but they do such things peacefully.

Practices of consultation, persuasion, and negotiation

In order to export its model of regional governance, Europe developed practices of consultation, persuasion, and negotiation that might instill in other nations and across civilizations "dependable expectations of peaceful change." The EU leads the world in "ratifying cosmopolitan international treaties" (Manners 2006a) – for example, on (1) human rights, most prominently the European Convention of Human Rights (ECHR); (2) democracy and liberty, as advanced by the case law of the ECHR and the Council of Europe's normative injunctions and treaties; (3) peaceful change, as exemplified by the EU's reliance on and constant references to the UN Charter, the 1975 Helsinki Final Act, and the objectives of the 1990 Paris Charter; and (4) social rights solidarity, exemplified by the 1989 Community Charter on the Fundamental Rights of Workers.

Beyond binding treaties, however, the EU also adopted and refined "soft" law practices, some of which come under the rubric of the Open Method of Coordination, which introduce non-binding and non-enforceable voluntary obligations and are "mostly concerned with immaterial exchange of information and best practices" (Barani 2006: 6). The diffusion of civilizational meanings through normative power is particularly amenable to soft-law practices, whereas consultation, persuasion, and negotiation between Europe and its "neighbors" and partners need not be enacted only in hard-law treaties but also in confidence-building and human-rights protection practices, and through participation in EU's economic and technological programs.

Since the 1980s, the EU has also fought to abolish the death penalty world-wide (Diez and Manners 2007: 176), played a leading role in trying to uphold the Kyoto treaty on global warming, attempting to persuade other states to accept legally binding emission standards, and strongly adhered to international law principles by offering united support and defence of the International Criminal Court (ICC). "The ICC and the Kyoto cases," argue Sibylle Scheipers and Daniela Sicurelli (2007: 452), "provide evidence of an emerging EU identity as a credible normative power."

Postnational citizenship practices

European normative power and the way it represents itself in the world is also deeply affected by European post-national-type citizenship. According to Delanty (2007a: 65), the EU is one of the few "examples of a polity based exclusively on rights as opposed to substantive notions of peoplehood." The EU's model of post-national citizenship is important from a civilizational perspective, first, because the EU has acquired the capacity to effect change at the national level – for example, enhancing the social rights of workers, equality for women, and more recently anti-discrimination for minorities. As such, it promotes regional integration and a distinct standard of "domestic" governance, which can be emulated across civilizations. Second, it establishes citizenship on a mixture of republican principles – both rights and political participation – and (still incipient) cosmopolitan principles – which look less at the polity of which one is a member than to a wider community, allegiance to which is based on mutually agreed rights. This mixed type of citizenship may serve as a model for dealing with civilizational encounters.

Finally, this model of citizenship legitimizes the projection of normative power. Because European nationals are citizens of their respective member states and the Union, the model eases up the negotiation of community norms in multilateral institutional frameworks – characterized by open deliberation and consultation – and justifies why increasingly the "European" interest is as important as national interests. Moreover, it is easier and more legitimate to negotiate European norms and governance principles among materially unequal members when those on whose behalf the negotiation takes place are citizens of both their respective nation-states and the larger community.

Common Foreign and Security Policy (CFSP) practices

Multilateralism is at the centre of CFSP practices. Both the US and the EU have been involved in multilateral diplomacy and pioneered multilateral practices and organizations. But while the practice of multilateralism is viewed in Europe as an "end in itself," and works there almost like a social norm, in the US it is more a means to an end. European multilateralism is inherently "communitarian," in the sense that it relies on practices of collective-identity formation to expand its civilizational community of practice and inclusive forms of security. Multilateral diplomacy and the decentralized but authoritative networks of deliberative forums, so characteristic to the EU (Mitzen 2006: 276), socialize and persuade others to adopt EU norms and, most important, are *the* mechanism through which practices diffuse. Multilateral forums are thus a medium for both the attraction of members of other civilizations to EU norms and the spread of the community of practice from the Western European core to the borderlands, where European civilization was born out of the encounter between Christendom, Islam, and Christian Orthodoxy.

To understand better how multilateral practices are deployed on behalf of peaceful change, we need to look more closely at the relationship between Europe's civilizational community of practice and the world it wants to affect in its own image by spreading its practices. I cannot improve on Jennifer Mitzen (2006: 281), who argued that

> a crucial function of the EU deliberative routines is to manage or tame the anarchic space that remains between the European states themselves. . . . because the habit of deliberation tames anarchy "inside," it also produces the potential to civilize EU relations with the "outside". . . . This does not mean that the EU will be an effective actor, or even successfully implement a given policy. But it does mean that it will be difficult to take security actions that are inconsistent with an internationally accepted notion of what it means to be civilized.

Civilized *security* policy, from the EU perspective, is based mainly on self-restraint, so it means "cooperative security." Cooperative security, which is also comprehensive and indivisible, refers to a "model of interstate relations in which disputes are expected to occur, but they are expected to do so within the limits of agreed upon norms and established procedures" (Nolan 1994: 5). Thus, it is the "natural" security practice of security communities. More specifically, cooperative security is a collection of security practices, adopted mainly by multilateral institutions, on the premise that threats to the community's security are best handled by confidence-building, preventive diplomacy, peacekeeping, dialogue, cooperative quality-of-life measures, the promotion of regional identities, and the inclusion of neighboring states into the community as members or partners. By offering security and economic partnerships, the community's multilateral institutions entice and teach partners to adopt the community's core standards and practices, thereby promoting strategic stability and peaceful change.

Among the EU's core practices, we should especially mention preventive diplomacy and peacekeeping, anti-terrorist practices, and mechanisms for regular political dialogue. These mechanisms include, for example, the CFSP's high commissioner, special delegations of the EU Commission, the special representative (EUSR) to conflict-ridden areas, the Early Warning Unit within the European Council's Secretariat, and the Political Security

Committee, which defines follow-up measures in crisis situations. With regard, for example, to EUSRs, who aim to facilitate conflict resolution and build consensus between the parties, the personalities involved and the office in question are less important than the practices of deliberation, which EUSRs instill on conflicting parties. In the case of the Middle East conflict, the EUSR provides "active support to actions and initiatives leading to a final settlement of the conflict and contributes to the implementation of international agreements reached between the parties and engages with them in the event of non-compliance with these agreements." While the EUSR or, for that matter, Javier Solana, the EU high commissioner, may carry less political weight with the parties than the American secretary of state, they nevertheless work "to reproduce what the EU stands for in its role as an external actor in border conflict situations" (Diez and Pace 2007: 6). The EU also uses its trade and development institutions and practices to help stabilize the region; "the EU is the biggest donor to the Palestinians, and the biggest trading partner and major economic, scientific and research partner of Israel" (Solana 2005: 35).

European Security and Defense Policy (ESDP) practices

In recent years, its increasing military role has made the EU a player in conflict management – for example, in the Republic of Macedonia in 2003 (Operation Concordia), in Bosnia-Herzegovina in 2004 (Operation Althea), and in peacekeeping operations in Africa, especially in the Congo in 2003 (Operation Artemis). Five out of six of ESDP's operations are civilian (Manners 2006b: 189) – for example, the European Union Police Mission (EUPM), which worked with police forces in Bosnia and Herzegovina to upgrade police-force skills and equipment. While an increased number and type of EU military missions may undermine normative power Europe, I agree with Mitzen (2006: 271–5) that fears of "great power Europe" undermining European normative power are unwarranted because Europe's collective identity as a normative power is anchored in intra-European foreign policy practices that permit deliberation and reflection.

It is thus important to place ESDP operations in context, not only of new or enhanced security challenges, such as suicide terrorism, but also of the drastic changes in military identity, practices, and routines that have taken place in Europe's new civilizational phase. This is especially so compared with the time not so long ago when European armies marched all over the continent to conquer and win military contests. While it is undeniable that, in addition to its NATO role, the EU is slowly – perhaps too slowly for the taste of many – developing a military arm as part of its ESDP, European military these days are trained to *prevent* conflict rather than to *win* it, and to keep and make *peace* rather than to make *war* as the highest of military skills and patriotic endeavors.

This is exemplified by Europe's anti-terrorism approach and the 2003

European Security Strategy (ESS). Combating terrorism effectively, says the "Counter-Terrorism Strategy" (Council of the European Union 2005), requires the EU to increase cooperation "with third countries ... respect human rights ... prevent new recruits to terrorism, pursue and investigate members of existing networks, and improve capability to respond to and manage the consequences of terrorist attacks." A more recent official document adds that European anti-terrorist measures should include impeding violent radicalization and terrorists' access to financial resources, protecting critical infrastructure, improving the exchange of information, supporting victims, and encouraging research and technological development (Commission of the European Communities 2007). Many pundits outside Europe dismiss this approach as soft (Kagan 2003) or, at best, identify the approach with a policing and defensive framing of terrorism, in contradistinction to former President George W. Bush's "war on terror." Europe's anti-terrorist strategy, however, makes sense from a normative power perspective because, in addition to the preventive and defensive measures of rigor, it aims at drying up the swamp that produces terrorism. Europe's good governance practices are probably better poised at this goal than American power-politics practices.

The normative power nature of European security practices becomes even clearer when it comes to the ESS, especially compared with its American counterpart, President Bush's 2002 National Security Strategy (NSS) (White House 2002). According to Mitzen (2006: 282–3), there are four differences between the ESS and the NSS. First, "the ESS situates Europe's role as arising from its own past, using that history of rivalry and conflict as a source of critical self reflection." Second, "threats of terrorism, rogue states and WMD do not 'dominate' the document the way they do the NSS." Third, "where specific threats are considered, they are not 'expelled' from Europe itself." Finally, "for dealing with these threats, cooperation and multilateralism are crucial."[10]

The ESS, therefore, identifies Europe's underlying sources of insecurity as bad government, the dark side of globalization, and power politics – that is, disdain for international treaties, international law, and human rights. To counter these threats, the ESS refers to developing an international order based on effective multilateralism, promoting an environment of well-governed democratic states, upholding and developing international law, resolving regional conflicts, spreading good governance, supporting social and political reform, and dealing with corruption and abuse of power. The ESS also refers to preventive action, but not in the sense of the American NSS, as it was militarily implemented in Iraq and Afghanistan, but mainly as crisis prevention (Council of the European Union 2003).

Decades ago, Arnold Wolfers wrote that states may have either "possession goals" (possessing something or dispossessing others from their possession) or "milieu goals" (changing the environment so *it* can be "nice" to self) (Wolfers 1962: 67–80). The ESS takes milieu goals to the civilizational level. Europe would like to change the world in its own good-governance civilizational image – through spreading its practices – so *it* could be nice to Europe. What is good for Europe, Europeans believe, will be good for the world. But, because the anarchic international system is still not ready to be shaped and shoved by Europe's self-image, it tries to shape and shove Europe in its own image instead.

Challenges to normative power Europe: the Muslim world and the United States

Some of the most difficult questions Europe's second phase of civilization now faces are whether it can integrate the Muslim "other" in its midst as "self" without ceasing to be "itself," and whether it can engage wider Muslim civilization beyond Europe's shadowy and expanding borders with practices of peaceful change. And can Europe, because of its normative power-based international governance practices, recapture its common civilizational roots and destiny with the US?

Before I briefly address European civilization's relations with the Muslim world and the US, it is important to remember that this chapter is about the reinvention of European civilization *because* its first phase failed miserably and collapsed with colonialism, the two world wars, and the Holocaust. I am not suggesting a naïve defense of European civilization across history or saying that European civilization is better than others. Nor, in the wake of resurgent xenophobia, anti-Semitism, and the strengthening of quasi-fascist parties to extirpate the "other" from Europe, am I suggesting that, because of its normative power practices, Europe has become the epitome of moral behavior and Kantian peace. Rather, my limited point is that Europe's normative power security-community practices may potentially transcend power politics. This section is about Europe trying to turn this potential into reality and the systemic environment resisting this move.

Europe and the Muslim world

The key question in the minds of 500 million Europeans, and of Muslims now living in Europe (close to 20 million) or elsewhere, is whether this latest chapter of interaction between European civilization and the Muslim world will result in the Europeanization of Muslims in Europe or in the Islamization of Europeans. The unwillingness of some European Muslims to abandon sharia or Islamic law and jihad, along with Islamic terrorism, proselytizing non-Muslims, social and economic polarization in Europe and the creation of a Muslim underclass – which engenders a heavy dose of crime – and Turkey's bid to join the European Union – which would augment the number of Muslim European citizens to roughly 90 million – raise the question whether the Muslim world, with which Europe interacts, is, or should be, part of "us," "them," or none of these.

Leaving aside radical extremes that advocate either extricating the

"Muslim danger" from Europe or turning Europe into an intrinsic part of "Dar al-Islam" through demography, but, if necessary, also through jihad, we can find several distinctive approaches to the challenge. Post-colonial arguments make the case that, in order to reinvent itself as a civilization, Europe must confront its colonial past. This means, in Edward Said's terms, abandoning "Orientalism" (Said 1979) and adopting an attitude that defines Europe less as unity than as dynamic difference.

Liberal European arguments, instead, make the case for a multicultural Europe, which, standing on the foundations of a shared supranational or post-national European identity and a European-type citizenship based mainly on rights, would make Muslims feel at "home" in Europe, without them having to abandon their cultures and religions (Limbach 2005; Delorme 2007). Adopting this point of view means conceiving

> a European public space and a European civility [that] could help us to go beyond the national scale and the confrontational definitions of civilization and focus on daily life experiences and interactions. Why not imagine European public space as an ethical and physical frame that enables us to develop a common civility drawn from liberal pluralism as well as a plurality of religious experiences?
>
> (Göle 2007)

A slightly different version of this position would attune Muslim religion more to European values and, rather than allowing foreign imams to teach Islam in Europe, would have the EU create institutions to supervise Islamic education. This has indeed begun to happen at the national and EU levels with the creation of Islamic councils in France and the Netherlands and the establishment of the Dublin-based European Council on Fatwa and Research.

Bassam Tibi, a well-known German scholar of Syrian descent, has put on the table a different, if bold, solution to the encounter of European and Muslim civilizations this time around: the Europeanization of Islam in Europe, and only in Europe, or what he calls "Euro-Islam" (Tibi 2007). Emanuele Ottolenghi (2005: 4), however, representing a widely held view, believes that moderating Islam and narrowing socioeconomic inequalities will not be enough, because "in the absence of successful absorption policies the alternative to a weak and unappealing European identity will increasingly be Islam." Europe, thus, will be better off if it goes back to reinforcing rather than overcoming national and nationalist allegiances.

I join this debate from a civilizational perspective and, more concretely, from the perspective of a historical quid pro quo. Thus, I maintain that Ottolenghi's medicine may kill the patient; it certainly would put a stop to Europe's second civilization phase. Europe should change itself enough to make Muslims feel truly European, and European Muslims should join Europe's community of practice, including the norms and values on which the practices are based. The key for normative power Europe's civilizational success lies in the deployment of normative power for the deconstruction and reconstruction of rigid social structures, which Europeans themselves engendered in the past with colonialism, the way territories were arbitrarily divided in the Middle East, and the role Europeans played in engendering conflicting identities between Muslims and Jews in Israel and Palestine. Europe's new civilizational key to success lies also in engaging Turkey, perhaps first as partner, but later as member, of the EU, if indeed this is what Turks actually desire. Admitting Turkey to the EU may become a most significant normative power experiment whose results will affect Europe and other civilizations. The opportunities here lie not only in engaging Islam to become Europeanized, as Tibi (2007) says, but also in constructing a Mediterranean identity that would be neither entirely Judeo-Christian European, nor solely Muslim, but a civilizational crossroad where communities of practice learn from each other. Europe in its new civilizational phase would contribute self-restraint regional-governance practices and, thus, also security community expectations of peaceful change.

Europe's normative power, then, can help find the historical compromise between Europe and Muslim civilization at the level of neighborhoods in Paris or Amsterdam, and at the crossing points or borderlands between civilizations, which according to Huntington are supposed to experience a violent and bloody clash. First, the existence of supranational European institutions and practices softens nationalist and religious pressures that may arise from the engagement between civilizations on Europe's territory. Second, normative power Europe can use its practices and agency to construct new regional orders in the Mediterranean and beyond with the aim of pluralistically integrating the different cultural communities.

Europe's second civilizational phase therefore requires transforming its idea of progress. According to the Enlightenment view of progress, power, knowledge, well-being and security would all follow reason and modernity, as interpreted in the West. A regenerated European idea of progress would not only allow for the merging of alternative modernities – as expressed by different religious creeds and norm codes. Rather it should also make possible the day-to-day mutual coexistence between alternative modernities and post-modernity, which transcends power politics with security-community practices.

Neither Venus nor Mars, but different branches of the same trunk

The deterioration of relations between Europe and the US that took place as Europe increasingly became more comfortable with normative power, and the US, under President Bush, increasingly behaved according to the crudest power-politics practices, produced a sense of malaise in diplomatic, economic, and cultural relations. In other words, European and American communities of practice seemed to have diverged and ceased being different manifestations of a broader Western civilizational constellation (Delanty 2003; Katzenstein in this volume). If, at the practical level, cracks in the special relationship of the Euro-Atlantic security community appeared only at the surface, at the intellectual level the cracks became tectonic fractures that went to the bottom of the earth. These were exemplified, on the one hand, by "realist" American disdain for normative power Europe (Kagan 2003), or suspicion that Europe was after modern superpower status (Kupchan 2002), and, on the other hand, by arguments of key European intellectuals, such as Jürgen Habermas and Jacques Derrida (2005), which established European independence from, and civilizational superiority over, the US (Kumar 2008).

We must, however, place the practical and intellectual "clashes" between Europe and the US in the last decade in the context of the Euro-Atlantic security community, of which they are both members, and which is strongly institutionalized in NATO. While it is true that, at the height of the American invasion of Iraq, a sizable number of European scholars thought the Euro-Atlantic security community was dead or dying (Cox 2003), others adduced that the differences were clearly a result of the Bush administration's practices, and therefore that the security community would survive (Risse 2004). While it is still unclear whether the key issue was and still is domestic politics, it is clearer that the Euro-Atlantic security community did not disintegrate, and that relations between Europe and the US, especially after the election of President Barack Obama, seem to be better than they have been in years. Thus, not only do normative power Europe and "exceptional US" still seem to "share a fundamentally similar Western inheritance" (Kumar 2008: 91), but also intellectuals' attempts to construct each other in terms of the "other" seem to have failed.

The key question for the future, therefore, is what type of constellation can be constructed between normative power Europe's community of practice, which aims to limit sovereignty at the domestic and international levels, and the US's community of practice, whose practices aim mainly to protect international relations modernity and its related institutions and practices, such as the nation-state, sovereignty, and, if necessary, military power projection. It is clear how Europe would like to reinvent itself from a civilizational perspective. It is less clear what civilizational entity the US wants to, and will, become.

In this context, European normative power practices may appeal to President Obama's needs of a new domestic and global agenda of change. This agenda, mind you, emerges not only because of technological developments, globalization, economic crisis, the rise of China, and so on, but also because the nature of the security threats ahead may be tackled better with a combination of normative power and power-politics practices. The more the Euro-Atlantic security community buys into normative power Europe practices – NATO has partly begun doing this (Adler 2008) – the more Europe and the US will cease to balance each other's practices (Adler and Crawford

2006), as they did in the last eight years, and will thus reconstitute themselves into one community of practice, or a constellation of closely related communities of practices. Moreover, as Adler and Greve (2009) show, security-community mechanisms and power-politics mechanisms, such as the balance of power, may temporally and functionally overlap at the regional level. Thus, US and EU practices may be able to coexist, and decision-making procedures and new practices will be needed to determine how and when to use one kind or the other, and when their combination may bring about the best results.

Whether Europe and the US will find a practical common ground, however, will depend to a large extent on domestic developments in Europe and the US as well as global challenges, such as global terrorism, weapons of mass destruction, global crime, and so on, which are precisely the security challenges that Europe chose to confront, at least partly, with normative power. The more both the US and the EU come jointly to rely on normative power practices and adhere to the rule of law, democratic governance, and multilateral practices, the more European civilization and American civilization will be able to confront jointly the task of taming anarchy and the dangers of war.

Conclusion: a mediterranean civilizational "roundabout"

Between 756 and 1492 CE the Ummayad Muslims and their descendants ruled at "al-Andalus" or "ha-Sefarad," in what is today Spanish Andalusia. According to a widely accepted, perhaps partly mythical, historical reading, despite "intractable differences and enduring hostilities," Muslims, Jews, and Christians abided in al-Andalus in a culture of tolerance that resulted from learning how to live with contradictions (Menocal 2002). According to historian Mark Cohen (1995), Jewish historians transformed this idyllic perception in the nineteenth century into a "historical postulate" and subsequently European liberals embraced it.

The myth of interfaith utopia (Cohen 1995: 3) did not go unchallenged. Bernard Lewis (1987: 4), for example, argued that it "is only very recently that some defenders of Islam have begun to assert that their society in the past accorded equal status to non-Muslims." Because of the Israeli–Palestinian conflict and, recently, the resurgence of radical Islam, the academic controversy over al-Andalus was "kidnapped" for political purposes. Many Muslims believe that al-Andalus proves that Jews can live peacefully in Palestine under Muslim rule. Others argue that not only Spain but also Europe should become the site of their future caliphate. Israelis, Jews, and Europeans suspicious of Muslims' intentions believe that a tolerant al-Andalus is a myth and proof that Muslims will stop at nothing to turn Europe into an Arab protectorate (Ye'or 2005).

While I am agnostic about the controversy surrounding this fascinating historical/academic and political chapter,[11] I mention al-Andalus because, regardless of whether it was tolerant, it was definitely a case of what Toynbee (1988) and Puchala (1997) called a "cultural roundabout," or cross-fertilizing meeting point between civilizations. Cultural roundabouts such as al-Andalus are characterized by "a mixing of cultures" that "produce hybrids of great originality" and which can link "civilizations by transferring artifacts, ideas and institutions" (ibid.: 20–21). Like global cities of the twenty-first century – for example, New York and London – the "historical result of inter-civilizational intermingling within and via cultural roundabouts" is *creative cross-fertilization.*" At the libraries of Cordoba and Toledo, where Arabic was lingua franca for Arabs, Christians, and Jews, the classic Greek texts, which the Abbasids translated, became a mechanism of civilization transmission from the old to the new world (Menocal 2002). There, the arts, philosophy, and scholarship (a cultural renaissance cannot take place without some measure of tolerance) flourished, becoming a signpost for future civilizational encounters.

While improbable, it is still possible, and highly desirable, that, if normative power Europe practices of self-restraint (Elias 2000) and security communities diffuse and attract (Collins 2004) practitioners from other civilizations, a new cultural roundabout could develop in the Mediterranean. This would mark perhaps the first time that an encounter of civilizations in the Mediterranean would be based not only on tolerance, if it ever was, but also on peaceful change grounded in self-restraint. A new civilizational encounter would depend less on a dialogue between religions, let alone their convergence, than on shared security-community practices characterized by self-restraint. Were a civilizational cultural roundabout to develop around shared practices of self-restraint, European civilization might achieve what the Ummayads perhaps did not – a *peaceful* cultural roundabout. It would be incumbent on the second phase of European civilization, however, to establish a civilizational encounter on mutual tolerance while developing a truly meaningful two-way cross-fertilization civilizational process.

Where else to develop a new cultural roundabout than in the Mediterranean, where normative power Europe and Muslim cultural practices exert their greatest influence? We should therefore see otherwise seemingly useless talk-shop European initiatives, such as the Euro-Mediterranean Partnership and the more recent Union of the Mediterranean, from a long-range civilizational perspective, namely, as opportunities for practices of self-restraint to constitute intercivilization encounters. Turning the Union of the Mediterranean into a laboratory for the first post-modern encounter of civilizations, therefore, will be one of the supreme tests of normative power Europe. Needless to say, it will take at least several generations to know whether it works.

How would and should this experiment differ from past questionable European "civilizing" experiments? First, the diffusion outward of a European community of practice based on self-restraint practices would not be aimed at attaining material goods and at culturally colonizing "inferior civilizations," but rather at ensuring peaceful change. Second, this experiment would be progressive because some practices are better, or less bad, than others. To my mind, practices of self-restraint and mutual tolerance are not only better practices than colonialism and imperialism – they also suggest the opportunity to establish civilizational encounters on mutual dignity and respect.

Notes

1 I thank Peter Katzenstein, Patrick Jackson, Daniel Nexon, and Antje Wiener for their valuable comments and my outstanding research assistant Orit Gazit for her invaluable help and suggestions.
2 The anarchical world includes not only the US and Muslim civilization but also India, China, and Russia, which act according to classical international relations' notions of power politics. The focus on the US stems from the fact that Europe is developing in relation to it. Muslim civilization is posed here in relation to European civilization since their encounter will undoubtedly influence the future of Europe.
3 Reifying the concept of civilizations, clashing very much as states do, as Huntington posited, sits uncomfortably with the heterogeneity within civilizations (Ajami 1993).
4 For a study taking nations as a category of practice, see Brubaker (1996).
5 For example, ancient Greece and ancient China were characterized by a chasm between the transcendental and the mundane order (Eisenstadt 1987).
6 In contrast, the US, which after World War II tried to impose its own institutions on other states and somewhat succeeded in doing so, hardly tried (if at all) to change the nature of the intercivilizational game.
7 It is worth noting that Elias distinguishes between, on the one hand, the transformation within European society toward self-restraint and, on the other, the tendency toward violence in the engagement with other political entities which are not considered part of the group (Elias 2000; Linklater 2004; Katzenstein in this volume, p. 20). I acknowledge the fact that social and political entities always "civilize" in relation to some "other" from which they try to distinguish themselves, yet contend that today's Europe is very different from the one Elias first wrote of in 1939. Normative power Europe of today aims at spreading the practice of self-restraint to its near and further surroundings. This, in turn, creates resistance among some political entities to which it tries to "sell its merchandise," but is absorbed and well received among others. I contend that today we speak of a mixed rather than "zero-sum" interaction between Europe and other civilizations.
8 For the relationship between self-restraint practices and the spread of security communities, see Adler (2008).
9 See also Commission of the European Communities (2003). "European Neighborhood Policy" includes Ukraine, Moldova, Belarus, Algeria, Egypt, Israel, Jordan, Lebanon, Libya, Morocco, the Palestinian Authority, Syria, and Tunisia. It is also supposed to reinforce the EU–Russia partnership.
10 Manners argues that the ESS has taken a "sharp turn away from the normative path of sustainable peace towards a full spectrum of instruments for robust intervention" (Manners 2006b: 189).
11 I nonetheless find persuasive Cohen's (1995: ix) erudite conclusion that Jews enjoyed more security in al-Andalus than under Christendom.

4 Civilization and state formation in the shadow of China

David C. Kang

What was the role of civilization in early modern East Asia? China as hegemon – and its main philosophy, Confucianism – had a powerful effect on the rest of East Asian domestic and international politics, even while what it meant to be Chinese and how best to organize society and government was continually modified and debated within China itself. China as civilization and the most powerful state in the region was inescapable, and most states and societies were forced to deal with China in their own way. Domestically, China influenced state-formation and societal practices, from language and religion to political institutions and economic activity. In international relations, the Chinese developed a Confucian order that was explicit and formally unequal but informally equal: secondary states were not allowed to call themselves equal with China yet had substantial latitude in their actual behavior. China stood at the top of the hierarchy, and there was no intellectual challenge to the idea of what constituted civilization until the nineteenth century and the arrival of the Western powers. Korean, Vietnamese, and even Japanese elites consciously copied Chinese institutional and discursive practices in part to craft stable relations with China, not to challenge it.

Although there has been a great deal of historiography about this era, there is little scholarship that has focused directly on war in early modern East Asia or that has put China and East Asian states in a comparative context, leading to a view of China as "empire without neighbors" (Hevia 1995: 15). Chinese civilization had an enduring impact on all the political units in the region, and examining the range of societies and states provides a better understanding of its effect and consequences.

Yet China lacked a messianic vision of transforming the world and managed to craft remarkably stable relations with many – but not all – of its surrounding neighbors. That is, China had little interest in actively exporting its own ideals and values, preferring instead to focus on the practice of foreign relations. This allowed the surrounding peoples and polities to contest, modify, and adapt Chinese ideas to their own ends. Some states, such as Korea and Vietnam, closely copied China in a range of practices. Others, such as Japan, experimented with some yet not all Chinese ideas. Still other societies – such as the diverse semi-nomadic peoples of the northern and western frontiers – resisted almost all cultural and political ideas, but still interacted with China, occasionally using Chinese practices and ideas in their foreign relations.[1]

Creating civilization also entailed creating the contrasting idea of an other, or "barbarian." This had implications for war and peace among and between the various political units of the region. In this way, the research presented here extends Iain Johnston's pioneering work about the sources of Chinese grand strategy, where he identifies two deeply enduring Chinese worldviews that encompass central paradigmatic assumptions about the nature of conflict, the inevitability of violence, and the enemy. Calling one "Confucian" and the other "parabellum," he argues that China and nomads operated in a parabellum strategic culture in which it was considered that "the best way of dealing with security threats [was] to eliminate them through the use of force" (Johnston 1995: x). Yet, important as Johnston's work is, he does not address a key issue: why those threats arose mainly from actors on China's northern and western frontiers instead of from powerful states to the east and south, such as Korea, Japan, and Vietnam. These Sinic states, which shared China's "Confucian" worldviews, had far more stable and peaceful relations with China. Early modern East Asia – like nineteenth-century Europe – operated in two very different international societies based on two different sets of rules: one which included the Sinicized states and one which regulated relations with the "uncivilized" nomadic world (Keene 2002).

This chapter focuses on the main enduring states of East Asia and makes three central arguments. First, there is no eternal unchanging China, and there have been multiple strands and an ever evolving notion of what is civilization, as much invented in the present as inherited from the past at any point in time. Second, the main secondary states of East Asia chose Confucianism and Chinese ideas more for their own reasons than from Chinese pressure. In Korea, Vietnam, and Japan, the debate about how to organize government and society occurred between warriors and scholars, with the Confucian literati winning in Korea and Vietnam and warriors ultimately winning in Japan. Although Chinese ideas were deeply embedded from the founding of these states, just as significantly, Chinese ideas were grafted onto vibrant indigenous cultures, and the two coexisted – sometimes uncomfortably – resulting in only partial Sinicization. Third, the Confucian international order was hierarchic and formally unequal, while allowing substantial informal equality and independence. Chinese ideas presented East Asian states with a range of domestic and international institutional and discursive practices that were hierarchic and flexible, and there was far more peace and stability among Confucian states than between Confucian and "barbarian" ones.

Civilization and the idea of China

Civilization and state formation were intertwined in East Asia. Yet the two were distinct, both conceptually and in practice. The East Asian experiment with governance also began quite early, with the emergence of China and its main philosophy of Confucianism during the Axial Age (800–200 BCE). China had been unified by 221 BCE, and a nascent notion of Hua-Hsia (or Chinese) community existed during the Warring States period. Nicola Di Cosmo (2002: 94) quotes the *Hsun-tzu*: "All the states of Hsia share the same territorial zones and the same customs: Man, Yi, Jung, and Ti share the same territorial zones, but have different institutions." Over the centuries, these ideas continually evolved and became more full and complete, and a central government ruled much of what is China today for almost two millennia. China has expanded and contracted, depending on local conditions and the strength of the political center, and, as Mark Edward Lewis (2007: 1) notes, "China owes its ability to endure across time, and to re-form itself again and again after periods of disunity, to a fundamental reshaping of Chinese culture by the earliest dynasties, the Qin and the Han." Yet, according to Naomi Standen (2007: 30), "we should not doubt . . . that many people in the tenth century did have a clear sense of belonging within a particular cultural nexus."

Certainly, a long-standing question within China itself was over what constituted civilization and what constituted barbarian. People within what is today known as China used the term civilization as early as 2,000 years ago, and as Charles Keyes (2002: 1171) remarks, "from Han times on . . . those who lived on the frontiers of the empire were considered to be barbarians . . . that is, they had not yet accepted the order presided over by the emperor or the authority of a literature written in Chinese." Throughout the next two millenia, the concepts of "Chinese" and "barbarian" were subject to debate and interpretation, and there was never a fixed definition (Brindley 2003; Giersch 2001; Abramson 2008). But the ideas have been present throughout Chinese history, and Mark Strange maintains that

> running through the periods (and surviving even to the present day) are a core set of defining concepts: that China is a unified sovereign state; that the Chinese polity draws legitimacy from a dominant cultural tradition, which founds itself on the value system of a core canon of authoritative texts; and that this cultural and moral tradition has close associations with an ethnic identity.
>
> (Strange 2007: 237)

However, we should be cautious of implying too direct or linear a path toward modern China or toward a Confucian civilization. Cultural ideas influenced the various states that rose and fell over time, but modification, adaptation, and debate existed at every point. As Standen (2007: 30) reminds us, "we should not . . . foreclose the issue, by adopting terms and categories, like ethnicity, that imply the inevitability of the modern Chinese nation-state and posit a linear development toward it." Indeed, some traits have historical roots, others do not, and all are constantly evolving depending on the circumstance, situation, institutional constraints, and political and economic exigencies, as well as a host of other factors.

Chinese civilization as it evolved consisted of both institutional and discursive practices, and, although discussion of civilization tends to focus on the latter, the former were arguably more present and direct means of extending Chinese ideas to various parts of East Asia. Scholars continually debated and revised ideas about the role of government, the organization of society, proper relations between groups and peoples, and the role of religion in public and private life. Literature, art, and culture were also important aspects of this larger process of civilization, although they are not our focus here.

It was arguably the Tang dynasty (618–907 CE) that made the most direct advances in governance, by introducing a key institutional experiment: a government based on talent, not on heredity, with civil servants being selected through a public competition open (in theory) to all males, and held at regular, fixed intervals, that assessed the candidates' qualifications. As Alexander Woodside notes:

> The eighth century, indeed, would make a good choice as the first century in world history of the politically "early modern." It was in this century that the Chinese court first gained what it thought was a capacity to impose massive, consolidating, central tax reforms from the top down, which few European monarchies would have thought possible before the French revolution, given their privileged towns, provinces, nobles, and clergy.
>
> (Woodside 2006: 1)

This was an important innovation – most coutries of the world have been governed by an aristocracy that chose rulers on the basis of hereditary ties. The examinations themselves were held in public spaces, and some sites – such as that in Jiangnan – held up to 16,000 candidates in brick huts. During the Qing dynasty, when Emperor Qianlong realized that Mongol and Manchu nobles on his frontiers could not read court edicts, he "tried to restore communications with his Mongol nobles by ordering a 'back to basics' reform of examination-system writing" (ibid.: 6). There was even affirmative action: in 1777, the central government allowed border students a special amnesty of thirty years during which they shold learn the "Central Domain" speech tones necessary for poetry examinations.

In addition to the civil examinations, bureaucratic administration in China involved a complex system of administration and governance. Chinese central administration was composed of six major ministries: personnel and appointments, finance and taxes, rites and education, war, justice and punishment, and public works. Ming-era China, too, was centrally organized into administrative districts down to the province level, with appointments made from the capital for most tax, commercial, and judicial posts (Mote 1988). The Chinese court (and the Korean, Vietnamese, and Japanese courts) also produced "veritable records" of government activities (Chinese: *shilu*; Korean: *sillok*; Vietnamese: *thuc loc*), sometimes on a daily basis. China introduced land reform as early as the Tang dynasty in an attempt to create more landholding farmers. A national tax system had emerged before the Tang dynasty, with the ideal tax rate of 10 percent. Yang Yang (727–81) was the author of China's famous "two tax" law of 780, which consolidated taxes into two semi-annual payments and shifted the focus away from people and onto property size (Woodside 2006: 62). William McNeill (1992: 106) argues that this eighth-century reform was a "pioneering shift" from a command economy to a market-based economy. Tang China also introduced a system of granaries to provide in the event of famine.

Yet there was no dedicated, linear, and focused march toward "civilization." Writing about the tenth century, Noami Standen points out that

> during those two hundred years [after the Tang dynasty collapsed] nobody knew that a Chinese empire would ever again be the dominant power in East Asia . . . the radically different world of the late Tang and Five Dynasties (907–60) . . . saw multiple power centers within the same territory interacting on an entirely different basis.
>
> (Standen 2007: 1)

In fact, the various – and numerous – foreign influences also left a profound imprint on Chinese ideas. For example, the three centuries preceding the Ming dynasty (1368–1644) witnessed the breakdown of central control in China, the Mongol Yuan invasions, and widespread instability throughout the region (Rossabi 1983; Barfield 1989; Jagchid and Symons 1989). Yet the Yuan set the stage for the subsequent five centuries by reestablishing "centralized, unified rule in China, laying the foundation for the provinces of modern China . . . and restoring a single tax and legal system on the country" (Crossley 2008: 7). By the time of the Manchu Qing dynasty, China had again developed a centralized process by which the government attempted to react to food shortages. R. Bin Wong (1997: 98–9) notes that these "[state-sponsored] granaries represented official commitments to material welfare beyond anything imaginable, let alone achieved, in Europe. . . . To think of state concerns for popular welfare as a very recent political practice makes sense only if we again limit ourselves to Western examples."

In short, identifying a coherent Chinese civilization is as difficult as identifying a European one. Throughout Chinese history there has been contestation and change, adaptation and innovation. Yet at the same time there has been considerable continuity over many centuries, and state institutional structures and social ideas in the nineteenth century would have been identifiable to those in the eighth century.

Sinic states: Korea, Vietnam, and Japan

Influenced by China and its civilization, the states of Korea, Vietnam, and Japan emerged over a thousand years ago as centralized political units, territorial states with internal control that conducted formal, legal international relations with each other, and for whom international recognition as a legitimate nation was an important component of their existence. State formation and civilization were deeply intertwined in East Asia, the nature of their relationship reflected in the formal, hierarchic, and institutionalized manner in which both developed.

The states of Korea, Vietnam, and Japan that emerged between the seventh and tenth centuries CE are still recognizable today as roughly the same political units. These states constituted the inner core of the regional system where Chinese cultural, economic, and political influence was direct and pervasive. As Kären Wigen notes:

> Compared to most countries in the late twentieth century... China, Korea, and Japan are among the most venerable nations in the world; although their boundaries have shifted over time, and the style of their imagining has been continually debated, the notion of nationhood has resonated long and deeply with the majority of each country's inhabitants... this sense of region is quite different from what might be encountered elsewhere in Eurasia or Africa, where national space is often complicated . . . by cross-cutting affiliations from a colonial or pre-colonial past.
>
> (Wigen 1999: 1187)

These three East Asian states were centrally administered bureaucratic systems based on the Chinese model. They developed complex bureaucratic structures and bear more than a "family resemblance" in their organization and cultures and outlooks. This form of government, including the calendar, language and writing system, bureaucratic system, and educational system, was derived from the Chinese experience, and the civil service examination in these countries emphasized knowledge of Chinese political philosophy, classics, and culture. Table 4.1 outlines the various political entities over the past six centuries in East Asia.

Table 4.1 East Asian states and their dynasties, 1300–1900

	1300	1400	1500	1600	1700	1800
China	1368–1644: Ming			1644–1911: Qing		
Japan	1333–1573: Ashikiga			1600–1868: Tokugawa		
Korea	1392–1910: Chosŏn					
Vietnam	1225–1400: Tran	1428–1778: Le (Trinh and Nguyen factions: 1543–1778)			Nguyen 1792–1883	

Yet while Confucian China was a pervasive influence, there was no messianic, transformative vision from China and little pressure on subordinate states to conform to Chinese ways. Second, imposition of Chinese civilization was intertwined with state formation and was a top-down affair driven by elites. Finally, multiple traditions survived – Sinicization was never complete or thorough.

Voluntary emulation

Despite the overwhelming centrality of Chinese ideas to the region, China's foreign relations were not marked by transformative or interventionist attempts to change the basic practices of other states. Indeed, pragmatism characterized its relations with its neighbors. China was more concerned with stability on its borders and, as long as stability was maintained and there was no threat to itself, it was content to leave neighboring countries alone. Of course, there was variation: Korea and Vietnam were most comfortable with the Chinese-oriented system, while Japan has always been most conflicted about its relationship with China – genuine cultural admiration, and yet a sense of unease and even competition. However, despite its reservations and sense of rivalry, Japan was willing to go along enough to help maintain a remarkably stable, peaceful, and durable China-oriented East Asian order.

Although Japan was less influenced by China than were Korea or Vietnam, there is really no difference in China's approach to Japan on the one hand and Korea and Vietnam on the other. Even for the latter two, which had regular tributary relations with China, China in general and Chinese as individuals seldom thought of these tributes as anything but validations of their own self-esteem. Yet Korea and Vietnam could not forget about China for a day! Japan was no different, except that its relationship was more cultural and economic, much less political, and military not at all, and the cultural relationship was with Chinese literature, not with China itself.

Neighboring states emulated Chinese practices for a number of reasons, one of which was as a means of domestic political and social control and another was to manage foreign relations with China. This adaptation occurred as much for domestic political reasons as from any Chinese attempt to change how they operated or from international considerations. Indeed, there is little evidence that the aim was to build up capabilities in order to match and rein in Chinese power. On the contrary, emulation actually had the opposite effect of ramifying the Chinese-dominated order.

One clear example of the Chinese influence is in language, with the wholesale importation of Chinese script and vocabulary into these three other cultures (Cho 2002). For example, the Korean, Vietnamese, and Japanese word for "country" (Chinese: *kuo*; Korean: *kuk*; Vietnamese: *quoc*; Japanese: *koku* or *kuni*) is the same, and was derived from the same Chinese character. These were not "feudal" states, organized around hereditary aristocratic power. Alexander Woodside (2006: 6) notes that, in these East Asian countries, "the monarch . . . largely governed through texts composed for them by mandarins, rather than by more personal (and perhaps more feudal) means of persuasive human contact." The "presented scholar" degree, based on examinations (Chinese: *jinshi*; Korean: *chinsa*; Vietnamese: *tien si*), created a set of civil servants responsible to the throne, unencumbered (mostly) by aristocratic claims.

Although the Korean Koryŏ dynasty (918–1392) was Buddhist in many respects, the dynasty's founder, Wang Kŏn (T'aejo, r. 918–43), remarked that "We in the East have long admired Tang ways. In culture, ritual, and music we are entirely following its model" (Deuchler 1992: 29). Interestingly, even though the Mongols conquered Koryŏ in 1259 and ruled through intermarriage for more than a century,

> the almost one hundred years of Mongol domination of Korean affairs . . . seem to have left but a light imprint. The Mongols were admired for their military organization and prowess; but apart from some fancy fashions, they seem to have furnished little of substance for imitation.
>
> (Ibid.: 83)

Chosŏn dynasty (1392–1910) court dress was identical with the court dress of the Ming dynasty officials, with the exception that in Korea the identical dress and emblems were two ranks (in the nine-rank scheme) lower. That is, the court dress of a Rank I (the highest rank) Chosŏn official was identical to that of a Rank III official at the Ming court (Ledyard 2006). Korea patterned itself closely after the Chinese model, and Korea used the same six ministries (*yukcho*) and a similar state council (*pibyŏnsa*) as in China. The six ministries covered taxation, military affairs, punishments, public works, personnel, and rites (Deuchler 1992; Lieberman 2003). Yet China simply did not "dominate" Korea during at least two millennia before 1900; Korea was de facto independent, and its Sinicization was most pronounced when that was quite self-consciously imposed on the country as an ideology by Korean neo-Confucians, apart from whatever the Chinese might have wanted. As Gari Ledyard (2006) argued:

> Chinese "control" was hardly absolute. While the Koreans had to play the hand they were dealt, they repeatedly prevailed in diplomacy and argument . . . and convinced China to retreat from an aggressive position. In other words, the tributary system did provide for effective communication, and Chinese and Korean officialdom spoke from a common Confucian vocabulary. In that front, the relationship was equal, if not at times actually in Korea's favor.

As with the Korean state, Vietnam adopted many Chinese practices in order to preserve Vietnamese autonomy and independence by presenting itself to

China as a recognizably similar political unit, one worthy in accomplishments and sophistication of treatment as a state. Vietnamese centralization of authority also was not a cause or effect of war; indeed, emergence as a state had more to do with domestic ideas about how best to govern. Victor Lieberman's (1993: 539) long survey of Southeast Asia concludes that "Interaction with China was probably more important in shaping Vietnamese self-identity than warfare with Chams, Khmers, or Thais."

Although independent, Vietnam borrowed heavily from China. The bureaucratic examination system, for example, was used by Vietnam under the Han and, when the French arrived in the nineteenth century, success in the civil service examination still required use of Chinese characters and knowledge of Confucianism. The Chinese had also introduced administrative districts and built roads, ports, canals, dikes, and dams. Chinese immigrants introduced Chinese-style schools, marriage rites and social customs, agriculture, and law. Confucianism penetrated to the level of economic and family organization at the village level, affecting patrilineal inheritance and even dress. The Vietnamese retained their indigenous language for unofficial uses and also indigenous social and religious customs, chief among them Buddhism.

The civil service examination system in Vietnam grew directly from the Chinese experience. By the eleventh century, three-stage regional examinations were held on successive weeks of the seventh lunar month, there were word limits (for example, 300 words for policy questions at the regional level), and winners were publicly announced in order of excellence. As with the Chinese and Korean systems, attempts to keep the process as fair and transparent as possible included measures such as prohibitions against examiners meeting with each other privately, and special care was taken to ensure that families of candidates – fathers, sons, and uncles, for example – were not colluding while taking the test. By the fifteenth century, up to 30,000 men took the regional examinations each year, and by the sixteenth century some 70,000 men were eligible for the first level of examination (Whitmore 1997: 675). Yet between 1554 and 1673, no more than thirty-one ever passed the exam in a given year (Taylor 1987: 23).

The Vietnamese, like the Koreans, adopted Chinese practices both from genuine emulation and as a means of diplomacy. As for emulation, cultural borrowing from the most advanced state is not surprising. As Brantly Womack observes,

> The Chinese court innovated and refined its institutions and ideology to face the challenge of preserving central order for the common good . . . [Vietnamese rulers] faced the same problem, and China provided an agenda of "best practices." . . . it should be emphasized that if China were still an active threat, then Vietnam's political task would have been military cohesion, and its intellectual task would have been one of differentiation from China [not emulation].

(Womack 2006: 132–3)

Victor Lieberman (1993: 513) notes that "Convincing China that Vietnam was 'civilized', and therefore not in need of Chinese occupation and instruction, presented another practical benefit of self-Confucianization." The complexity of emulation and difference is reflected in famous Vietnamese nationalist poems from the eleventh and fifteenth centuries. These poems celebrated victories over China even while they were written in Chinese using a Chinese literary style and employing China as a basis for defining what was Vietnam (Vuving 2001).

China has always loomed large for Japan, which has always had a difficult relationship with its mainland neighbor. The Japanese state that developed was in many ways influenced by China. David Pollack (1986: 3) writes that "until modern times the Chinese rarely troubled themselves about Japan; the Japanese, however, were preoccupied with China from the beginning of their recorded history until the opening of the West in the last century." According to Donald Keene (1974: 383), "The central factor of Japanese literature – if not the entire traditional culture – was the love for and the rejection of Chinese influence."[2] And Pollack (1986: 3) notes that, "for the Japanese, what was 'Japanese' had always to be considered in relation to what was thought to be 'Chinese.'" Indeed, China dominated as myth and reality in Japanese history.

Early in its history, Japan experimented with a Chinese-style governance system. Its university system in the eleventh century was based on a curriculum that studied the Chinese classics, as was the organization of its bureaucracy, and the capital city of Kyoto was modeled after the Tang dynasty capital in China (Shiveley and McCullough 1999). Yet early attempts to import Chinese bureaucratic approaches in the eleventh century failed in the smaller, more backward environment of Japan (Farris 1998; Grossberg 1976a). Japan was clearly a state as early as the Nara era, but the Chinese influence – although constant and powerful – was mitigated and had less an impact there than in either Korea or Vietnam. With the promulgation of the Taiho Code in 701, Japan during the Heian era (749–1185) introduced a Chinese-style government utilizing a bureaucratic system that relied heavily on imported Tang dynasty institutions, norms, and practices (Farris 1998).

However, the Chinese example as a normative precedent remained very important even for the Tokugawa Japanese. Japan and China continued to trade informally, with up to ninety Chinese ships visiting Japan each year during the seventeenth and eighteenth centuries, and Japan imported over 1,000 Chinese books each year (Osamu 1980). When Tokugawa shoguns were looking for legal and institutional models for how to structure their own government and society, "they were usually Chinese in origin," such as the "Six Maxims" first issued by Ming founder T'ai-tsu in 1398, as well as Qing and even Tang and Song legal and administrative codes (Jansen 1992: 65, 228). Indeed, the *Tokugawa jikki* (the official annals of the Tokugawa era) contains numerous references to Japanese legal scholars consulting with Chinese and Korean scholars as they attempted to interpret various Chinese laws and precedents and modify them for Tokugawa use. By the time of Tokugawa Japan, "educational institutions at every level across the nation followed a similar curriculum of Japanese and Chinese texts... the *Tangshixuan* collection of Chinese poetry was a required text, where it was regarded as a canonical work." Chinese literature was so in demand that between 1727 and 1814 one publisher – Suwaraya Shinbei – put out twenty-seven editions of the *Tangshixuan* (Toby 2001: 228).

Although the Japanese studied Chinese institutions in all periods, they did not import the names and terminology, but rather the *ideas* that those institutions reflected. There were no "six ministries," for example, in Japan. In this respect, the Japanese were much less slavish than their East Asian state counterparts.

Civilization and state formation: imposition from above

Chinese ideas tended to be imposed top-down by states as they attempted to centralize authority and extend control over their territories. In domestic politics, smaller states would borrow from China because it was a model that offered solutions to practical problems faced by elites, and because relations with China offered legitimacy at home and access to trade abroad. In Korea, Vietnam, and Japan, the process of importation was essentially a conflict between warriors and scholars. In the case of Korea and Vietnam, the "neo-Confucian" revolution of the fifteenth century came about as these states actively consolidated their rules. This conflict, between state and society and between scholar and warrior, marked all three of the Sinicized East Asian states. In Japan, the scholars lost out. In Korea and Vietnam they triumphed.

The Mongol invasions of Korea in the thirteenth century, *wako* pirate incursions along the coast, and a resurgent Ming China might have prompted a full militarization of the new Korean Chosŏn dynasty. Yet the opposite occurred: Confucian scholars increasingly became influential, and the military was increasingly marginalized, as the new dynasty sought to establish domestic order and international stability. Its founders were not outsiders rebelling against an established order – in fact, they came from the educated elite – and their dissatisfaction was driven by a desire to intensify neo-Confucian practices, not overturn them. Deuchler (1992: 107) notes that, "To the social architects of early Chosŏn, the adoption of ancient Chinese institutions was not an arbitrary measure to restore law and order, but the revitalization of a link with the past in which Korea itself had a prominent part." With the establishment of the Chosŏn dynasty and the intensification of neo-Confucian practices, "scholar-officials... became directly involved in policymaking at all levels" (ibid.: 292).

The original Vietnamese Ly dynasty (1009–1225) was nominally Chinese in its organization, but it was the Tran dynasty (1225–1400) that set up Chinese-style population registers for each village and a "National College (*Quoc Hoc Vien/Quoc Tu Vien*)... [where] scholars were ordered to focus on the classical Chinese texts" (Whitmore 2006: 117). After a Ming Chinese interregnum of two decades, state building continued when Le Loi founded the Le dynasty (1427–1788) and began a series of neo-Confucian reforms, including a Le law code that regulated land sales, debt interest, and relief for peasants (Lieberman 2003: 381). Although the Ming occupation was relatively short, it had a lasting effect on Vietnam, hastening the centralization and organization of the state. Whitmore (1997: 675) remarks that, "while the Vietnamese violently rejected Ming political control, these literati equated Ming models with modernity."

Of the four major states in early modern East Asia, Japan had the most conflicted relations with China. The Ashikaga shoguns of the fourteenth century encouraged the growth of Kyoto and the commerce, Zen monasteries, and diplomatic, cultural, and economic ties with China. The *bakufu* also developed a civil service and employed bureaucrats, although not on the scale of China and Korea. Known as *bugyonin*, these bureaucrats were used by the Muromachi *bakufu* to administer public finance and tax collection, adjudicate lawsuits, process land claims, and deal with other shogunal decrees (Grossberg 1976b). Although those on the lowest rungs of society were often subject to personalistic rule by local magistrates,

> if you were a civil, military, or ecclesiastical landlord, or a steward of such a person, then the system looked reliable, even modern . . . "law" was a salient feature of the Japanese medieval era: groups had rights and litigation was not yet suppressed, legal experts flourished both in the bakufu and the imperial system.
>
> (Steenstrup 1991: 239)

According to Batten (2003: 42), although central control broke down during the warring states era (*sengoku*: 1467–1568), "the idea of 'Japan' as a single country remained fairly strong." Tellingly, at no time did any of the potential *daimyō* attempt to create an independent state. Indeed, they all remained explicitly committed to the emperor as ruler of Japan – the only issue being who would be the most powerful actor, not who would reign. When one of them won enough power, he would declare himself "shogun," not emperor. This belief in "Japan" as particularly exemplified by the emperor is most starkly revealed by the institutional contortions that various shoguns went through in order to be eligible – for example, adoption of sons.

Hideyoshi conducted a national land survey and implemented a national system of taxation in the late sixteenth century. The Tokugawa *bakufu* continued the centralizing trend. Although there remained important exceptions to centralized power, the Tokugawa *bakufu* had complete authority in foreign affairs and military matters, and control both of the currency and national highway system and over the religious life of Japan. Land registers and maps and a national census were implemented continually from 1716 onward (Toby 2001: 202). Products were marketed nationally because of a national currency. The Tokugawa *bakufu* changed the national maps to representations based on provinces and districts rather than the *daimyō* domains. Even the larger domains of Satsuma and Tosa were subject to these regulations, and they complied. Bruce Batten highlights the range of instruments under state control and the centralization of power in Ashikaga and Tokugawa Japan, connected rather than isolated by the sea to the world around it (Batten 2003).

Each of these states had a sizeable permanent military and/or long military traditions. So, if they were not fighting each other, what were these armies doing? Putting down rebellions, guarding the central government, and maintaining essential systems. In Korea the units of the army that were the best trained and the most dependable were always in Seoul to protect the palace and the bureaucracy. Each province had at least two major towns with military garrisons and, in the important southern provinces, naval units. The military ran the land and sea transport for grain taxes and other government logistics, and also communication (including the fire towers for overnight links to the capital – weather permitting!) and postal facilities, which were almost entirely for official use. Every commoner was in the reserves up to the age of sixty and his household had to pay the cloth tax which supported the military (Park 2006). The military handled the routine duties quite well, but sadly proved worthless against foreign invasions.

Here too, Japanese was the exception. In the shogunal system, military resources were under the separate and individual control of many *daimyō* in addition to the shogun. Mobilizing them was a mere extension of politics (it could be easy, difficult, or risky, depending). But since the participation of the *daimyō* was essential, he had a political stake in success, and since this factor provided for a special bond between commander and troops, military effectiveness could be enhanced. Heroism could be locally recognized and the rewards locally applicable to life's opportunities.[3]

Multiple traditions

Despite the obvious Chinese influence in all aspects of government and society, none of these countries was an exact replica of China: they al employed Chinese-language culture and political systems, yet retained their own unique indigenous cultures as well. This is best exemplified by their diglossic linguistic traditions: the Chinese language was used for writing in Korea, Vietnam, and Japan during the entire time under study, even while these countries retained their own indigenous languages and, in some cases, script (Cho 2002). These systems were mixed: rationalized attempts at centralized and national governance coincided and coexisted with traditional elements, such as hereditary monarchies and slaveholding.

Confucianism was grafted onto quite different social and cultural patterns in these other countries. During the first millennium CE a rough division had obtained, with Confucian ideas influencing governance and Buddhist ideas influencing social norms. Yet Confucianism slowly began to influence and transform both state *and* society – and was largely a top-down process carried out by elites. This process accelerated in the fifteenth century with the neo-Confucian revolution in Korea and Vietnam. However, although Confucianism permeated deeply into the social fabric of society, it never fully eradicated Buddhism or indigenous social practices in any of the societies. This transformation was neither quick nor complete, and even today there are elements of indigenous culture and Buddhist ideas that coexist with grafted-on Chinese ideas about family life and social structure, the proper role of societal actors, and their relationship to the state.

Although Korea was deeply influenced by Chinese culture and ideas, this influence was laid over an indigenous culture and society, and the two coexisted without truly synthesizing. Thus, although Koreans used Chinese characters for writing and borrowed a large portion of their vocabulary from China, indigenous Korean writing and vocabulary continue to exist to today, and often a concept will be illustrated by two words – one Chinese, one Korean. Similarly, culture and society borrowed many Chinese customs while retaining many uniquely Korean customs. As Martina Deuchler (1992: 292) comments, "[Korean] Confucian scholar-officials emerged from the old aristocratic matrix and carried over some distinct elements of this heritage, notably an acute consciousness of status and descent."

The creation of modern Vietnam involved essentially the interweaving of Chinese ideas with indigenous Vietnamese ideas. As in Korea, a tension existed between military and court men, who viewed kinship, Buddhism, and aristocratic ties as important for Vietnamese order, and scholars, who emphasized Confucianism, education, and impersonal state institutions as the bases of leadership. Numerous scholars have noted the flexible, syncretic nature of Vietnamese social and political institutions, and Mahayana Buddhism was the prevailing religion well into the Le dynasty. Although royal succession in the Tran and Le dynasties was determined by strict patrilineage, primogeniture did not become deeply rooted until the neo-Confucian reforms of the fifteenth century, for example (Wolters 1976). As Keith Taylor (1983: 300) concludes, "Vietnamese became experts at surviving in the shadow of the mightiest empire on earth . . . [they] retained their own language and, with it, memories of their pre-Chinese civilization . . . it means that . . . Vietnam remained distinct and separate from the Chinese sphere of thought."

Ambivalence toward China was more powerful in Japan than in Korea. The Japanese stopped sending envoys to China in 890 and did not resume until the mid-fourteenth century, and then only for a hundred years. They had a visceral resistance to the subordinating rituals required by the formal tributary conditions that China laid down, and internal criticism along those lines forced the Ashikaga shoguns to discontinue tribute relations after a short bout in the fifteenth century. During the Tokugawa era, most trade between China and Japan was conducted in the Philippines or in Southeast

Asian ports, although there were periods when Chinese ships could visit Nagasaki.

However, by the time of the Tokugawa shogunate, the civil service had become much smaller and a warrior caste had grown up. David Pollack (1986: 7) notes that, throughout language, culture, arts, government, and economics, China either as model or as context "exerted a powerful pressure on every act of culture." Even a quintessentially Japanese product such as the *Tale of Genji* – a Heian masterpiece – was "everywhere underlaid by a structure of Chinese archetype." In Tokugawa Japan there were Chinatowns peopled with up to 5,000 Chinese not only in Nagasaki; numerous artists, scholars, religious leaders, and other artisans lived in Edo, Kyoto, and other cities. For example, the abbots at Mampukuji temple in Uji (near Kyoto) were Chinese from the Fujian "parent temple" from its founding in 1661 until 1740, and after that the abbots alternated with their Japanese counterparts until 1800 (Jansen 1992: 56).

Multiple traditions have always existed in East Asia, with Buddhism, Confucianism, and indigenous ideas mixing, interacting, and evolving, but rarely seamlessly blending.

The Confucian international order

Chinese civilization had an enduring and transformative effect on the domestic politics and societies of many surrounding states. But it also constituted an international order. Indeed, it is increasingly accepted that "every international system or society has a set of rules or norms that define actors and appropriate behavior" (Krasner 2001: 173), which Christopher Reus-Smit (1997: 557) calls the "elementary rules of practice that states formulate to solve the coordination and collaboration problems associated with coexistence under anarchy." In this respect, the Confucian international order that arose from Chinese civilization had a pronounced effect on the relations between these states. This Confucian international order in East Asia encompassed a regionally shared set of formal and informal norms and expectations that guided relations and yielded substantial stability. With the main institution of the "tribute system," the Confucian order emphasized formal hierarchy among nations while allowing considerable informal equality (Keyes 2002; Fiskesjo 1999). As long as hierarchy was observed, and China was recognized as dominant, there was little need for interstate war. Sinic states, and even many nomadic tribes, used some of its rules and institutions when interacting with each other. Status as much as power defined one's place in the hierarchy: China sat highest, and secondary states were ranked by how culturally similar they were to China rather than by their relative power. This social order also contained restraint by China and benefits to the secondary states.

Hierarchy and authority

A key element of hierarchy is the proscription of certain behaviors by subordinate states. These limits on behavior can involve both coercion and legitimacy. In early modern East Asia, although states were largely free to do as they pleased, there were some limits on their actions. Perhaps most significant was the explicit recognition that China was at the top of the hierarchy. Other states were not allowed to call themselves the equal of China, although this had little impact on their daily functioning.

This proscription was formalized in two key elements of tributary diplomacy: recognition by China, known as "investiture," and the sending of embassy envoys to Beijing. Investiture involved explicit acceptance of subordinate tributary status, and was a diplomatic protocol by which the Chinese emperor recognized the status of the king in tributary states as the legitimate ruler of those states (Yoo 2004). Envoys to China followed numerous rituals and used the Chinese calendar, marking events such as birthdays or other significant events. Investiture and envoys were also practical, however – embassies were frequently a means for extensive trade between China and tributaries, and investiture was important both for domestic legitimacy in the tribute state, as well as confirmation of their status with China.

This hierarchy was rank-ordered, based in part on how culturally similar these states were with China. Korea and Vietnam were no stronger than Japan, but they were viewed more highly by virtue of their relations with China and their more thorough adoption of Chinese ideas, Korea being seen as a "model" tributary (Yun 1998; Choi 1997). Vietnam first entered into a tributary relationship with China upon its independence in the tenth century, and from that time on "Song [Chinese] rulers unquestionably placed the Vietnamese kingdom at the top of a hierarchical system of relationships with leaders along the southern frontier" (Anderson 2007: 8). Wills (n.d.) notes that "the [Vietnamese] Le kings sent regular tribute embassies, were meticulous in the use of seals and terminology, and prepared their own tribute memorials and accompanying documents in quite respectable literary Chinese."

Yet, beyond these measures, China exercised little authority over other states: "When envoys bowed before the Chinese emperor, they were in effect acknowledging the *cultural* superiority of the Chinese emperor, not his *political* authority over their states" (Smits 1999: 36). Relations with China did not involve much loss of independence, as these states were largely free to run their domestic affairs as they saw fit and could also conduct foreign policy independently from China (Son 1994; Kang 1997: 6–9). They also replicated these rank orders in their own relations with other political units. Korea, for example, explicitly ranked its relations with other countries: various Mongol tribes were rank 4, the Ryukyus rank 5 (Robinson 2000; Kang 1997: 50–51). Swope (2002: 763) notes that "when addressing states such as Ryukyu they [Korea] considered to be inferior in status within the Chinese tributary system, they implied . . . paramountcy. Japan they regarded as an equal or as an inferior depending upon the occasion."

Stability within the Confucian order

The Confucian order yielded considerable stability. Significantly, between 1368 and 1894 – five centuries – there were only two wars between China, Korea, Vietnam, and Japan: China's invasion of Vietnam (1407–28) and Japan's invasion of Korea (1592–8). These four major Confucian states of East Asia developed stable, peaceful, and long-lasting relations with each other. The more powerful they became, the more stable were their relations. China was clearly the dominant military, technological, and economic power in the system, and it had written the international "rules of the game," but its goals did not include expansion against its established neighboring states. The smaller states emulated Chinese practices and to varying degrees explicitly accepted Chinese centrality in the region.

This central claim does not imply, however, that violence was rare in East Asia. There was plenty of violence, but it tended to occur between Sinicized states and other, generally non-state actors, such as the semi-nomadic northern peoples, in the form of border skirmishes, piracy, and the slow expansion and frontier consolidation of some states (such as China) at the expense of non-state units. While the *frequency* of skirmishes between China and nomads may have been high, the *scale* of those skirmishes was generally quite low. Although the nomads were generally more nuisance than threat, on the few occasions that they managed to form state-like structures, they became powerful and dangerous to the settled states.

The status quo orientation of China and established boundaries had much to do with the period of peace. That is, the culmination of successful state-building produced peace, much as status quo orientations and resolution of border conflicts has led to peace in contemporary Europe. Rational calculation on the part of China and the secondary states resulted in an international system that was remarkably long-lived and stable. Although a clear distribution of power was one element of this system, just as important was a clear status hierarchy. China had written the international rules of the game (known as the "tribute system") and stood at the top of the hierarchy, and there were few challenges to the order. Korean, Vietnamese, and even Japanese elites consciously copied Chinese institutional and discursive practices in part to craft stable relations with China, not to challenge it. Even the nomadic tribes valued Chinese stability, and, according to Perdue (2005: 521): "The collapse of a Chinese dynasty threatened the stability of the steppe empire. This relationship explains why, for example, the Uighurs intervened to keep the Tang dynasty alive."

By the tenth century, Korea and China had established the Yalu river as their border, and it was affirmation of this border and Korean acceptance of tributary status in the fourteenth century that precluded a war between the new Ming Chinese and Chosŏn Korean dynasties. Near the beginning of the Ming dynasty in 1389, the Ming had sent an expedition against the Koryŏ dynasty (918–1392) to recover territory that it alleged had been annexed by the Mongols, whom the Ming had already driven from China. The Koryŏ decided to fight the Ming over the demarcation of the border, and it was this campaign, and General Yi Sŏnggye's unwillingness to fight it (preferring negotiation), that led to the fall of the Koryŏ and, three years later, the creation of a new dynasty, the Chosŏn (Kim 2006; Roh 1993; Lee 2004; Ha 1994). Yi immediately opened negotiations with China, and the Ming did indeed settle for the Chosŏn's tributary status. Significantly, in exchange for entering into tribute status with China, Chosŏn Korea retained all territory previously held by the Koryŏ, and relations between China and Korea were close and stable for 250 years, with the two sides exchanging numerous envoys and regularly trading.

These Confucian norms regulated Chinese–Vietnamese relations as well. After a Chinese occupation of two decades in the early fifteenth century, Vietnam immediately entered back into a tributary relationship and continued to send envoys to China on a regular basis until the late nineteenth century. Had its independence been based purely on military power, there would have been no reason for Vietnam to have conducted such elaborate rituals, nor explicitly to have acknowledged China as dominant, nor to have continued sending scholars to study in China. Embassy missions were a vital part of the tributary relationship, and the Le dynasty (1428–1778) initially sent embassies every year, which eventually settled into a pattern of one embassy every three years (Whitmore 2005: 6). As Victor Lieberman (1993: 513) notes, "Convincing China that Vietnam was 'civilized,' and therefore not in need of Chinese occupation and instruction, presented another practical benefit of self-Confucianization." Even when Vietnam was riven by internal factionalism, both sides retained the royal throne, which had been invested by China. Although Vietnam fought numerous wars with its Southeast Asian counterparts, relations between China and Vietnam remained stable and peaceful until the twentieth century.

In over four centuries, Japan challenged its place in the Confucian order only once, in 1592. The Japanese invasion of Korea drew on half a million men and over 700 ships and "easily dwarfed those of their European contemporaries," involving men and material ten times the scale of the Spanish Armada of 1588 (Swope 2005: 13).[4] After the Japanese initially routed sparse Korean forces and drove north past Pyongyang, China intervened and pushed the Japanese all the way back down the peninsula, and it soon became clear to both sides that Japan could not hope to conquer Korea, much less China (Hawley 2005: 409; Swope 2002).

Why Hideyoshi decided to invade Korea remains unclear, but most evidence points to status, economic, or domestic political considerations. Japan accepted as given the larger international order and rules of the game; it challenged its place within the existing order, but not the structure itself.

Berry sees a desire for greater status: "He [Hideyoshi] was clearly less interested in military dominion abroad than in fame" (Berry 1982: 216); while Swope (2002) notes that Hideyoshi demanded a dynastic marriage with one of the Chinese emperor's daughters along with the resumption of tribute trade. Deng (1997: 254) sees a Japanese desire to reenter into tribute status with China: "Trade is also shown because of the fighting over the ability by tributary states to pay tribute. Hideyoshi invaded Korea, a Ming vassal state, to force China to allow Japan to resume a tributary relationship, and threatened that a refusal would lead to invasion of China itself." Hawley (2005: 22–4, 76) emphasizes continual war as a way for Hideyoshi to quell internal dissension among his followers. Notably absent is a Japanese assessment of the relative military capabilities of the two sides, and Berry (1982: 278) concludes that "there is no evidence that he systematically researched either the geographical problem or the problem of Chinese military organization."

The Chinese would never acknowledge equality, but did consider granting Japan investiture at a status similar to certain Mongol leaders and below that of Korea and Vietnam (Swope 2002: 769). Korea – and China – sent minor officials to negotiate with the Japanese, because "the Koreans valued highly the tributary system and their place within the first rank of tributary states. As the Japanese held lower rank, the Koreans would have jeopardized their status had they sent royalty as envoys" (ibid.: 780). According to Kenneth Swope:

> Hideyoshi could have extracted trade concessions had he accommodated himself to the established rules. Hideyoshi, however, in bidding for recognition as the equal of the Ming, was trying to alter an established system; the Ming were not willing, and could not yet be forced, to agree to such changes.
>
> (Ibid.)

In 1598 Japan retreated from Korea without gaining anything.

Thus Japan's sole revisionist attempt was a disaster. Thereafter, although Japan remained formally outside the tribute system, it did not challenge that system. As Alex Roland (2005) notes, "The Tokugawa shogunate turned inward and gave up war, not the gun." Swope (2002: 781) concludes that, "because the Tokugawa maintained order in Japan, piracy was not the problem it had been in the past and the two states co-existed in relative peace until the late nineteenth century."

Arrighi and his colleagues argued:

> the China-centered tributary-trade system can often mediate inter-state relations and articulate hierarchies with minimal recourse to war. Japan and Vietnam, being peripheral members of this system, seemed more content to replicate this hierarchical relationship within their own sub-systems than vie directly against China in the larger order.
>
> (Arrighi *et al.*: 2003: 269)

Thus, even though Japan accepted tributary status only sporadically, the system as a whole was stable because Japan assented to Chinese political, economic, and cultural centrality in the system, and also benefited from international trade and the general stability it brought.

Indeed, it was only with the arrival of Western imperial powers and the implosion of the China-dominated system in the late nineteenth century that Japan challenged China's position again. Yet, even into the twentieth century, scholars such as Hamashita (2008) have explored the nature of the economic and diplomatic linkages made in East Asia and argued that Japan challenged China within the Confucian international order, not outside of it. According to Hamashita, prosperity from the post-Imjin War economic boom, smuggling, and commercialism that prospered outside the tribute trade system framework was not a collapse of the system, but a sign of its success, which resulted from strong demand for Chinese goods. Refuting the commonly held view that the arrival of the Western great power politics in Asia marked a sharp disjuncture from the traditional Sino-centric order, he argues that the tribute trade system was far stickier and more persistent than is normally assumed. Based on the examination of a series of treaties signed during this period,[5] he makes a further claim that not only were the tribute trade system and the Western-style treaty order compatible, but also that the tribute concept tended to subsume the Western treaty concept even into the twentieth century.

Civilization and the Other: "nomads"

Coexisting with these major Sinicized states were many different types of political units that resisted China's civilizational allure, most notably the various pastoral, highly mobile tribes and semi-nomadic peoples in the northern steppes (variously known as Mongols, Khitans, Uighurs, and others). A thorough discussion of these peoples and their foreign policies is beyond the scope of this chapter, and the main point here is to contrast their cultures and identities with those of the Sinicized states. The nomads were less centrally organized on account of the ecology of the steppes, which favored mobility and thus made tribal domination difficult. What centralization did exist was mainly a result of the personal charisma and strength of the ruler, and thus "tribal rivalries and fragmentation were common" (Perdue 2005: 520; Crossley 1997). Even the Zunghar empire that emerged in the late seventeenth century had only "an increasingly 'statelike' apparatus of rule" and never developed the same centralization or institutionalization as did the Sinicized states (Perdue 2005: 518).

China and nomads existed along a vast frontier zone, and the disparate political and cultural ecology of the various nomads and China itself led to a relationship that, although mostly symbiotic, was never as institutionalized and hence was less stable than were relations between the Sinicized states. These nomads had vastly different worldviews and political structures from the Sinicized states: they rejected Chinese ideas of civilization such as written texts or settled agriculture and they were playing a different international game by different rules; thus crafting enduring or stable relations was difficult. The frontier was only turned into a border when other states such as Russia began to expand eastward in the eighteenth century, and the nomads were left with nowhere to move.

The major exception were the Manchus, descended from Jurchens and more settled than the Mongols to their west. The Manchu state emerged quickly in the early seventeenth century when Nurhaci (originally a Ming vassal) centralized control over a number of disparate tribes to the northeast of China (Crossley 1997). The Jurchens and Manchus were never Mongols, and for long stretches of time their economic agenda was comparable to Chosŏn, Ming, and other more settled societies. Indeed, the Manchu conquest of the Ming was more opportunism than design, and, while ruling China and absorbing some of the traditional Han institutions, they retained unique Manchu elements as well. Although Qing worldviews and identity never completely Sinicized, the Qing used many of the institutional forms and discursive style of traditional Chinese dynasties in dealing with the neighboring states.

As David Wright (2002: 58) asks, "Why all the fighting?" Although popular imagination sees the nomads prowling like hungry wolves outside the Great Wall, attacking randomly and whenever possible, there was in fact a logic to Chinese (and Korean) interactions with the nomads.

At its core, the Chinese–nomad relationship was about trade. Nomads needed three things from agricultural China – grains, metals, and textiles – and they would trade, raid, or engage in tribute to gain them. Peter Perdue (2005: 520) notes that "it was almost never the ambition of a steppe leader to conquer China itself. Steppe leaders staged raids on the Chinese frontier to plunder it for their own purposes." For its part, China used offense (as Johnston emphasizes), defense (the Great Wall), trade, and diplomacy in attempting to deal with the nomads. Thomas Barfield (1989) argues that, when trade was more advantageous, the nomads traded; when trade was difficult or restricted, they raided China's frontier towns to get the goods they needed (Khazanov 1984). The Chinese weighed the costs of warring with the nomads against the problems of trading with them. As Sechin Jagchid and Van Jay Symons (1989: 1) write, "when the nomads felt they were getting too little or the Chinese felt they were giving too much compared to the relative power of each participant, war broke out."

However, endemic frontier skirmishes took place not only for material reasons but also for reasons of identity and deeply held cultural beliefs. Nomads were willing to trade with the Chinese and Koreans, but they had no intention of truly taking on Chinese norms and cultures as did Korea, Vietnam, and Japan. This led to a "chasm between Chinese and nomadic perceptions of themselves and each other" (Jagchid and Symons 1989: 4). David Wright concludes that:

China's failure to solve its barbarian problem definitively before the advent of the Manchu Qing dynasty was a function neither of Chinese administrative incompetence nor of barbarian pugnacity, but of the incompatibility and fixed proximity between very different societies, ecologies, and worldviews. Many statements in historical records strongly suggest that the Chinese and the Nomads had clear ideas of their differences and were committed to preserving them against whatever threats the other side posed.

(Wright 2002: 76)

Chinese–nomad relations highlight the importance of ideas to the outbreak of violence. Material power is important, but just as important are the beliefs and identities that serve to define a group, state, or people. China was able to develop stable relations with other units that adopted similar civilizational identities: states that conducted diplomacy in the Chinese style, and states that were recognizable and legitimate to the Chinese. It was much harder to establish stable relations with political units that rejected China's vision of the world.

Conclusion

Chinese civilization had an enduring and wide-ranging political, social, and cultural impact on surrounding states and peoples. States emulated China in order to deal more effectively with the massive presence that it presented, and Chinese ideas were grafted – sometimes uncomfortably – onto and into vibrant indigenous cultures and societies. These Chinese practices also provided a range of institutional and discursive tools which were hierarchic and compromised sovereignty with which to moderate and avoid conflict.

The argument presented here extends Iain Johnston's work in two ways. First, it rebalances scholarly inquiry about war and historical East Asian international relations away from a focus mainly on China–nomad relations to include both nomads and Sinic states. It is understandable why scholars such as Johnston (1995) or Chua (2007) focused on nomads, because that is where most of the fighting occurred. But explaining East Asia requires explaining both war and peace – and the stable relations between Sinicized states is just as important as the endemic violence on China's northern borders. Second, the argument in this chapter emphasizes one of Johnston's oft-overlooked points: that East Asia operated with two international orders: a civilization encompassing the Sinic states and a different international order that regulated relations between the Sinic states and "barbarians."

The East Asian experience also contrasts with a widely held idea about the link between states and war. After all, Charles Tilly (1975: 42) famously wrote that "war made the state, and the state made war," and it is common to view warmaking and state-making as inextricably intertwined. Yet, in contrast to Europe, where states developed in the context of continual threats to their existence, in East Asia states developed in part in order to ensure their continued survival with respect to China. All states use force if they deem it effective for dealing with threats, and East Asia was no different from Europe in this regard. What was quite different, however, was the source of threats. While in Europe the more powerful states became, the more they fought with each other, in East Asia the more powerful states became, the more stable were their relations. It was the most centralized and enduring states that crafted the most stable relations with each other, and violence and instability tended to arise between states and non-state actors. Furthermore, the East Asian states emerged centuries before their counterparts in Europe, and they survived much longer. While these Sinicized states crafted stable and enduring relations with each other, they were unable to do the same with the nomads, who had different identities, goals, and political organization. Exploring why this is the case has the potential to advance our theories of international relations in a number of ways.

Although China may have been the source of a long-lasting civilization in East Asia in the distant past, today it has no more civilizational influence than does modern Greece. Few states or people in East Asia look to China for ideas, for example, or for practical solutions to present problems. Yet there does exist a historical thread from the past to the present: as China has grown increasingly powerful and self-confident, speculation about how it might act in the present has increased. Most notable are questions about whether it can adjust itself to the Western international norms that have dominated the world for the past few centuries. Yet we should also ask whether there exists any thread that links contemporary Chinese behavior to the past. If, for example, it has few messianic impulses today and instead focuses on pragmatic relations with its neighbors, the world can probably adjust more easily to a powerful China than to a China that sets out to remake the world in its own image.

Notes

1 An extraordinary diversity of peoples, cultures, and polities existed on the northern steppes, and for expositional ease I refer to these in the text as "nomads," although the term is far from satisfactory.
2 Quoted in Pollack (1986: 3).
3 Thanks to Gari Ledyard for these insights.
4 The Spanish armada consisted of 30,000 troops on 130 ships, and was defeated by 20,000 English troops (Hawley 2005: xii; Turnbull 2002; Lee 1999).
5 They include the 1876 Treaty of Kangwha between Korea and Japan, the 1882 Regulations for Maritime and Overland Trade between Chinese and Korean Subjects, and the 1885 Tianjin Treaty between China and Japan.

5 The Samurai ride to Huntington's rescue

Japan ponders its global and regional roles

David Leheny

In November 2004, members of Japan's Second Middle Eastern Cultural Exchange and Dialogue Mission, headed by leading area specialist Yamauchi Masayuki,[1] made a pitch for Tokyo's global influence based in part on an expectation, referencing Samuel Huntington, that its distinctiveness might allow it to sidestep the civilizational battles then raging in the Middle East. The mission released its report while the Koizumi cabinet, in the face of increasing violence in Baghdad and deep misgivings among Japanese voters, famously held its unpopular line on supporting the American mission in Iraq. The report explained the suicide bombings as the results of the "clash of civilizations" (MOFA 2004: 9), but argued that Japan would have a clear role in allowing the region to move beyond it. In this report, "soft power" (rendered as "*sofuto pawā*") is defined as "cultural power," and the authors stipulate that it should flow from Japan's modernizing experience, making it appealing both to the Middle East and to other developing nations:

> Like last year, people showed great interest in Japan's experience as a non-Western nation that had rapidly modernized, but maintained its own traditional culture while doing so. It is a longstanding desire of lesser developed countries to maintain their cultural identities even in the midst of the process of globalization.
>
> (Ibid.: 3)

This is a familiar narrative in Japanese debates about its international role. The country developed quickly but did not fully Westernize in doing so; it has valuable experience that it can share with others, in terms both of economic growth and the maintenance of a distinctive cultural identity. If there is anything unfamiliar about the claims, it is the geographical focus: in the 1980s and 1990s, these were predominantly heard in the "Asian values" arguments that frequently stipulated a special relationship, based on cultural closeness, between Japan and the countries of East and Southeast Asia. But with the rise of China, whose claim to cultural closeness with Asia is potentially greater than that of Japan, the juxtaposition of Japan's modernity to that of the West is no longer a clear selling point for Japanese influence in the region, at least in a manner that easily distinguishes it from its continental rival. Those arguing for Japan's soft power, its civilizational role, or its cultural importance in international affairs have been using these memorable and common tropes in new ways, combining them with new motifs and applying them beyond the Asia-Pacific. But these debates also expose tensions between different readings of the word "civilization," whether referring to culturally distinctive units or groupings or to a process of development and refinement.

In this chapter, I take this volume's theme of "civilizational states" to reflect on changing debates within Japan about what Japan is and what it represents to the world. But I take issue with the idea that civilizations or civilizational states can be defined and deployed as part of an explanatory framework for international politics. Instead, I suggest that there have been narratives about a cultural essence (which cannot easily be divorced from notions of "civilization," and which are now inseparable from Japan's subordinate position in the American imperium) responsible for a durable Japanese way of approaching the world, and that these narratives are contested even as they continue to provide the basis for strategic visions about Japan's international role. As Peter Katzenstein notes in his introductory chapter to this volume, arguments about civilizations in world politics run the gamut from Huntingtonian claims about cultural dispositions to (Patrick) Jacksonian discursive investigations of the construction and use of civilizational tropes by states and political elites. Often described as an ethnically homogeneous island nation (populated by a culturally unique people) willing to act as an economic giant but a political pygmy, Japan would seem to be ideal for the dispositional case; surely, there must be something in the water to make the Japanese so, well, Japanese both at home and abroad.

Needless to say, a civilizational perspective need not be so crude. Katzenstein's depiction of "multiple modernities . . . and multiple zones of prestige," drawing respectively from S. N. Eisenstadt and Randall Collins, eschews cultural essentialism and leaves space for the analysis of agency and mechanisms that produce behavior. But I argue that what is most distinctive about Japan's international stance is not any clear pattern of behavior or style or diplomacy, but rather the durability of the idea of Japanese distinctiveness, or of Japan as a weirdly liminal space that bridges the modern and the traditional, the East and the West, and other Orientalist/Occidentalist binaries. Indeed, no matter what Japan does (or what Japanese analysts and political figures want it to do), it might still be described, both positively and negatively, as a country that respects tradition while modernizing or as one that has turned hybridity into an art form, effortlessly "Japanizing" foreign practices and adopting them as part of a cultural core. The practices change, but the discourses endure. As Jackson notes in his conclusion to this volume, the notion of distinctive civilizations may be powerful and consequential as a rhetorical device, but it is less helpful when imagined as a discrete cause (or a framing device for investigating causes) of the messy business of international relations.

I proceed in five parts. First, I examine Japan's postwar international relations, drawing attention to Japanese articulations of the country's global and regional roles and to the broader external perception that something broad and almost primordial about the country itself – not just the strategies of individual leaders or only the specific policies of the state – has been responsible for its particular behavior. I then discuss Japanese debates about "civilization," showing that these have largely been subordinate to claims about national culture and have also rendered the notion of a distinctive Japan a difficult concept for use in Japanese debates about the country's role. Third, I connect these debates about culture and concerns about civilization to intellectual and social trends in post-Bubble Japan, following Tomiko Yoda's (2006) argument about fear that Japan's collective "agency" may have disappeared. I then examine recent arguments by Japanese conservatives about the country's global and regional roles, focusing especially on one highly popular account that emphasizes Japan's need to return to its cultural roots. Finally, I provide a brief sketch of recent discussions of Japan's soft power, pointing out that, while there is widespread support for the idea that Japan should have and employ soft power resources, there is little precision in these accounts regarding what Japanese values are or why they should be appealing. They are, however, marked by certain discursive continuities more than a coherent vision of how Japan affects the larger world.

Japanese civilization in Asia

Before the Middle East mission articulated a vision of Japan's special role in the Arab world, most observers focused on the shape of Japanese connections to the Pacific Rim. In an essay in a popular and well-received volume published during the heyday of concerns about Japan's growing clout in the Bubble era, Shafiqul Islam wrote that the "growing Japanese economic presence in East Asia is fueling the perception that since the 1980s Japan has begun to do with peaceful economic means what it could not do by violent military means in the 1930s" (Islam 1993: 352). This oft-repeated view was more of an absent-minded shorthand in diplomatic and political economic circles than a carefully considered statement about Japanese diplomacy and economic activity in the years following the Plaza Accord. After all, despite the connections to Japan's prewar fascist regime among the leadership of its postwar Liberal Democratic Party (LDP), and however unsettling Prime Minister Nakasone Yasuhiro's occasional forays into racial theorizing,[2] it would be hard to suggest that the Japan of 1988 was really no different from that of 1945, except for its choice of weapons. But, still, the shorthand persisted.

Islam was merely referring to the perception, not espousing it himself; he ultimately argued that Japan's economic behavior in the 1980s was unexceptional, aimed by different actors as a rational way to maximize economic and diplomatic benefits while minimizing costs. But his references to the then popular but now moribund notion of "Japan Inc." remind us of one of the key stories about Japan that emerged during the spectacular transformation of its international image, from timid American ally to a voluble and even menacing global presence. Japan had, in this popular version, learned methodological lessons in World War II, but had not really changed its goals. Military means for regional domination had failed, but economic tools might carry the day, through the conquering of foreign import markets and the rapid spread of Japanese capital around the Asia-Pacific. In this version, other postwar transformations – the consolidation of democratic institutions, the development of large-scale and sometimes combative social movements, the spread of wealth across a broad (but not as broad as often described) middle class – were rendered less important than the idea of some kind of durable Japanese drive for power, one seemingly determined less by the agency of individual actors, or by the structure of the regional state system, than by an unspoken but collective will. For American and European exporters, mid-level local managers in Japanese-owned businesses in Asia, and pundits concerned about the potential decline of American primacy in the face of this Asian challenge, the notion of Japan Inc. or of a Japanese "system" (see van Wolferen 1990), one that could replace the seemingly inapt use of the simple idea of a "state," helped to explain the otherwise inexplicable replacement of American power by a country without an overseas military presence or a visibly strategy-minded leader.

This perception was very much of its era, and the resulting fights over "Japan-bashing," racism, and the structure of Japanese politics have exposed most of the tensions in it, just as the end of the Bubble economy has consigned the most alarmist claims to the dustbin of history, or at of least poorly researched history. It was not, however, without roots in Japanese political and social discourse. Only the most aggressive of Japanese writers (such as, most notably, the right-wing novelist turned politician Ishihara Shintarō) would argue that Japan should aim to supplant American power. But many others were relatively comfortable with the idea of a Japanese essence – a culture, a spirit, a soul – that could not be boiled down to the agency of specific leaders and their decisions, or even of a common set of political principles and institutions. The evidence for this unique essence lay less in a comprehensive assessment of global cultures, with Japan in a distinctive spot, than in the construction of an imagined, modern West, and of Japan as its authentic counterpart that could speak for the equally authentic if less modernized peoples of Asia.

Japan's postwar "Asianism" draws many of its roots from the prewar era, in part because the intellectual core of the argument could be meaningfully separated from issues of war responsibility, guilt, or prewar aims. Whether one believes that the Japanese government was on a brutal, militaristic campaign of colonization, or on the misdirected but noble mission of liberating the countries of Asia from Western imperialism, one could still have faith in legitimate cultural ties between Japanese and other Asians, particularly when compared to Soviet expansion or America's informal postwar empire (Koschmann 1997). And so Japan's postwar diplomatic initiatives in the region, particularly its efforts at economic leadership, could be understood in terms of a "flying geese" metaphor developed by economist Akamatsu Kaname in the 1930s. The complexity of Akamatsu's argument, which hinged on a form of product cycle theory, was in many ways less important than the symbolic role it played in legitimizing the "Greater East Asian Coprosperity Sphere," by implying that other Asian countries would be drawn along to modernity by following Japan and allowing it to fight through the headwinds (see Cumings 1984; Kasahara 2004; Bernard and Ravenhill 1995; Samuels 2007). Indeed, Japanese aid schemes to the rest of Asia through much of the postwar era were premised on ideas of a regional industrial complex that functioned, in part, as a hierarchical division of labor, but rationalized by the understanding that other Asian countries would develop by cooperating with and learning from Japan (for example, Hatch and Yamamura 1996). Divergent notions of the region's economic success thus informed the contested 1993 World Bank Report *The East Asian Miracle*, with American economists emphasizing the neo-liberal policies and Japanese economists and contributors emphasizing an East Asian developmental model requiring the active hand of the state (Wade 1996). Aid scholar David Seddon (2005: 64) describes it as "replete with contradictions."

This struggle over the report represents more than a simple intellectual tiff. It instead is emblematic of a struggle to legitimize internationally the notion of Asian difference (or, alternatively, of modern Western universalism) – something occasionally construed institutionally, sometimes culturally, sometimes historically – that could be politically exploitable. In Japan, the idea of an East Asian model has never been separable from the idea of a Japanese model that has shaped the rest of the region. Usually it is voiced less clumsily than Foreign Minister Asō Tarō's strange comment that Taiwan's educational successes demonstrated the positive outcomes of Japanese imperialism there; the remark "had the unique effect of uniting both China and Taiwan" in its denunciation (Kang 2007: 172). Sometimes, however, its articulation has been general enough to be defensible to Japan's neighbors. Malaysian Prime Minister Mahathir Mohammed's "Look East" policy in the 1990s lionized Japan's success as a model for the region, arguing that there was much his own country could learn from the Japanese. This might, of course, have been a cagey effort to extract more guarantees of development assistance and of training visas for underemployed Malaysians to enter Japan, but it was also a part of Mahathir's own efforts to express Asian unity against Western influence (see Leheny 2003: 133–4); he co-authored, with the right-wing provocateur Ishihara, *The Asia that Can Say No* – as in "no" to the United States.

The perception that Shafiqul Islam describes might then be seen wholly in negative terms: a country that dominated Asia in the past wants to do it again. Singaporean leader Lee Kuan Yew famously suggested that allowing

Japan to send its troops on peacekeeping missions would be like giving whiskey-filled chocolates to an alcoholic. But it might also – as it was usually in Japan – be seen more positively. There was something about Japan that it shared with Asia, distinguishing both from the homogenizing effects of Western modernity, and even establishing Japan as the effective barrier. For leftists, Japan's postwar pacifism was deeply rooted in cultural soil it shared with an Asia to which the country bore special responsibilities; for conservatives, Japan's success demonstrated that it had one-upped the West and could lead a grateful Asia more effectively. Japan's simultaneous, if potentially contradictory, distinctiveness and connections to Asia were therefore institutionalized and taken for granted, similar to the ways in which "liberty" and "rights" are taken for granted in the United States. There is remarkably little disagreement on the basic ideas, but they are readily exploitable for myriad actors seeking, in Japan's case, to renounce military force or to embrace it, or, in the American case, to support gay marriage or universal access to assault weapons. The notion of a Japanese essence – a culture, a civilization, or a collective will – has been as common in Japanese political discourse as it was among those who looked at the purchase of the Rockefeller Center and compared it, without irony, to the attack on Pearl Harbor.

Civilizational analysis in and about Japan

When Japanese professional baseball adopted interleague play in 2005, with Central and Pacific League teams now battling it out in the regular season, the monthly *Yakyū Kozō* (*Baseball Kid*) titled its April issue "*Se-Pa bunmei no shōtotsu*" ("The Central-Pacific Clash of Civilizations"), showing just how far Samuel Huntington's terminology had permeated Japanese popular lingo.[3] *The Clash of Civilizations*, when translated, was a bestseller in Japan as it was in many other nations, spurring the Tokyo publisher Shūeisha to request that Huntington add a short volume (*shinsho*) just for Japanese audiences; *Bunmei no shōtotsu to 21-seiki no nihon* (*The Clash of Civilizations and 21st Century Japan*) was published in 2000, arguing that Japan would ultimately have to choose between supporting the United States or tying itself more closely to China. Crucially, his description of Japan as its own civilization – distinct somehow from the "Confucian" civilization that emanates from China and covers much of the rest of East Asia – fitted well with long-term debates over Japanese uniqueness and particularity. Like observers elsewhere, Japanese writers have struggled with competing ideas of civilization as a universal, teleological project of development and as a form of differentiation between civilizations. In part because many constructions of Japanese national identity have been built largely around ideas both of cultural uniqueness and of rapid modernization, Japanese debates have focused chiefly on parallel forms of development that allow the country to match an imagined West (and, in particular, the postwar American imperium) but without ever really becoming part of it. In some ways, the complex and open-ended nature of recent English-language studies of Japan from civilizational perspectives has made them difficult to use either in assertions of Japanese particularism or in critiques of these discourses.

The most famous Japanese source on "civilization" is the classic treatise by Fukuzawa Yukichi, the leading Meiji-era intellectual and educational theorist, who published *Bunmeiron no gairyaku* (*Outline of a Theory of Civilization*) in 1876.[4] In Fukuzawa's view, civilization referred both to progress and to differentiation; Japanese civilization was different from that of "the West" (*seiyō*), but was also on a timeline of progress that could in large part be measured with reference to Western modernity and to Asian backwardness. Crucially, for Fukuzawa, civilizing Japan meant not only the construction of individual citizens in line with Enlightenment principles from the West, but also the construction of a "national subject," a nation with a collective will that could support the new Meiji state that had emerged after the 1868 "restoration" and toppling of the Tokugawa regime (Koschmann 2006: 126; Yonetani 2006; Tanaka 1993: 36–40). In this version, the notion was inseparable both from Japan's sudden emergence into an international political system dominated by Western conceptions of progress and from the domestic debates about how Japan had to respond to the threat from the West, whether by resisting it through cultivation of presumably indigenous characteristics or by accommodation through emulation of foreign institutions.

With the international spread of sociological and anthropological studies of "civilizations" in the 1970s and 1980s, Japanese scholars struggled to fit this notion into existing debates about the nature of Japaneseness. Starting in 1979, Japan's National Museum of Ethnology began to sponsor annual international symposia on key themes in ethnology, and in 1983 hosted one on "Japanese Civilization in the Modern World." In his introduction to the volume resulting from the symposium, the museum's chief, Umesao Tadao, engaged the differences between culture and civilization directly. Without going so far as to say that studies of culture emphasized only specific aspects of a broad social milieu, he argued that "civilizational analysis" should be understood as, in effect, a form of "systems analysis," broadly connecting the interaction of a people with their physical environment, and particularly in terms of the material cultures they ultimately produced. In this view, this approach – to grasp and to label its internal functions and interdependencies – is to work at an extraordinary and unnatural intellectual distance, making the "study of civilizations as knowledge from outer space" (*uchūteki ninshiki to shite no bunmeigaku*) (Umesao 1984: 16–28, at 16). Other chapters in the volume somewhat predictably involved efforts to define what "civilizational analysis" actually meant or to shoehorn apparently existing research agendas into the framework of comparative civilizational studies. Despite the familiarity of the term "civilization," the volume did not serve as a harbinger of things to come.

The pre-Huntington neglect of the concept of "civilizations" in popular Japanese debates, particularly ones that dealt with politics, may also have resulted from the sense that "civilization," viewed either in terms of broad comparisons or as modernization and progress, seemed to privilege external influences on Japan. Partly for this reason, throughout much of the postwar era, *bunmei* (civilization) was overtaken in Japan by *bunka* (culture). As has been well documented elsewhere, Ruth Benedict's *The Chrysanthemum and the Sword*, published shortly after World War II, became an immediate and durable touchstone for postwar Japanese debates regarding the meaning of "Japaneseness." Japanese authors such as Nakane Chie and Doi Takeo created bestselling images of a Japan distinguished by its vertically oriented society with "village" characteristics (Nakane) or by the dependence of Japanese on the embracing love of their mothers and, by extension, other Japanese (Doi). Particularly after the publication in English of volumes such as Ezra Vogel's *Japan as Number One* and the rise of Japanese studies at American universities, these cultural accounts, which owed a great deal to Orientalist claims of American researchers such as Benedict, boomeranged back into popular American discourse, having been validated by the now translated works by Japanese scholars.

Armchair etymology has particular risks in discussions of Asian politics. The *reductio ad absurdum* inherent in the frequent statement that "the Chinese character for 'crisis' also means 'opportunity'" simultaneously fossilizes the meanings of words and essentializes ideas as "Asian" or "non-Western"; American oil companies presumably did not need to learn classical Chinese to figure out that the crisis in Iraq meant new opportunities for them. I am usually reluctant to take the "the Japanese have a word for . . ." route, but the crucial similarity and difference of the words for "civilization" and "culture" bear some scrutiny, at least in terms of the extraordinary attention to the latter and relative lack to the former in popular debates. As Umesao (1984: 11–13) notes, their rendering in Japanese as, respectively, *bunmei* and *bunka* suggests a potential connection between them, in that both begin with "*bun*" (letters or literature): 文明 and 文化. But Umesao does not go on to analyze the subsequent characters, instead shifting immediately to the debates over the relationship of the compounds. Here, however, the varied use of the subsequent characters would render any generalization of their meaning nearly impossible. Civilization's "*mei*" refers to clarity, light, and revelation, which might suggest a process of illumination. Culture's "*ka*" means "shape" or "quality." But it too is frequently used in compounds that delineate processes (for example, *sangyōka*, or industrialization; *jiyūka*, or liberalization) with teleological implications that do not differ radically from the idea of enlightenment.

In his genealogical study of the intellectual and environmental influences on Japanese architecture, Kawazoe Noboru follows the idea of a "systems" (*shisutemu, kei*) approach, referring to physical "hardware" and institutional "software" – in effect, the uses to which devices are put – to conceptualize civilizational difference; for example, he describes Japanese civilization in terms of *girei taikei*, or "systems of courtesy," by examining the development of shrines and other buildings (Kawazoe 1994: 46–54). But he acknowledges that one of the problems in using the term *bunmei* is that it emphasizes the external sources of Japanese social behavior, leaving *bunka* to cover indigenous or autonomous Japanese practices; "civilization" is thus the "Chinese civilization" or "Western civilization" from which Japan adopted so many institutions, and "culture" is the Japanese core (ibid.: 23). Kawazoe's goal is analytical, not prescriptive or evaluative, but his depiction echoes the German *Kultur/Zivilisation* debates from the early twentieth century, in which the "distinctiveness of German thought and *Kultur*" might be juxtaposed with the "decrepit *Zivilisation* of its [Western] enemies" (Jackson 2006: 96).[5]

As a result, "civilization," while used mostly in a positive sense, can also imply the loss of some kind of authenticity. Conservative politicians in the United States and Japan might refer to "Western civilization" or "Japanese civilization" but would describe one set of Americans or Japanese as "civilized" only in a form of anti-elitist sarcasm; one would be careful not to praise the "civilized" city dwellers, drinking chardonnay and lattes, while disparaging their "less civilized" counterparts back in rural areas, who are presumably too busy noodling for catfish in the American south or jostling in loincloths in a festival in Saga prefecture to have time to TiVo *Mad Men*. The crucial difference here is in the word "culture," which, as Eisenstadt himself notes, has extraordinary implications in Japanese social and political discourse; like "liberty" and "rights" in the United States, the idea of culture – or, more specifically, of "Japanese culture" – is utterly essential to notions of Japanese difference. The "discourses of Japaneseness" (*nihonjinron*, or, more literally, "discourses about Japanese people") that stipulate that Japanese are collectivists – or tied especially tightly to their mothers' indulgence, or embedded in a "shame" rather than "guilt" culture, or preternaturally respectful of authority, and so forth – are less frequently but still recognizably called *nihonbunkaron*, or "discourses about Japanese culture." These have, as has been widely noted, been crucial to the construction and maintenance of postwar political identity and legitimacy, differentiating the Japanese primarily from an imagined West and, with the partial exception of other Asian cultures, from the rest of the world as well.[6]

Indeed, the relative failure of "civilizational analysis" in Japanese intellectual circles might have prepared readers for the limited appreciation in Japan of S. N. Eisenstadt's (1996) *Japanese Civilization: A Comparative View* and Johann Arnason's (1997) *Social Theory and the Japanese Experience*. Although translated into Japanese and scheduled for publication in three volumes by Iwanami (volumes 1 and 2 appeared in 2004 and 2006), and despite the dedication of a 1998 symposium to his approach at the International Research Center for Japanese Studies (*Nichibunken*), Eisenstadt's work appears to have had a limited impact in Japan.[7] Some of this is no doubt due in part to the complexity of his ideas, which makes them less likely to be adopted by political pundits than the Wagnerian drama in Huntington's book; it is harder to describe interleague play in baseball, even with the requisite irony, as an Axial break than to suggest something timelessly different about the Central and Pacific leagues.

Even if written more simply and concisely, however, Eisenstadt's views of Japanese distinctiveness – always a potential plus in marketing – are mixed with critical analysis of the *nihonjinron* ("theories of Japaneseness") that have long typified public discussions of Japanese culture.[8] That is, in making the case for a comparative civilizational approach, Eisenstadt distanced himself deliberately from the spokespeople of essential Japaneseness.[9] In his view, whatever value in-group trust (a key feature in his analysis) has for Japan has to be understood not as the outcome of a metaphysical decency or the aesthetic judgment of the Japanese but rather as the result of a polity molded without transcendental religious claims about authority that had to be over-come in the (Axial) moment of secular transformation. This is hard to describe in the 20,000 words or so that usually constitute a bestselling *shinsho* such as Huntington's Japan-oriented sequel to *The Clash of Civilizations*. The concept of civilization may furthermore lose some of its magic and appeal when rendered in terms that make cultural distinctiveness seem epiphenom-enal, and perhaps even an afterthought.

Civilization as identity and its loss

This does not make civilization an unimportant discourse in Japan, but it is just that: a discourse that builds on specific constructions of how Japanese history has unfolded. In discussions of global politics (even when written by Japanese scholars), the country's history is usually broken down into four and a half basic stages. In the premodern era, Japanese warlords competed to control different parts of the archipelago partly shaped by cultural influences from China, as David Kang notes in his contribution to this volume. The Tokugawa shogunate ended that period by unifying the country in a polity marked by a warrior-led status hierarchy, a policy of national isolation (*sakoku*) to ward off colonial incursions and technological transformation too slow to match up against the West. Commodore Perry's "black ships" inaugurate the third period, "opening" Japan and leading to its rapid economic and political modernization, but also to the development of state corporatism and militarism, and culminating in the national cataclysm of World War II. The United States once again played a crucial role in shaping Japan's fourth, "postwar" period, with the country pacified, democratized (if a bit fixated on leadership from one party), and mobilized for "miraculous" economic growth with relatively egalitarian distribution. Finally (and incom-pletely), there is a long-term economic slowdown, conspicuous in its genera-tion of widespread fears of national decline, a reactive nationalism that has fueled the desire for remilitarization, and the zany cool of Japanese pop culture. More impressionistically, this version moves from competing samurai houses to the creation of the Tokugawa government in Edo around 1600; from a decaying Tokugawa economy to the arrival of Commodore

Perry in 1853; from the Meiji Restoration of 1868 to the Manchurian Incident of 1931, and to the dropping of two atomic bombs in 1945; from the ashes of defeat to the image of a highly successful and egalitarian "Japan Inc." in the late 1980s; and then through the recession, the Aum attack, and the Kobe earthquake of 1995 to *Sailor Moon*, and to Koizumi Junichiro's Elvis impersonation and his controversial visits to Yasukuni Shrine.

As shorthand, this is no more inaccurate than most national histories, but the rigid periodization and definitive labeling together efface the complexity of the country's past and provide the opportunity for politically self-serving lessons that might be drawn by different observers about where Japan went right or wrong. They allow for the post facto articulation of continuities that simplify Japan's historical path and miss the contingencies and choices shaping the institutions that define today's Japan. For example, trade barriers were occasionally explained (or even justified) in the 1970s and 1980s by referring to the country's long-term purported xenophobia, ostensibly growing from eighteenth-century national isolation, forgetting that the policy was never as complete as often stated, not to mention that it ended over a century earlier (Hellyer 2002). US pundits who confidently predicted that an Iraq under American domination could be democratized as easily and successfully as Japan had forgotten (or probably never knew) that Japan had extensive, if largely dysfunctional, democratic institutions before World War II (Dower 2002), as well as a party system that military leaders destroyed only through resort to terrorism and assassination. Similarly, the overwhelming image of postwar Japan's meritocracy and a wide middle class hid remarkable and durable gaps in educational and employment access (Ishida 1993). And, as hyped as it has been in the media, the post-Bubble nationalism seems to have extended only as far as a new willingness to consider UN peacekeeping missions and more defensive capabilities in Japan, not even to broad public support for tougher talk against China (Oros 2008).

But Japan's "long postwar"[10] has entailed the construction of several broad templates for public discussion of the country, involving contributions from politicians, scholars, journalists, and others seeking to make sense of what Japan is and what it has become. Like observers elsewhere, they deploy – sometimes reflexively and sometimes deliberately – common tropes of national history that provide well-understood precedents, symbols of a long and successful process of modernization (even if interrupted by the militarist hiccup of the 1930s and 1940s), and the legitimacy associated with a shared set of references. One was cultural distinctiveness. Indeed, while Japan's most famous postwar political intellectual, Maruyama Masao, famously mined Japanese intellectual history to find the cultural roots that allowed Japan to slide so easily into fascism (see Bellah 2003), *nihonjinron* theorists such as Doi tried to resuscitate "humanist" elements from prewar claims about Japan's uniqueness (and superiority) that could still separate Japan effectively from the America that had occupied it and from the industrialized West that served as the only non-communist model of postwar development (Borovoy 2008).

Even during the period of Japanese high-speed growth, marked by broadly optimistic views of Japan's future, there was considerable debate about the country's past, and about what ought to be maintained. To be sure, legitimate postwar discourse required a distancing from the prewar militarist regime (a difficult task for those politicians who, like Prime Minister Kishi Nobusuke, had been among its leading figures), but, beyond that, history was malleable. Just as samurai imagery had been useful to wartime leaders building martial images of valor and loyalty, postwar film directors such as Okamoto Kihachi and Kobayashi Masaki made samurai classics about independent-minded rebels bucking the system. Japanese traditions – kimono, tea ceremonies, village festivals, cherry-blossom viewing – could be meaningfully separated from the militarist regime that had also put them to ideological use.

The problem, of course, was that Japan's postwar economic growth had arguably come at a high price: the country's essence or soul. Wartime leaders had vilified their American and European enemies by mocking their cruelty, their racism, their philistine materialism, and their decadence. But the cornerstone of LDP rule in the postwar era, the country's miraculous economic expansion, had taken place under the extraordinary shadow of the American imperium. Japanese intellectuals could (and did) emphasize that the Japanese economy had grown far more rapidly than that of the United States and, particularly by the 1980s, that the country had achieved something that no other nation ever had. But they could not avoid the extent to which Japan had been shaped and controlled by the United States during this time. They ultimately could not avoid the fear that Japan had been Americanized, a charge leveled particularly at young people (especially women) whose behavior seemed not to fit traditional mores, but often attached more casually to the population as a whole.

With the country's extraordinary economic success, which became most apparent in the freewheeling 1980s, leaders such as Prime Minister Nakasone Yasuhiro could make an interesting counter-claim; Japan had succeeded not by forgetting its past, but rather by modernizing while retaining its distinctively Japanese roots. Nakasone – himself deeply influenced by the presidential stature of Ronald Reagan and the intellectual clout of Margaret Thatcher – sought to make Japan a more patriotic and proud nation in part through the valorization of an imagined past. With the "*furusato* [hometown] movement," the Japanese government encouraged smaller cities and rural areas around Japan to promote their local characteristics (a traditional food, festival, or the like) that served as the core emotional tie between themselves and the Tokyo (or perhaps Osaka or Kyoto) dwellers who themselves had roots in Aomori, Shimane, or Wakayama prefectures (Robertson 1988; see also Ivy 1995). City dwellers were all understood to have come from somewhere else, and, in part through local tourism and family visits once or twice a year, they would be encouraged to remember their ties to an authentic, pre-urban Japan, one that was closer to the soil and therefore to their cultural roots. Tokyo, a cosmopolitan giant, was not exactly seen as non-Japanese, but, whatever a source of national pride its financial districts and booming skyscrapers might have been, the city reflected something about a civilizing process that threatened to leave tradition – and, for that reason, the "real" Japan – in the past.

But during the long recession of the 1990s, which coincided with disasters such as the Aum Shinrikyo attack on the Tokyo subway and the government's appallingly slow response to the Kobe earthquake of 1995, Japan did not seem like the modern, civilized, focused nation that had created its own economic miracle. Neither did it seem, with its millenarian cults and garish youth fashions, like a sanctuary of cultural tradition. In popular discourse, it became easier to make the argument that Japan had fundamentally lost its path (Leheny 2006b: 27–47). Japan's problems were increasingly judged to be not simply disconnected maladies but, rather, symptomatic of a larger Japanese malaise, a torpor from which, as left-leaning author Yamada Taiichi put it, the country would need some kind of shock to be woken out of:

> The highest value in Japan is for calm [*heion*]. So if we don't experience a real decline [that can shake things up], our sense of values will become completely ambiguous. It's gotten so that we're not really working for ourselves or for our own standards, but rather, since the end of the war, for this unchanging goal [of economic development]. And now the downside of this approach is continuing to become more apparent. But we don't have any ability on our own to change this paradigm. I think most Japanese are subconsciously hoping for foreign pressure or for national decline [*shūmatsu*], something from outside that will force us to change.
>
> (Yamada and Kawamoto 1995: 33)

At stake, therefore, was not just the solution to Japan's problems, or growing doubts about the success of the Japanese postwar economy that had fueled notions of what Japan could offer a grateful Asia; it was instead confidence in the national community that could lead the region. As literature scholar Tomiko Yoda puts it, the deep anxiety surrounding Japanese social and political debates in the 1990s involved "the terrifying prospect of disappearance, not so much of the master narrative but of the desire (and agency) that used to generate it" (Yoda 2006: 49). And the recent debates about Japan's role in Asia must be viewed in the context of Japanese writers, politicians, and scholars who are trying to define what contemporary Japan is, and how it connects to the country's past, or at least the appropriate or laudatory parts of it.

Samurai as diplomats

What would a Japan imbued with a rejuvenated sense of agency, rather than a lying-on-the-sofa-watching-television depression, look like? Few things represent agency more viscerally than a sword-wielding samurai refusing to bow to modernity. In late 2003, when *The Last Samurai* was released in Tokyo, I was initially stunned at its success in Japan; Tokyo critics can be prickly about foreign observations about Japan, particularly when their inaccuracies suggest something about the inability or unwillingness of outside observers to get the country right. What was one to make of a film, in essence about the rebellious Meiji leader Saigo Takamori, that ended with Tom Cruise lecturing the Meiji emperor in English about the meaning of Japaneseness, then going off to marry Saigo's sister? Had a Chinese film ended, no less preposterously, with Jet Li lecturing George Washington in Mandarin about the meaning of America before going off to marry, say, Patrick Henry's sister, my strong assumption is that it would mostly be treated by American critics as a farce. And yet the film was extremely popular, even prompting right-wing writers on Channel 2 (Japan's massive, comprehensive Internet chat room) to extol its rapturous discussion of the *bushidō* (way of the warrior).

As most Japanese are aware, the book *Bushidō: The Soul of Japan* was written in English by Nitobe Inazō, a Japanese convert to Christianity (and later to Quakerism); less often discussed is that he crafted *bushidō* as, in effect, the Japanese response to *kishidō* (knighthood), which explains the book's focus on the idea of Japanese "chivalry."[11] That is, the whole point of the book *Bushidō*, which deeply informed *The Last Samurai* and many modern discussions of samurai honor, was to render Japanese codes of honor in "civilized" terms, to make Japan's past as honorable as Europe's ostensibly was, at least for early twentieth-century readers in the United States and Europe. Indeed, while notions of honor profoundly affected samurai life, it was a deeply malleable and contested concept, no more determining of how people ultimately behaved than the word "freedom" is among Americans.[12]

The resuscitation of the *bushidō* goes far beyond a Tom Cruise film and some obsessive-compulsive shut-ins writing online. In 2005, mathematician Fujiwara Masahiko published his bestselling *Kokka no hinkaku* (*The Dignity of a Nation*, though "*kokka*," or "national house," is an equally precise translation of the word "state"). Although the aging Fujiwara comes from a distinguished family of writers (as the author's note at the end of the book reminds readers), and had earlier published other books on his experiences teaching in the United States (at the University of Colorado) and on a fellowship at Cambridge, there was far more than the author's reputation at work in making this short volume one of the bestselling Japanese books of the past decade. The book is a frontal assault on "American" ideas, starting with "pure logic" but proceeding to critique notions of democracy and equality, and an expression of the need for Japanese to rediscover the *bushidō* so that they can recapture their dignity and soul. The book justifies some (but not all) of Japan's previous military exploits, even as it avoids the sort of knee-jerk patriotism one might associate with nationalism; it explicitly suggests that Japan should not be following the United States on its military adventures. It is, in many ways and on many levels, a remarkable piece of work.

But not intellectually: it would be pointless to challenge Fujiwara's position, since he himself uses a dodge-and-weave style of argument that would invalidate virtually any critique. For example, he lists four reasons that "pure logic will make the world fail" (*ronri dake de wa sekai ga hatan suru*), a crucial point, because Western societies fetishize pure logic while Japanese society is based more on emotion:

1   "There are limits to logic," which we know because American schoolchildren, having been taught that typing is more important than writing by hand, no longer know how to spell; just as American children should learn fundamentals rather than typing, Japanese children should spend time learning fundamentals rather than English (Fujiwara 2005: 35–44).

2   "The most important things cannot be explained purely with logic," by which he means moral choices, including the idea that "murder is wrong" (ibid.: 44–50).

3   "For logic to work, one needs a starting point," such as the moral premise upon which a logical claim has to proceed: because murder is wrong, X then Y, and so on (ibid.: 50–55).

4   Pure logic cannot deal with complexity (*riron wa nagaku narienai*), emphasizing that long causal chains, indeterminacies, and ambiguities make hash of overly rigid logical analyses (ibid.: 55–64).

Immediately after making these arguments, Fujiwara writes: "*kore wa ōbeijin ni wa nakanaka rikai dekinai yō desu*," or "these are things that I wouldn't expect Westerners to understand" (ibid.: 65). To put the matter as delicately as possible, "Dignity of a Nation" is not exactly Kant's *Critique of Pure Reason*.

It is, however, a cultural touchstone in Japan, and that bears some scrutiny. Presumably some readers were drawn to his anti-American argument, rendered without the rage of rightists such as Tokyo governor Ishihara Shintarō or the *manga* author Kobayashi Yoshinori. Fujiwara's writing style is pedantic but warm, not hectoring and belligerent; if his anger at the United States is as apparent but more muted than theirs, his argument about Japanese spirit appears to have resonated with the reading public. In this view, Japan has lost something profound in its near colonization (Fujiwara occasionally uses the term *shokuminchi*, or "colony"), with its qualities and dignity diminished through its subservience to a materialistic, soulless, and increasingly feeble-minded United States; indeed, the closing chapter, really meant to seal his argument, opens with a discussion of the nearly apocalyptic degradation of Japanese students' math skills, which are now at about the same level as that of the Americans (Fujiwara 2005: 159–60). There is a way back, but it has to start with a reconstruction of Japan's essence and a turn away from the adoption of American values and institutions. For Fujiwara, the *bushidō* has to be understood as a way of benevolence, one certainly based on authority and hierarchy, but also implying duties and even kindness for the warriors who were on top of Tokugawa Japan's status pyramid. Traditional Japan's attention both to aesthetic and behavioral form or shape (*katachi*) and to the importance of even restrained emotion (*jōsho*) distinguish it from a West that respects only material power, self-interest, and the logical pursuit of both.

Although the publicity materials surrounding the book describe Fujiwara's contribution as his articulation of Japan's status as a "civilization with emotion and form" (*jōsho to katachi no bunmei*),[13] he rarely uses the word "civilization," usually employing terms such as culture or spirit (*seishin*, as in *bushidō seishin*). When he does turn to an explicit discussion of civilizations, it is only as a brief comment on Samuel Huntington, with whom he expresses agreement for recognizing Japan as a separate civilization (Fujiwara 2005: 181). Fujiwara insists that Japan has something distinctive to offer the world. Unlike the tyranny of neo-liberal economics or the demand for specific types of democratic institutions, both of which are symbolized by the United States, Japanese culture offers a benevolent, non-judgmental kindness: a respect of human emotion and of communal togetherness, values that are just as universal as the liberty and democracy promoted by the United States (ibid.: 177–80). For this to work, however, the Japanese must express a new pride in and love for their country. This is not the allegiance to the government, the focus on the "national interest" (*kokueki*) implied in the English term "nationalism." For Fujiwara, Japanese should adopt *sokokushugi*, which he defines as love for the "culture, tradition, emotion, and natural environment of one's own country" (ibid.: 113). He compares it to the word "patriotism" in English, which is not entirely inapt. But it might just as easily be translated as love for a non-gendered parent country, something between a motherland and a fatherland.

"*Dignity of a Nation*" is but one of a recent spate of conservative books aimed at making sense of Japan's global and regional roles. Abe Shinzō's much-discussed *Utsukushii kuni e* (*Toward a Beautiful Country*), published just on the cusp of his arrival as prime minister, also describes the effect that a rejuvenated Japan can have on the world, though his stress is on a strong government with a powerful military and loyal, patriotic citizens – potentially including immigrants – that resembles other advanced industrial powers. While he too aims at reconstructing Japanese history, particularly the immediate postwar era that saw his grandfather Kishi Nobusuke jailed as a Class "A" war criminal, his goal is a semblance of diplomatic normality, at least as defined by the practices of other leading democracies that can easily deploy their militaries overseas (Abe 2006). Asō Tarō's book *Totetsumonai Nihon* (*Japan the Tremendous*) shares some of Abe's diplomatic and military goals, but bases it instead on a new Asianism, in which Japan is culturally related to a cohesive Asia, but also its leader, guiding it toward a new, democratic modernity. Eschewing the principled hectoring typified by other nations (presumably, the United States), Japan will be a "coach" in the "never-ending marathon" (Asō 2007: 157–80), mentoring an Asia that is not exactly Western, but more democratic than China would have it.

Each of these books, like Fujiwara's, struggles with a dual notion of civilization – a Japan that has somehow modernized and progressed toward civilization, and yet a Japan that exists as a distinctive civilization unto itself (with some connection to Asia). These conservative books, while highly popular, do not dictate the full range of Japanese opinion. They coexist with the rabid nationalism of *manga* artist Kobayashi Yoshinori; the pragmatic, highly literate, pro-Asian progressivism of University of Tokyo international relations professor Fujiwara Kiichi (no relation to Fujiwara Masahiko); and the multicultural, left-leaning idealism of his University of Tokyo colleague, political scientist Kang Sang-jung, a *zainichi* Korean who was born and raised in Japan. Like anyone else writing about contemporary Japan, all of these authors must grapple with the widespread notion of a traditional Japan that somehow modernized, or of the maintenance of an essence that merged with or perhaps was polluted by the onrush of modernity.

Japanese soft power as discourse

Among democracies, Japan is hardly unusual in the virulence of its debates between cosmopolitan scholars and angry nativists, all of them articulating – generally to completely different audiences, and with varied levels of fidelity to logic and internal coherence – their visions of their country and its future. In these arguments, the outside world can operate as a kind of funhouse mirror, reflecting onto Japan almost whatever its participants want to see: a scary world that demands Japanese military engagement; a developing world grateful for Japanese guidance; or a war-torn world looking to Japan's iconic stature as a peaceful nation with special understanding of the horrors of nuclear war. Indeed, recent debates about Japan – including a semi-official description by one of the country's cultural ambassadors – demonstrate how discourses about Japanese civilization can be used, virtually without any evidence or outside reference point, to simplify and dictate the meaning of Japan's global presence.

The debates are recent in part because, until 2002, many Japanese analysts (for example Aoki 2001) seemed to accept Joseph Nye's initial (1990a) argument that soft power was an American currency, not something easily available to unique, insular, misunderstood Japan. But Douglas McGray's article "Japan's Gross National Cool" in *Foreign Policy* (2002) inspired a flurry of excitement in Tokyo's government and business circles. At a time of continuing economic uncertainty, but also of growing aspirations for an international role, McGray's account of Japan's vibrant pop culture scene and its tentacles across Asia made it fashionable to discuss the country's potential for soft power across the region, focusing both on the spread of its entertainment industries and on the potential for new "public diplomacy," including the creation in 2004 of a new office in MOFA dedicated specifically to Japan's global image (Lam 2007). I have analyzed elsewhere (Leheny 2006a) the Japanese discourses surrounding McGray's "cool Japan" argument, and feel no particular need to revise my central claim: that the term "soft power" was open-ended enough to allow a wide variety of political actors, from those on the pacifist left to those on the pro-military right, to suggest that Japan needed to build its soft power resources. On the left, Japan's "soft power" was taken almost as a replacement for "hard power" (conceptualized mostly as cultural/economic versus military tools, which was not how Nye differentiated them), whereas, on the right, "soft power" would reduce resistance to a more assertive Japan, because people watching *anime* or reading *manga* would realize that even a well-armed Japan could be trusted. Most importantly, this discussion took place mostly without any examination of the actual meanings inferred by foreign audiences from the Japanese source material; like most analyses of American soft power, it was primarily an ideological rather than an academic debate. The broad assumption was that others – particularly Asians – would appreciate and understand Japanese pop culture in the same way that Japanese did, an assumption that at once constructed a cohesive "Japanese" way of understanding pop culture and implied a distinctive and exclusive connection to the Asia-Pacific.

Fascinatingly, there is actually very little analysis of what messages are communicated via Japanese pop culture. Some observers lamented that it shied so far away from clear meanings and from national identifiers that it might as well be "non-national" (*mukokuseki*) or culturally "odorless" (Iwabuchi 2002). In the rapidly increasing English-language literature on the subject, there seems to be growing doubt that Japan's pop culture resources will actually amount to much in terms of national power. One scholar has suggested that the Japanese pop culture scene has shaped the institutional contours for the region's entertainment industries, but that the influence probably does not extend much further than that (Otmazgin 2008). The editors of a recent volume (Watanabe and McConnell 2008) furthermore suggest that Japan's cultural consequences may not greatly enhance national power. Another line of argument has it that the spread of Japanese pop culture across Asia has affected understandings of a normal middle-class existence, meaning that power may reside in the metonymical world of ideal lifestyles, represented by flat-screen televisions and sushi takeout, rather than in the hands of instrumentally oriented state actors (see Shiraishi 2006; also Leheny 2006a: 230–32; Aoki 1999: 43–91).

To the extent that a consensus has emerged among foreign observers and moderate to liberal Japanese analysts regarding regional political influence, it is that the spread of Japanese pop culture in Asia may produce some diplomatic benefits for Tokyo, but that these successes are rapidly undone by prime ministerial visits to Yasukuni Shrine or by controversial statements about Japan's wartime responsibility (for example, Lam 2007). Nye has himself said that the Yasukuni visits would lead Japan "to squander its soft power" (Nye 2006: 3). Journalist Yuasa Hiroshi, of the right-wing *Sankei Shimbun*, argues in a magazine article (2006: 173–5) that this is an ideological and self-serving argument, generated more by Nye's interest in seeing Japan

remain a "civilian power" under American tutelage rather than as an independent military power; there are other ways, he suggests, to mollify China
than to accept Beijing's distorted (in his view) version of Japan's wartime
behavior.

For the most part, however, the discussions of Japanese soft power have
involved public opinion polls showing that people like or do not like Japan,
or basic data on J-Pop or video-game sales, or references to *anime* fan clubs
overseas. In one of the few semi-official statements of what is actually
conveyed through Japanese pop culture, Japan's ambassador to UNESCO,
Kondo Seiichi, writes in a manner that partly echoes Samuel Huntington's
account of a post-ideological world that gives rise to a potential clash of civilizations. But it also echoes parts of Fujiwara Mashiko's depiction of
Japanese openness, acceptance, and tolerance in comparison with the hyper-
rational and selfish materialism of the West. Virtually every aspect of what
Japan is in this view is familiar: a civilization that is modern but not like an
idealized cold, rational, neo-liberal America; an exemplar without being a
values bully; a country that maintains its identity in the face of the pressure of
modernization. In a discussion about the global impact of *anime*, Kondo
implicitly but unmistakably compares Japan to a United States that had
promoted democratic ideals as a counterweight to an "axis of evil":

> One of the reasons why Japanese anime appeals to young people around
> the world today may be that the end of the Cold War has liberated human
> beings from ideological confrontation, creating an environment where
> they can freely pursue diverse cultures. Many people in the world now
> prefer contemporary expressions in art and culture instead of the
> missionary preaching of ideals. This is a situation apparently favorable
> to Japan, which is not good at projecting ideals. . . . The most important
> factor on the receiving side probably has to do with the psychology of
> contemporary human beings. While enjoying the freedom and material
> prosperity that are the fruits of modern rationalism, people feel perplexed
> at the growing divide between rich and poor, cutthroat market competi-
> tion, environmental destruction, and identity crises, as well as the social
> unrest and terrorism that have arisen partly because of their inability to
> resolve these issues. For those who have some doubts about modern life
> but cannot articulate them, the messages from Japanese anime empha-
> sizing human complexity and the importance of coexistence with nature
> may appear to offer some hints for problem-solving options superior to
> reliance on the simple dichotomy of rewarding good and punishing evil.
>
> (Kondo 2008: 199)

My point here is not to criticize Kondo's interpretation, which relies on a
veritable mountain of unverifiable assumptions but on virtually no evidence.
Instead, I call attention to his possibly intentional reference to Huntington's
notion of a world driven by something other than ideology, and also his clear

statement that there is a pure modernity somewhere out there in the world – rational, dehumanizing, and cold – against which Japan's modernity can be favorably compared. Kondo's wishful thinking certainly seems less pernicious than that of the American leaders who confidently predicted a speedy and bloodless transition to pro-American democracy in Iraq. But it is no less instructive in displaying a popular and even quasi-official account of what Japan offers to a world that eagerly awaits its message. This account is, of course, far more intimately connected to long-term internal debates about Japan than it is to any effort to study or understand the effect that Japan has on the outside world.

The return of the Samurai

At least in some Japanese views, the "clash of civilizations" offers an opportunity. It affords Japan the chance to spread its own soft power because of the sense that different civilizations co-exist, and that Japan's particular stance makes it a less confrontational model of development than does that of the United States. Yamauchi Masayuki, the Arab specialist noted in the introduction to this chapter, implicitly made this case in a 2004 article in the moderately liberal monthly opinion journal *Ronza*:

> One cannot quickly introduce a Swiss-style federation or American-style democracy into the multiethnic, multi-religious states of the Middle East. In societies that have pride in their history and tradition like the Arab-Islamic civilization (*arabu-isurām bunmei*), even if one tries to inject Anglo-Saxon-style liberal democracy or free market principles, the transplantation simply is not easy. It might be difficult for the Americans who promised a speedy reformation of Iraq to accept that notions of soft power must be premised on the existence of multiple civilizations.
>
> (Yamauchi 2004: 32)

But what does Japan offer? Merely the experience of rapid development? Of rapid development that coexists with traditional society? And, in Japan's myriad international activities, how do we determine which we might use to establish some kind of pattern, theme, or modality to understand Japan's soft or social power? For a civilizational analysis to account for Japan's international stance, it would presumably have to rest on a dispositional perspective that would encompass an extraordinary array of public and private initiatives, even if stylistically, across time. It would have to relate Japan's uneasy stance toward Asia after the Meiji Restoration to the practices of Japanese firms and political elites (sometimes nearly indistinguishable from one another) in the 1930s; to the brutality of Japanese forces during World War II; to the "Yoshida Doctrine" and Japan's aid initiatives from the 1960s onward; to the four "non-nuclear principles" articulated by Prime Minister Sato; to the hand-wringing over troop deployments to the Persian Gulf in 1991; and to the deployment of troops in 2004 to Iraq. It would have to account both for Prime Minister Fukuda's 1977 decision to pay a $6 million ransom to Japan Red Army members to secure the release of a hijacked Japanese airliner in Bangladesh and for the refusal by Prime Minister Koizumi (and Fukuda's own son, then serving as Koizumi's chief cabinet secretary) to withdraw troops from Iraq to save the lives of three Japanese taken hostage by the Saraya al-Mujahideen. It would for that matter have to account for the decision by Takato Nahoko, one of those three hostages, to move to Iraq to rescue "street children" (often teenagers) vulnerable to drugs, crime, and abuse. This is, of course, an absurd amount of material for any particular perspective to cover, but it seems equally impossible to establish persuasive (let alone rigorous) criteria that would differentiate between those aspects of a country's international relations important enough to merit discussion. Takato and her fellow left-wing hostages are as Japanese as Yoshida and Koizumi, and dispositional perspectives presumably must treat them all equally or suggest the ways in which observers might categorize and consolidate Japanese behavior to make it amenable to explanation.

And this is why I turn instead to a discursive approach to civilization. If there is anything that unites a broad swath of Japanese comments about the country's place in the world – and this is a very big if – I would argue that it is a common sense that the country is trying to find its way in a world not of its making, a world in which the rules were made by someone else (probably Western). But this sense too is constructed in a discursive environment that emphasizes a distinctive history, a radical rupture with the past occasioned by an "opening" to the world, and a continuing vulnerability to the vicissitudes of others' choices. This argument is, however, deeply malleable. It might mean, as I think it does to Fujiwara Masahiko, that, because of Japan, another, better world is possible – if only Japan could remember the civilization that it abandoned. It might mean, as I think it does to Abe Shinzō, that the current world is about as good as it gets, and Japan needs to follow the normal rules by becoming a more normal, decisive, active, and powerful actor. It might mean, as I think it does to Asō Tarō, that a better world is possible, but only a more active and normal Japan can provide the appropriate leadership. But this is hardly a disposition, no more defining of how Japanese live their lives than would be claims of Japanese modesty for a nationalist such as Kobayashi or of Japanese obedience for a provocative critic such as Fujiwara Kiichi. It is instead a set of discourses that embed a long and complicated past in an understandable narrative that allows people to make sense of their own lives while legitimating their different claims about what kind of security, trade, or diplomatic policy their government ought to follow.

But the narrative is durable, and perhaps that, more than any disposition or style, has the potential to travel. In a report on Japan's efforts that must have been music to the ears of Tokyo's diplomats, an *Al-Ahram* journalist wrote in 2005:

No doubt what happened to Japan during the 20th century is nothing short of a miracle. During the first part of the century they became a military superpower in the Far East, feared by their neighbours for the ferocity and fearlessness of their soldiers. After World War II they became an economic superpower and were equally feared and respected for their economic might.

Arabs and Muslims always ask, why were the Japanese able to change, adapt, and draw strength from their values, traditions, and heritage, and transform their ancient warriors into modern soldiers or corporate employees while we in the Arab, Islamic world have failed to do the same?

(El Desouky 2005)

It is an inspiring story, and Japan's wealth, stability, and security surely could make it an extraordinarily appealing model for others. But this oft-retold story, with myriad inflections and uses that depend on the narrator and the audience, has little to say about the internal misgivings about what Japan has become in its path to modernity. Japan may, in this view, be the country that most perfectly represents the ability to merge the traditional with the modern, to civilize without losing the distinctiveness of its own civilization. But it is also a country in which one can sell hundreds of thousands of books by suggesting that the move away from the way of the samurai – those "ancient warriors" that were somehow transformed – may have been a terrible mistake.

Notes

1 All translations from Japanese are by the author unless otherwise noted. Japanese names are given in Japanese order (FAMILY–given; for example, ABE Shinzō) except where the authors themselves have produced English-language texts, when they are given in Western order (for example, Tomiko YODA and Takashi SHIRAISHI).

2 For example, in one speech he favorably compared the intelligence of Japan to that of the United States because "in America there are many blacks, Puerto Ricans and Mexicans" (Bowen 1986).

3 *Baseball Kid's* homepage is http://www.byakuya-shobo.co.jp/kozo/.

4 Fukuzawa founded Keio University, which now hosts a web version of the full text of this classic, at http://www.slis.keio.ac.jp/~ueda/bunmei-1.html. The book has also been translated and published in English, cited in the bibliography here as Fukuzawa (1973). For a summary, see Nishikawa ([1993] 2000).

5 I thank Patrick Jackson and an anonymous reviewer for making this connection.

6 I have written elsewhere (Leheny 2003: 38–40) about *nihonjinron* in Japanese politics. The most comprehensive source on *nihonjinron* is Oguma (1995).

7 The symposium's proceedings were published by Nichibunken in English, but even some of the authors, auch as Ueyama Shunpei (1999), in his paper that immediately follows Eisenstadt's overview chapter, admit to only a passing familiarity with Eisenstadt's work. See Sonoda and Eisenstadt (1999).

8 For reasons of space as well as relevance, I do not discuss critical reactions among foreign researchers of Japan to Eisenstadt's and Arnason's books, which tend to focus on doubts about the linearity and continuity of social processes begun

hundreds or even thousands of years ago to ideology and practice today (see, for example, Botsman 2004/2005). My own concerns revolve in particular around Eisenstadt's somewhat selective use of anthropological accounts to provide a depiction of contemporary Japanese culture (for example, Eisenstadt 1996: 341–4) that feels more connected to the Japan I have read about in the popular media than to the one in which I have lived.

9　Interestingly, in an account that deliberately aligns itself with Eisenstadt, Bellah (2003: 59) is notably more sympathetic to some of the precepts of cultural unique-ness, arguing, "it has been the deep implication of nonaxial structures of power determined to prevent the full institutionalization of axial premises that explains their persistence." That is, cultural uniqueness is neither deniable nor merely the result of state-led ideology, but rather the outcome of broad intellectual and social claims that guide national flexibility and collective will.

10　I draw both the terminology and its conceptualizaton from Gluck (1991) and Harootunian (2006).

11　I thank William Kelly for making this point to me in earlier discussions.

12　On the ambiguity of samurai honor, see Ikegami (1997).

13　See, for example, http://www.shinchosha.co.jp/book/610141/.

6 Four variants of Indian civilization

Susanne Hoeber Rudolph

This chapter is about the role civilizational discourse has played in the perception of India. Before tackling this many-sided subject, I want to stipulate some uses of the term "civilization." The uses take at least two ideal-typical forms. The first invokes singularity and holism. Civilization is construed as an internally homogeneous cultural program with firm boundaries. Its "essence" can be articulated. Those within its borders understand those outside the borders as distinctively other (Huntington 1993). The second ideal-type invokes civilization as a heterogeneous and pluralist concept. Constituted of multiple components, its attributes are contested, its borders are permeable, and it engages with other civilizations[1] whose members may share identities.

These contrasting visions have different implications. The closed homogeneous metaphor suggests that when two such entities encounter each other conflict is likely, if not inevitable. Opposed civilizations are characterized by mutual incomprehension. Other civilizations are viewed not only as different but also as threatening. Pluralist and open civilizations are prepared to learn from each other and to share attributes. "Civilizations," say Hall and Jackson, "are better understood as ongoing processes, and in particular, as ongoing processes through which boundaries are continually produced and reproduced" (Hall and Jackson 2007a: 6).

My role in this volume is to examine a civilization that has evolved in variant forms over time. Its dominant attribute in classical times was said to be a capacity for peaceful, non-conflictual diffusion in and beyond India. The image of the crusader militant, Christian or Muslim, which seems to lie behind the often reiterated concept of civilizational clash, misses the vast history of a civilization, silently and unresisted, making its way into new territory, either sharing ground with or superseding previous civilizational forms.

I have given this chapter its present form, four variants of Indian civilization, in order to emphasize that civilizations and their fluid and changing life forms are the creation of historical actors, rather than objective entities with boundaries and properties that can be registered in a gazetteer. I have four variants because dominant intellectual and cultural communities both inside and outside Indian civilization have worked on changing its image over time and in time.

Hindu civilization? Indian civilization?

The first theoretical problem my project encounters is that of naming the civilization I am about to discuss. Shall I talk about Hindu civilization, complying with Samuel Huntington's categories, which foreground religion, thus preempting the question of what defines civilization? Or shall I talk about Indian civilization, using language that foregrounds a geographic arena and leave open what defines the civilization?[2] "Hindu Civilization" suggests that one overarching cultural component, religion,[3] overrides all others. "Indian Civilization," by contrast, makes space for numerous cultural components and suggests contestation among them. John Hobson reminds readers that "civilizations are amalgams, insofar as they are never pure or pristine but are always impure or hybrid. And this occurs as they are social-ized through iterated interactions with other civilizations" (Hobson 2007: 150).[4] Indian secularists speak of a composite civilization.

There is another dimension to using the phrase "Indian Civilization" rather than "Hindu Civilization." The South Asian subcontinent as presently defined encompasses several nation-states – Pakistan, Bangladesh, Sri Lanka, Nepal, the Maldives, Bhutan and Afghanistan. Without sharing a religion – they practice Islam, Buddhism, Hinduism – these countries share enough linguistic, aesthetic, literary and religious characteristics that the idea of an Indian civilization provides a plausible summary for their commonality.[5]

In the constructions of Indian civilization, both insiders and outsiders play a role, *deshis* and *videshis*, those of the country and the distant tourist, travel writer, foreign service officer, and academic. What they choose to highlight shapes the continuing contestation over the meaning of Indian civilization. Versions of Indian civilization are like a volleyball being propelled by inside and outside contestants trying to score the decisive winning point. But the match has no end.

Explaining non-conflictual diffusion of civilization

Without conducting a systematic survey of the historical behavior of all civili-zations, I ventured the opinion above that the exemplars of a civilization, silently and unresisted making its way into new territory, are as likely to preponderate as those exemplars which focus on the frequency of conflicts.

One of the forces that historically lent coherence to Indian civilization was an overarching language. Sheldon Pollock, in his consideration of the "Sanskrit Cosmopolis" (1996), privileges language as a vehicle for the creation of a political/cultural whole. It is a force that is purely cultural, inde-pendent of state actors. Pollock allocates to language powers that go well beyond the community-creating or identity-forging or legitimating functions that come to the mind of the political scientist. His account of the constitutive role of language in the definition of what he calls the empire systems of pre-modernity in the first thousand years of the Common Era – Achamenid, Hellenic, Roman, Angkoran and Chola – transfers easily to civilizations. He underlines the qualities required of such a constitutive language, for which Sanskrit becomes a model:

> This had to be a language of trans-ethnic attraction; a language capable of making translocal claims . . . ; one not powerful so much because of its numinous qualities . . . but because of its aesthetic qualities, its ability somehow to make reality more real. . . . Furthermore, this had to be a language dignified and stabilized by grammar. The conceptual affinities between the order of Sanskrit poetry, the order of Sanskrit grammar, and the moral social and political order are profound indeed. . . . In 800 CE in Europe this language was Latin . . . from *c*. 1000 CE on in West Asia this language was New Persian . . . In South and Southeast Asia . . . this language was Sanskrit . . . Sanskrit performed the imperial function of spanning space and time and this enabled one to say things with lasting and pervasive power.
>
> (Pollock 1996: 239–40)

Pollock envisages a process of language diffusion which is the reverse of civilizational conflict, a silent, almost agentless,[6] process in which the Sanskrit cosmopolis or the "empire system of pre-modernity" spreads without conquest or the exercise of power. It diffuses in India from the north, where it originated, to the south, whose Dravidian-based linguistic traditions were quite different. It diffuses beyond India to much of Southeast Asia. It diffuses via the "empire-system [which] consisted in a relatively stable field of highly imitative behavior" (ibid.: 239): "How do we understand the processes by which whole social strata willingly abandon their linguistic routines and doxa, and submit, altogether voluntarily, to a new culture, especially one so mercilessly disciplined as that of Sanskrit?" (ibid.: 232).

Pollock asserts that there was no conqueror's prestige attached to the language, as there might have been to Latin and English in their respective spheres, no bureaucratic compulsion to Sanskritize as there was in the Roman administrative apparatus; there was no "center" (Mecca, Rome) to orchestrate the diffusion, no state in whose interest it was to propagate the language. Indeed, when Sanskrit became the language of high politics and sacred enunciations throughout much of Southeast Asia, there was no social or political entity on the mother continent to take an interest, to utilize the "soft power"[7] which the sending civilization (Pollock 1996: 238) could have harnessed to political ambition.

Pollock's elimination of alternative explanations leaves intact an explanation internal to the processes of the language, that Sanskrit can make transsocial claims due to its "constitutive features of representation, which creates the being by disclosing it, as fame is created by being named in poetry" (Pollock 1996: 239), or "that [its] purpose is to make the real somehow super-real by poetry" (ibid.: 242). His account underlines that "civilization" may develop, expand, or contract without significant agency by states and without significant conflict, let alone political conflict.

The fact that Sanskrit is the language used for articulating many of the texts that constitute Hinduism does not detract from its role in constituting "Indian" civilization in the sense of a pluralist, composite civilization. It creates a unified space that is at least partly filled in later centuries by high culture and political languages which also play a role in other civilizations, notably Persian (allied to Islamic civilization) and English (allied to Western civilization).

Civilization as ideology? Four variants

Civilization is an open-ended process, a discursive formation shaped by con-testations generated from within and from without. The dominant discourse changes over time, depending to a large extent upon who controls the discourse and to what end. Defining a civilization is partly a political process with political consequences. Civilizational discourses perform the work that ideologies were once said to perform. They create an image of humans and their relationship to each other, of society, of history and the hereafter. Over the 250 years between the mid-eighteenth century and the twenty-first century, I identify and characterize four variants of Indian civilization.

1   The Orientalist variant dominated the late eighteenth and early nineteenth centuries. It was shaped by East India Company officials resident in India with a commitment to classical learning. They announced the new civiliza-tion. They learned Sanskrit, translated India's great classical texts, and distributed their valuable findings to a world eager to hear of new civiliza-tions. Like the construction of Western civilization from the texts of long departed Greek and Roman authors, the classical Indian civilization of the Orientalists was based on knowledge grounded in an ancient past. The Indian authors of such texts were long departed; classics such as Shakuntala and the Bhagavad Gita dated to the pre-Christian era. The new learning was quickly elaborated by enthusiastic European recipients. Ex Oriente Lux appealed to literary Europeans and Americans such as Goethe, Heine, Emerson and Thoreau riding the wave of the romantic revival.

2   An Anglicist variant diametrically opposite to the Orientalist view of Indian civilization arose in the first quarter of the nineteenth century, a contrast Thomas Trautman has summed up as Indophilia and Indophobia. The image of the civilization was still owned mainly by Europeans. The voices were those of utilitarian and evangelical East India Company officials such as Thomas Babington Macaulay, Lord William Bentinck, and Charles Grant,

passionate reformers of a "degraded" Indian society. They began to be supported by the first and second generation of Indian players who had received a Western education – commentators who were using their new acquaintance with European alternatives to critique the inherited civilization. The outside creator of this dark view was an England that was passing from romanticism to utilitarianism and, in the second part of the century, to "race science" (Trautman 1997: 165 ff.).

The nineteenth-century, made-in-Europe image of Indian civilization is by no means uniform. Next to the much maligned monstrosities of the utilitarians (Mitter 1992), in the West in the second part of the century the romantic idealism of the early Orientalists persists in literature, music, and poetry. Added on is the interest in the West in the new spiritualism, of the sort expressed by the theosophists, who acquired a positive view of Indian religious possibilities.[8] They composed those whom Gandhi, recognizing the hegemony of the utilitarian/evangelical view, would call "the other West."

Part of what nationalism is about, as Benedict Anderson noted when he talked of "imagined communities" (1983), is the appropriation of the process of characterizing the nation. This process spills over into the production of civilizational markers. The two visions of Indian civilization that arise in the nationalist era are shaped primarily by Indian actors within India, although both visions are subject to and influenced by outside, extra-civilizational responses. In a colonized country such as India, the outsider is inside. The Englishman who collaborated on the civilizational image was an officer of the Indian Administrative Service running the local administration or a teacher teaching your son.

3   From the mid-nineteenth century, Indians increasingly become players in the construction of a civilizational image that had been mainly the product of the European imagination. The portrait of spirituality, asceticism, magic, transcendental wisdom and social hierarchy is contested by the plainly political faces of Gandhi and Nehru and by the image of an India fighting non-violently for freedom. A liberal nationalist variant begins to augment or supersede the classical construct of the Orientalists and the degraded image presented by the utilitarians/evangelicals. An element in this liberal nationalist variant was the image of India as pluralist and tolerant, shelter to multiple civilizational streams.

4   A Hindu nationalist variant of Indian civilization has been currently and for the last hundred years in contestation with the liberal nationalist variant. The nineteenth and early twentieth centuries saw the rise and consolidation of popular political movements that considered India as an expression of Hindu civilization. They began to develop conflictual versions of Indian history that designated Muslims as foreigners and tried to unravel the overlapping customary practices which characterize much of Indian religion, searching for a "pure" unadulterated Hindu civilization.

The historical career of these variants underlines the fact that civilizational images, like ideologies, are not merely pictures of a collective identity but programs for collective identities. They are constructed in part to sustain and advance certain modes of governance, the organization of society, and even the policies of everyday life. The Orientalist image of Indian civilization presumed that India had reached a high level of civilization. It was used, at the policy level, to support funding for education in classical and vernacular Indian languages. At the wider philosophical and global level, it contributed to the view that Graeco-Roman civilization was not the only or even the most excellent civilization. The contrasting Anglicist image of a degraded India was designed to support the idea that India needed to be transformed from a barbarian to a civilized condition, and that only an English-language education could achieve this goal.

The Orientalists bestow civilization on India

The concept "civilization" has become suspect in post-colonial writing. It is seen as yet another rhetorical device for sorting the non-West into lower slots in the historical ranking system, creating a science of imperial mastery. Hamid Dabashi writes:

> practically the entire scholarly apparatus at the service of civilizational studies of non-western civilizations was the handiwork of Orientalism as the intelligence arm of colonialism... these civilizational mirrors were all constructed to raise the western civilization as the normative achievement of world history and lower all others as its abnormal antecedents.
>
> (Dabashi 2004: 248)

There is indeed that in the career of the concept "civilization," especially when used – as by the Mills, James, and John Stuart – in connection with a theory of civilizational stages, that makes it the verbal tool of imperial master theory. But the concept has had several careers. The one developed by the post-colonial reading is just one.

The positive view of India constructed by servants of the eighteenth-century East India Company was made possible by the relatively symmetrical power relations between the company's agents and Indian rulers. As British rule over the subcontinent tightened; as the company extended its rule from the presidencies of Bengal, Madras, and Bombay to kingdoms throughout the subcontinent and imposed treaties of "subordinate cooperation"; as, in a word, the power equation became increasingly asymmetrical, the British view of Indian civilization was transformed from respect to contempt. Conflating power and culture, the imperial monitors of civilizational standing lowered the standing of those who lost power and elevated the standing of those who had gained power. The 1857 rebellion, when first the Indians massacred the

British and then the British massacred the Indians, froze the asymmetrical relationship in fear and distrust.

The concept of civilization was a way of organizing the increasingly widespread experience eighteenth-century Europeans had with a world east of Suez. Bruce Mazlish (2004b: 14) reminds us that the historical moment is one in which archaeological discoveries were extending the European world's historical horizon (Keay 2001) by revealing the innovations and achievements of previously unknown civilizations. There are archaeological finds in Egypt. The Rosetta Stone was recovered and translated in the 1790s. Decipherment of Brahmi script in 1837 made the Ashokan Pillars accessible. "The process was clearly facilitated," says Mazlish, "by western civilization seeking to define itself by excavating other civilizations and recognizing them as earlier counterparts (though generally seen as inferior)" (2004b: 16).

The scholarly servants of the East India Company in Calcutta who founded the Royal Asiatic Society were led by Sir William Jones. They came to be known as the Orientalists. The term's positive valence has been sufficiently reversed by Saidian post-colonial narrative that it is hard to return it to its eighteenth-century meaning. The Saidian post-colonial project asserts that the Orientalists' positive evaluation of Indian civilization is not what it seems, an evaluation based on scholarly passion for classical languages and texts. The Orientalists are said to have created knowledge about Indian civilization to make their rule more effective. Their ambition, according to Said, was to "gather in, to rope off, to domesticate the Orient and thereby turn it into a province of European learning" (1979: 79) What they had to say was said in the service of power and deprived Indians of voice and agency. On Said's word, the Asiatic Society Orientalists appropriated and absconded with Asian civilization in the interests of colonial power over the ruled.

What, then, does another story look like (Rudolph and Rudolph 1997)? The scholars, among whom Sir William Jones stands out, but who included Charles Wilkins, H. T. Colebrooke, James Prinsep, and others backed by Governor General Warren Hastings, were products of an intellectual setting that favored a civilizational epistemology. This saw history populated by huge coherent wholes defined by great languages and their classic texts. Gibbon's publication in 1776 of the first volume of his *The Decline and Fall of the Roman Empire* gave a powerful impetus to the civilizational idea already well developed in the mind of an era.

Most important, Graeco-Roman civilization was implicitly regarded as the only civilization. What the Orientalists did was to break the hold of Graeco-Roman on the concept of civilization. The "discovery" of other culturally sophisticated civilizations – sophisticated by being bearers of a complex language and culture – introduced an invigorating relativism into the interpretation of global phenomena. Graeco-Roman was not the only civilization, and those at a distance were not necessarily barbarian, but Persian, Indian, Arab. To the extent this move attached Asian civilizations to the "province Europe," it forced Europeans to share the civilizational space.

When Sir William Jones looked around from the deck of his ship, he imagined himself surrounded by civilizations that could elicit the respect and reverence commanded by the Graeco-Roman. Jones wrote:

> When I was at sea last August, I found one evening, on inspecting the observations of the day, that India lay before us, and Persia on the left, whilst a breeze from Arabia blew nearly on our stern. It gave me inexpressible pleasure to find myself in the midst of so noble an amphitheatre, almost encircled by the vast regions of Asia, which has ever been esteemed the nurse of sciences, the inventress of delightful useful arts, the scene of glorious actions, fertile in the productions of human genius, abounding in natural wonders, infinitely diversified in the form of religion and government, in the laws, manners, customs and languages, as well as in the features and complection of men.
>
> (Kejariwal 1988: 27–8)

It is O. P. Kejariwal, author of an influential book on the Asiatic Society of Bengal, who conveys the ontological effect of the "discovery" of other civilizations by calling it a Copernican revolution for history (ibid.: 28). Certainly it destabilized the mindset of Europeans who had seen themselves living in a world of barbarians and had now to deal with a new category, the idea of civilizations characterized by different sorts of "civilized" conduct.[9]

It was hardly surprising that, for the eighteenth century, the rational century of the Enlightenment, it was language rather than religion that proved to be the decisive marker of civilization. Here is Jones again:

> Sanskrit language, whatever be its antiquity, is of a wonderful structure, more perfect than the Greek, more copious than the Latin, and more exquisitely refined than either, yet bearing to both of them a stronger affinity, both in the roots of the verbs and in the forms of the grammar, than could positively have been produced by accident; so strong, indeed, that no philologer could examine them all three, without believing them to have sprung from some common source, which, perhaps, no longer exists.
>
> (Kejariwal 1988: 47)

It is not irrelevant that the British presence in India in the eighteenth century is more that of a trading company than an imperial power. The cultural setting seems to emphasize what Adam Smith, marking the gentling effect of trade, would have called *doux commerce*. Eighteenth-century Indologists do not speak of a clash of civilizations. On the contrary, Jones and his colleagues formulated a theory which gave the greatest importance to the complementarity of civilizations. The theory of Indo-European languages, the idea that Sanskrit and European languages had common origins, built an image of civilizations which emphasized overlap and convergence rather than conflict, closed boundaries and mutual exclusion.[10]

Thomas Trautman notes how this civilizational theory linked Indian history with the world's civilizations:

> The discovery of the Indo-European language family . . . has profoundly affected the way in which we now read the oldest writings of Rome, Greece, Iran, and India, and make it a principle of method that the illumination of any one must include, in part, comparison with the others.
>
> (Trautman 1997: 227)

Views about the excellence of Indian civilization were not confined to the East India Company's Orientalists. A positive Orientalism became the European fashion at the end of the eighteenth century, supplying an outside response to the inside, confirming that the shaping of a civilizational definition is interactive. Goethe (1749–1832) produced enthusiastic reviews of Indian literary forms:

> Wouldst thou the young year's blossoms and the fruits of its decline
> And all by which the soul is charmed, enraptured, feasted, fed,
> Wouldst thou the earth and heaven itself in one sole name combine?
> I name thee, O Sakuntala! and all at once is said.
>
> (von Herzfeld and Sym 1957)[11]

He also expressed his enthusiasm in more prosaic form:

> The first time I came across this inexhaustible work it aroused such enthusiasm in me and so held me that I could not stop studying it. I even felt impelled to make the impossible attempt to bring it in some form to the German stage.
>
> (Ibid.)

These testimonials suggest the interactive formation of civilizational images. They also confirm that in its early phases the concept of civilization was a European construction.

The Utilitarians rank civilizations

The Anglicists acquired their title when they triumphed over the Orientalists by establishing English rather than Indian languages as the means for educating Indians in the three government colleges that were set up in the first half of the nineteenth century. The new era's casual contempt for Indian civilization was famously expressed by Thomas Babington Macaulay in his role as law member of Governor General Bentinck's council. His "Minute on Education" held "that all the historical information which had been collected from all the books written in the Sanskrit language is less valuable than what may be found in the most paltry abridgments used at preparatory schools in England."[12]

Two overlapping constituencies contributed to the Anglicist thrust: Christian evangelicals who knew that India was heathen territory and philosophical sympathizers with Jeremy Bentham's utilitarianism (Stokes 1959). They collaborated in picturing Indian civilization as the obverse of the picture drawn by Jones's colleagues in the Asiatic Society of Bengal, as a civilization sufficiently depraved to be abominated. In the words of Charles Grant, a leading abominator:

> [the Indians] have had among themselves a complete despotism from the remotest antiquity; . . . it has pervaded their government, their religions, and their laws. It has formed by its various ramifications the essentials of the character which they have always had, as far as the light of history goes, and which they still possess; that character, which has made them a prey to every invader, indifferent to all their rulers, and easy in the change of them; as a people, void of public spirit, honour, attachment, and in society, base, dishonest and faithless.
>
> (Trautman 1997: 104)[13]

The Anglicist objective was unabashedly assimilationist – again Macaulay: to make of the Indians a class of persons "Indian in blood and color, but English in taste, in opinions, in morals, and in intellect" (Clive and Pinney 1972: 249). The depraved nature of the Indian civilization made such a project of improvement salutary.

The most vivid and explicit counter-vision of Indian civilization was elaborated by the most distinguished of the Benthamites, James Mill, philosopher, economist, and head of the office of examiner of Indian correspondence in the East India Company in London (Rudolph 2007). The highly paid and influential position followed his publication in 1817 of a well-received six-volume *History of India*. He wrote what quickly became the definitive view of India on the basis of the literature available in London, and in the absence of any personal acquaintance with the subcontinent. The volume became a critical entry in the debate between two visions of Indian civilization. Indeed, Francis Hutchins (1967) has argued plausibly that Mill's motive in writing the history was to prepare a justification for the permanent subjection of India.

Mill began his project with a critique of the lead proponent of the Orientalist vision:

> It was unfortunate that a mind so pure, so warm in the pursuit of truth, and so dedicated to oriental learning, as that of Sir William Jones, should have adopted the hypothesis of a high state of civilization in the principle countries of Asia.
>
> (Mill 1968: II, 138)

The activities of the "pure mind," however, were to be deplored:

> So crude were [Sir William's] ideas on the subject that the rhapsodies of
> Rousseau on the virtues of the savage life surpass not the panegyrics
> of Sir William on the wild, comfortless, predatory and ferocious state of
> the wandering Arab.
>
> (Ibid.: 140)

What was needed was a less crude and more systematic method for ranking
civilizations:

> It is not easy to describe the characteristics of the different stages of social
> progress. It is not from one feature, or from two, that a just conclusion
> can be drawn . . . It is from a joint view of all the great circumstances
> taken together, that their progress can be ascertained; and it is from an
> accurate comparison, grounded on these general views, that a scale of
> civilization can be formed, on which the relative position of nations may
> be accurately marked.
>
> (Ibid.: 138–9)

Accurate marking yields a conclusion: "the progress of knowledge . . .
demonstrated the necessity of regarding the actual state of the Hindus as little
removed from that of half-civilized nations" (ibid.: 144).

There is a good deal at stake in these passages beyond the question of
Indian civilization. They are part of a larger philosophical conversation
between romantics and utilitarians that included participants well beyond the
empire. For a time, due to the "progress of knowledge," the utilitarian side
seems to have had the advantage. At this point in the debate the Orientalists,
according to Mill, tried to save their view of Indian civilization by inducting a
spurious rhetorical device:

> The saving hypothesis however, was immediately adopted, that the situ-
> ation in which the Hindus are now beheld is a state of degeneration; that
> formerly they were in a high state of civilization; from which they had
> fallen through the miseries of foreign conquest and subjugation.
>
> (Mill 1968: II, 144)

And what about the leading civilization theory of Jones and the Orientalists,
the concept of a civilizational overlap, an Indo-European kinship, that
produced Indo-European languages? Charles Grant "completely suppressed
Jones' argument for the kinship between Europeans and Indians" and "said
nothing about the similarity of Sanskrit to Latin and Greek." James Mill, in
six volumes, maintained silence with respect to the Indo-European thesis
(Trautman 1997: 122).

Manipulation and modification of civilizational rankings continued to be a passionate pastime for nineteenth-century scholars and statesmen. The ranking process was further complicated by the addition of an evolutionary social theory that places winners of wars and lords of empires in a superior position. John Stuart Mill, less rabid than his father about the degeneracy of Indian civilization, and like his father in a position at the East India Company which called on him to address civilizational ranking, employed an additional, more optimistic measuring rod, one already developed by English liberal theorists from Locke on. "Childhood is a theme that runs through the writings of British liberals on India with unerring constancy," writes Uday Singh Mehta.[14] The childhood metaphor, with its implication of deep parental care and obligation, normatively aligns British dominance with the most sacred of spheres, that of the family (Mehta 1999). It implies a future in which the child will become the man and be freed of the leading strings that taught him to walk (Mill 1985). It also raises a temporary caution which can be infinitely extended: "not yet."

Inclusionary and exclusionary variants of Indian civilization

Before we proceed to the next two variants of Indian civilization, the liberal nationalist inclusionary form and the Hindu nationalist exclusionary form, I want to point to a circumstance that makes it difficult to pin these down. The Indian civilizational image in recent times is more unstable than it was in the nineteenth century. Many of the elements that were thought to constitute Indian civilization were located in a traditional society that has been eroded or erased. Change has been so swift that it is hard to capture characteristics that can be identified with Indian civilization.

Only yesterday Indian civilization was seen as a space of non-violence, asceticism, spirituality, and other-worldliness. Today, it is seen as the rising superpower, possessed of nuclear capability, the home of the IT revolution, lively this-worldly capitalism, the land of malls and consumerist passions. Only yesterday was it the land of famine and abject poverty; today, it is the land of a large and expanding middle class. Often the image features contradictory traits.

Nevertheless, in the midst of these recent transformations, certain features stand out and exhibit some continuity. I begin with the third variant, a liberal nationalist and inclusivist India that receives and naturalizes diverse cultural forms. The metaphor of a "composite civilization" captures the many religions, starting with Hinduism but continuing with Islam and Christianity, which found a home in India and suggests that all are acceptable. A striking formulation of this view, influential both outside and inside India, was uttered by Swami Vivekananda. He deeply influenced the European vision of Indian civilization via his widely reported representation of Hinduism at the World Parliament of Religion at Chicago on 11 September 1893:

There never was my religion and yours, my national religion or your national religion; there never existed many religions, there is only the one. One infinite religion existed all through eternity and will ever exist, and this religion is expressing itself in various countries in various ways. Therefore, we must respect all religions and we must try to accept them all as far as we can.

(Prasad 1994: ix)

The image of an open and tolerant civilization was enhanced by historical imagery that was propagated through school textbooks and which for a time became part of a standard national history (Rudolph and Rudolph 1983). I say for a time in that, when the Hindu nationalist Bharatiya Janta Party (BJP) came to power in some Indian states in the 1990s, and in the central government in 1998, textbooks were widely rewritten with an accent on Hindu nationalist heroes. Reshaping history and civilization were allied projects. In any case, the history of the emperors Ashoka and Akbar provided authoritative icons for the inclusive imagery of Indian civilization. Gandhi and Nehru as founders of the republic carried on the tradition of an open, tolerant civilization.

The (Buddhist) Emperor Ashoka (268–233 BCE), symbol of ancient toleration, had become available for civilizational construction in 1830. That year an Asiatic Society of Bengal scholar, James Prinsep, discovered and deciphered the rock edicts which the emperor had caused to be erected around the Indian periphery to publicize his views about tolerance and non-violence. The Ashokan wheel (*chakra*) was adopted in the Indian flag and the Ashokan Pillar became a mark of Indian sovereignty. Ashoka's words came to personify the pluralist state: "King Priyadarsi, beloved of the gods, honours the men of all religious communities with gifts and honours . . . other sects should be daily honoured in every way . . . " (quoted in Sircar 1975).

The noble laureate economist Amartya Sen, in the course of writing a book expressive of the intelligent, liberal, modern Indian's view of his civilization, as presented in *The Argumentative Indian*, invokes the icon on the side of inclusivity (Thapar 1961):

during the third century BCE [Ashoka] covered the country with inscriptions on stone tablets about good behavior and wise governance, including a demand for basic freedoms for all – indeed, he did not exclude women and slaves as Aristotle did.

(Sen 2005: 284)

Similarly, Sen invokes the Muslim emperor Akbar (1542–1605):

The politics of secularism received a tremendous boost from Akbar's championing of pluralist ideals . . . well exemplified even by his insistence on filling his court with non-Muslim intellectuals and artists . . . [and]

trusting a Hindu former king, who had been defeated earlier by Akbar, to serve as the general commander of his armed forces.

(Ibid.: 18)

Nehru and Gandhi made different contributions to the inclusivist civilizational image. Gandhi's was the inclusivity of the believer, for whom all religions contained truth. Nehru's was the contribution of the skeptic, whose tolerance is motivated by the Enlightenment conviction that religion is false knowledge destined to disappear. That meant the inclusivist variant of Indian civilization could draw on both spiritualist and rationalist versions.

There is a good deal of overlap between the inclusivist and the exclusivist versions of Indian civilization. The image of India as ascetic and spiritual still imbues both variants even as the image is challenged by the galloping hedonism and materialism of a resurgent Indian economy. The spiritualist, otherworldly, and ascetic features nurtured inside India were enacted and amplified "outside" by the New England transcendentalists Emerson and Thoreau, and by the German romantics. In the 1930s the response to Gandhi, and in the 1960s the beat generation's embrace of a spirituality defined as freedom from convention and a laid-back lifestyle, kept the idea of Indian spirituality alive. So too did serious questers from the "other West" (Rudolph and Rudolph 2007) in search of spirituality in Himalayan ashrams or in export ashrams run in the USA and Europe by Indian godmen.

The fourth variant: history as the vessel of civilization

The fourth variant of Indian civilization, the Hindu nationalist exclusivist variant, draws on history to support its image. For several generations Indians have fought ferocious battles over the representation of the history of the subcontinent and over control of the institutions that disseminate historical truth. The battles over representation begin with the origin of Indian civilization. How the story is told becomes a template for open versus closed versions of Indian civilization. Until the 1960s, the story that Indian civilization had its origins in an "Aryan invasion" – that is, an influx of peoples from West Asia using horse-drawn vehicles – was conventionally accepted by respectable historians and Indologists. So was the view that these Aryans were the authors of the Rigveda, of Hinduism's foundational texts. They were thought to have overrun the Indus civilization of ancient Harappa, a people hypothesized to have a different, possibly Dravidian, culture.[15] This history was compatible with the Orientalists' view that Indian and European cultures/languages derived from a common source.

On the other hand, the advocates of a Hindu nationalist or Hindutva[16] perspective have been assaulting the historical consensus. Working with a closed, self-contained civilization image, they assert that India's culture and people did not originate from invasion or migration. The Aryans were not a foreign people. They probably lived in Harappa. The undeciphered Harappan language will prove to be a form of Sanskrit. The Harappans were the indigenous source of the Rigveda.[17]

The debate had an inside dimension. The Harappa revision and other historical revisions were favored for public-school textbooks by Indian state governments controlled by the Hindu nationalist BJP. The debate also had an outside dimension. It was carried on before the California State Board of Education. The board was approached by diasporic Indian partisans of the indigenousness thesis with the request that it "correct" California public-school readers. (The board declined.)[18]

In the struggle for the control of history and the telling of civilization, the Hindu nationalist variant constructs a mirror image to that of the liberal inclusivists. Its targets are school textbooks, associations of professional historians, popular "vernacular" literature such as the 10 rupee historical comic books (*Amar chitrakathas*) that proliferate in corner bookshops, and, most recently, the Web. If the syncretic sympathies of the Mughal (and Muslim) Emperor Akbar and his Hindu generals and Hindu wives and Hindu architecture make good copy for the inclusivist vision, the Mughal Emperor Aurangzeb makes good copy for the Hindu nationalists. A pious Muslim, Aurangzeb rejected Akbar's openness and syncretism. He reinstituted the *jiziya*, the poll tax, on non-Muslims and allowed or instigated Hindu temple defacement or destruction. He at least partly abandoned the policy of including Hindus in court life and administration. In the Hindu nationalist vision of Indian civilization, Aurangzeb rather than Akbar becomes characteristic of the Mughal period.

But for an overall understanding of the exclusivist position such iconic particulars are less important – the same facts could be conceded by an inclusivist – than this variant's overall view of Indian history. In writing history, shall Muslim monarchs be treated as part of composite India or as enemies and foreigners? The canonical textbook by Majumdar, Raychaudhuri, and Datta (1973) explicitly treats the Mughals as foreigners, even while giving Akbar a benign face. Pakistani textbooks begin their history after the Mughals and avoid the loaded question whether Mughal syncretism should be acknowledged as part of Pakistan's inheritance. On the whole, Hindu nationalism rejects as repellant the assimilationist or syncretic processes that characterized the 600 years of Muslim rule.[19]

Yet the marks of syncretism and hybridity are everywhere. Invaders were Indianized and Indians reshaped by the civilizational encounter. Most of the Central Asian invaders – Kushans, Huns – were absorbed into the Hindu caste system (Ahmed 1966). The Brahmanic/Sanskritic ranking system was used to certify conquering invaders as *kshatriyas*, kings as understood by the Hindu *varna* system (Shah and Shroff 1972). For their part, the invaders successfully drew Indian peoples into Persian, Mughal, and/or Islamic cultural arenas in architecture, painting, and court ritual. The flexible Sufis who were the avant garde of conversionary Islam in Bengal, the influential Chishtaya who shaped Islam in North India, adopted Hindu iconic and social forms and local custom in ways that inflected the practice of Islam (Eaton 1993, 2000). It was common local practice, and to an extent still is, that revered (Muslim) Pirs and Hindu saints, as well as religious pilgrimages and festivals, were patronized by Hindus and Muslims. In "shatter zones," where religious cultures met and interlaced, syncretic sects emerged that are difficult to sort on the Muslim or Hindu side.[20] The devotional Hinduism of the *bhakti* sects produced saints, usually from lower castes, for whom all social distinctions, including those of Hindu or Muslim, melted before the force of loving devotion. The permeable lines between religious communities characteristic of South Asia make its Islam a very different phenomenon from the stern puritanical forms found in the Wahabi-based Islams of the Middle East.

Hindu nationalism seeks to disrupt the hybrid and syncretic legacies of these civilizational encounters in order to transform India into a homogeneous Hindu civilization. In the last twenty years, the family of Hindu organizations has undertaken a vigorous program of "reconversion." While some South Asian Muslims can trace their provenance to Persian or Pathan or Central Asian origins, most Indian Muslims and Christians are converts, residues of foreign invasions and occupations who must be brought back to their "true" condition. M. S. Gowalkar, former leader and theoretician of the Rashtriya Swayamsek Sangh (RSS), the cultural wing of the family of Hindu organizations, put it this way:

> They [Muslims] look to some foreign lands as their holy places. They call themselves "Sheiks" and "Syeds." Sheiks and Syeds are certain clans in Arabia. How then did these people come to feel that they are their descendants. That is because they have cut off all their ancestral national moorings of this land and mentally merged themselves with the aggressors. They still think that they have come here only to conquer and establish their kingdoms.
>
> (Gowalkar 1966: 128)

The exclusivist position holds that Hindutva – Hinduness – is the fundamental civilization of the subcontinent, and that variation must be subsumed under this fundamental. Hindutva is so wide and comprehensive that it encompasses not only Hindus but also the non-Hindu minorities. These are Hindu Muslims and Hindu Christians, all sorted in a subordinate position. Again Gowalkar:

> The foreign races in Hindusthan must either adopt the Hindu culture and language, must learn to respect and hold in reverence Hindu religion, must entertain no ideas but those of glorification of the Hindu race and culture . . . or may stay in the country, wholly subordinated to the Hindu nation, claiming nothing, deserving no privileges, far less any preferential treatment – not even citizens' rights.
>
> (Gowalkar 1939: 73)

The exclusivist variant of Indian civilization as presented above is not the end of the story. Exclusivist Hindutva has had to come to terms with the new historical context of post-independence democracy. Political Hinduism, which became a powerful force in the 1990s, began by using an extreme anti-Muslim vision to advance its political fortunes. But political constraints derailed extreme Hindu communalism. In order to lead coalition governments, the BJP has had to abandon its main exclusivist policies.[21] The coalition governments it formed in 1998 and 1999 included regional parties that depended on Muslim voters or held a pluralist view of Indian society that made a place for minorities. The BJP's coalition partners insisted on a Common Minimum Program that excluded three key Hindu nationalist planks.

The need to express its position in language closer to that of the secularist parties has affected public statements by members of the Sangh Parivar, the "family" of Hindu nationalist organizations. A recent restatement of RSS goals and beliefs by Ram Madhav, the RSS public spokesman, contrasts strikingly with the rhetoric Dr Gowalkar used fifty years earlier. The contemporary rhetoric appears to have passed through a process of discourse upgrading that rubs out blatant communal language, borrows objectivist turns of phrase from current social science, and recognizes that certain attitudes are no longer admissible in the public sphere:

> Issues of identity have exercised the RSS from its inception. India is a multi-religious country. With over 120 million Muslims, it has the world's second largest Islamic population. Christianity came to India in the 1st Century AD. Jews and Parsees have lived in India for hundreds of years, without fear or persecution.
>
> Yet the 850 million Hindus who comprise the vast majority of the Indian population are, to the RSS' mind, India's cultural mainstay. Hindu tradition and civilization, the shared values of family and community worship – a seamless, uninterrupted continuum for 5,000 years – are the sinews of the Indian nation. They give it its essential character.
>
> A year ago, Professor Samuel Huntington wrote a book, *Who Are We? America's Great Debate*. In his foreword, he said, "Anglo-Protestant culture has been central to American identity for three centuries... I believe one of the greatest achievements, perhaps the greatest achievement, of America is the extent to which it has eliminated the racial and ethnic components that historically were central to its identity... That has happened, I believe, because of the commitment successive generations of Americans have had to the Anglo-Protestant culture."[22]

The Huntington project in *Who Are We?* is not a defense of the "melting pot." It is not a defense of an assimilation process in which all identities contribute as they blend together. Nor is it a defense of multiculturalism. It is a sophisticated defense of white Protestant hegemony and, by derivation, is borrowed for a sophisticated defense of Hindu hegemony. Still, Ram Madhav's statement labors to present a modified and gentled approach, an approach that reflects a greater respect for pluralism. It appears to represent a strategic adaptation to the new political order. If it is not a genuine change of norms, it could be an opportunistic adaptation whose effect should not be underestimated. Words can commit by creating a discursive formation that makes for a transformed reality.

The reformulation of goals that the electoral process has forced upon Hindu nationalist politicians may modify their image of Indian civilization in ways that bring the liberal nationalist and Hindu nationalist variants closer together.

Notes

1 Robert Cox (2002a) speaks of "an amalgam of social forces and ideas that has achieved a certain coherence but is continually changing and developing in response to challenge from both within and from without."
2 The term "Indian" derives from the early naming of India by foreign visitors who encountered the lands of the Indus river.
3 An argument circulates in the Indian public sphere that "Hindu" or the related noun, Hindutva – Hinduness – is an adjective that has no specific religious referent, but a cultural one. Thus there are Muslim Hindus and Christian Hindus, and so on. Justice J. S. Verma and the Indian Supreme Court, in its decision in the Bombay election case *Prabhoo* v. *P. K. Kunte* (AIR 1996 SC 1113), took the view that Hindu referred to a broader cultural category, not just a religion.
4 Peter Mandaville also puts it well: "the history of civilizations, in this view, is one of competing claims by multiple actors within a given ideational-material complex to define, speak on behalf of, and articulate the meaning and parameters of that civilization" (Mandaville 2007: 136). An excellent essay reviewing the definitions of civilization is Akturk (2007). He reviews, among other sources, Braudel's understanding of civilization (Braudel 1995).
5 However, the Indian naming raises some questions for the smaller sovereignties that confront the Indian mega-polity in the South Asian Association for Regional Cooperation.
6 By agentless I mean there was no state or empire, no political entity, to power this process. There were of course other second-order agents, merchants and travelers and preaching ascetics who brought Sanskrit to Southeast Asia.
7 "[Soft power] is the ability to get what you want through attraction rather than coercion or payments. It arises from the attractiveness of a country's culture, political ideals, and policies. When our policies are seen as legitimate in the eyes of others, our soft power is enhanced" (Nye 2004: ii).
8 Such as Annie Besant (Taylor 1992) and Madame Blavatsky (Blavatsky 1972).
9 In their enthusiasm to indict the Orientalists as false speakers for colonized civilizations, post-colonial writers tend to miss this paradigm shift in perception of the other.
10 The Oxford professor Max Muller laid out the significance of the theory fifty years later:

> No authority could have been strong enough to persuade the Grecian army [of Alexander] that their gods and their hero-ancestors were the same as those of [the Indian] King Porus, or to convince the English soldier that the same

blood was running in his veins as in the veins of the dark Bengalese. And yet there is not an English jury now-a-days, which, after examining the hoary documents of language, would reject the claim of a common descent and a legitimate relationship between Hindu, Greek, and Teuton. . . . We challenge the seeming stranger, and whether he answers with the lips of a Greek, a German, or an Indian, we recognize him as one of ourselves.

(Muller 1855: 177).

11 Heinrich Heine (1797–1856), whose fame is also intercontinental, makes a similar contribution in his *Auf Flügeln des Gesanges* (*On the Wings of Song*):

At the Ganga the air is filled
with scent and light
And giant trees are flowering
And beautiful, quiet people
Kneel before lotus flowers.
(Singhal 1993: II, 234, 327)

12 The phrase is from his well-known *Minute on Indian Education* of 1835 (Clive and Pinney 1972: 249).

13 For a discussion of the Asian despotism debate, see Rudolph and Rudolph (1985); also Anderson (1977).

14 See also Nandy (1989).

15 For an exposition that was widely accepted in the mid-1990s, see Allchin (1995). Most historians now subscribe to the idea that, instead of an "invasion," there may have been a series of migrations and other less apocalyptic entries by outside peoples. See Thapar (2000). The debate about the origins of Hindu civilization peaked in the year 2000. *Frontline* published a series of articles by the proponents of the accepted view that peoples migrating into India had been the source of the Rigveda and other aspects of Hinduism. In addition to Romila Thapar, a historian retired from Jawaharlal Nehru University, Asko Porpola, a Finnish Indologist, Michael Witzel, a professor at Harvard, and Steve Farmer contributed articles to a debate in the Hindu (Witzel and Farmer 2000). The object of their critique was a book by N. Jha and N. S. Rajaram, *The Deciphered Indus Scripts: Methodology, Readings, Interpretations* (Jha and Rajaram 2000).

16 The term, propagated by Savarkar (1938), meaning Hinduness, has come to be associated with Hindu nationalist positions.

17 Among the recently contested issues was the claim by Rajaram that one of the Harappan seals depicts a horse. Because horses are associated with the Aryans, this is said to prove that the indigenous Harappans, not outsiders, are the historical Aryans who generated the Rigveda. Witzel and Farmer (2000) indict the Rajaram argument by pointing out that the photo of the Harappan horse seal used is computer enhanced, and, in any case, only one seal would not count as proof of a strong horse civilization.

18 The Hindu American Foundation (HAF) had filed a lawsuit against the California State Board of Education (SBE) because SBE refused to accept some of the changes demanded by HAF to the proposed new social science/history textbooks for the sixth grade. In a judgment delivered on 4 September 2006, Judge Marlette of the Superior Court of California upheld that the textbooks as approved by the SBE met all legal requirements of accuracy and neutrality, and denied HAF's demand that they be rescinded ("California Textbook Issue" 2006).

19 Counting from 1192, the battle of Tarain, when Mahmud of Ghur defeated a Rajput federation led by Prithviraj Chauhan, was followed by the conquest of much of North and East India by Muslim armies.

20 Examples include the Meos, whose lands lay between (Mughal) Delhi and

(Rajput) Jaipur (Mayaram 1997). Also on syncretic sects in Rajasthan, see Khan (1995) and Hollister (1979).

21 The planks were the building of a Ram temple on the site of the Babri Masjid, a mosque destroyed in 1992 by a Hindu mob; the abrogation of Article 370 of the Indian constitution, which provides a special, more autonomous, status to the (Muslim majority) state of Kashmir; and the enactment of a uniform civil code, which would supersede Muslim personal law.

22 Statement by Ram Madhav, national spokesman, Rashtriya Swayamsevak Sangh, 10 August 2008.

7　Islam in Afro-Eurasia

A bridge civilization

Bruce B. Lawrence

Why civilization?

In the most extensive effort yet mounted to trace civilization as a category of critical inquiry, the Dutch sociologist Johann Arnason invokes the pithy dictum of A. N. Whitehead: "Without metaphysical presupposition there can be no civilization" (Arnason 2003a: v). But which metaphysics, tracing which analytical trajectories, produce a consensus about the sources and patterns, the projects and ideologies that cluster as "civilization"?

The major distinction that characterizes Arnason's approach is to differentiate civilization as a unitary concept from civilizations as multiple units, none of which can be understood except through sustained, comparative analysis with their counterparts. He further distinguishes cultural from non-cultural approaches, citing well-known sociologists such as Weber, Durkheim, and Eisenstadt, or famed historians, such as Toynbee, Spengler, and Braudel, but also lesser luminaries, such as Borkenau, Patocka, and Krejci. Deftly he tries to move from civilizational discourse to subsequent debates about modernization, globalization, and post-colonialism. The comparative analysis of civilization, in his view, both anticipates and continues to permeate all macro-level reflection on human society, world history, and political theory.

The core issue remains culture, and it informs the provisional definition of civilization for my own chapter. I define civilization as the broadest, most capacious envelope of cultural traits related – directly or indirectly, explicitly or implicitly – to geographical location and temporal shifts. In a thumbnail definition, civilization equals culture writ large over space and time. Space predominates. The geographical lens of pre-modern civilization focuses on the ecumene, or the Eurasian ecumene (McNeill), or the Afro-Eurasian oikumene (Hodgson). Civilization presupposes cities, commerce, travel and trade, warfare and alliances. The ecumene is the known world connected through urban nodes, at once locally rooted and regionally, as also transregionally, linked to other nodes. Time becomes crucial in trying to chart change in modes of production and patterns of influence that characterize civilization from pre-modern to modern phases of world history.

The axial era looms large as the major temporal marking for all civilizational analysis. The "Axial Age," first coined by the philosopher Karl Jaspers, was developed extensively by Eisenstadt and Hodgson, among others. Cities preceded it, from 3000 to 800 BCE, but then in the middle of the Agrarian Age, from 800 to 200 BCE, "great bursts of creative and many-sided cultural innovation . . . resulted in an enduring geographical and cultural articulation of the citied zone of the Oikoumene into regions" (Hodgson 1974: 1, 112). The post-Axial Age persisted for two millennia, from 200 BCE to 1800 CE, when it was replaced by the Technical Age. The last major hinge of history is also the most complex. It is an age marked not only by the emergence of Occidental or Western dominance but also by a breakdown of the parity that had previously made possible the diffusion and adjustment to technical changes among Afro-Eurasian citied societies (ibid.: 3, 200).

In what Braudel terms *la longue durée*, or the broad expanse of historical time, there was no single civilization but multiple civilizations, and it is important to wrestle with the cultural envelope which each provides. The present chapter will focus on the distinctive cultural traits of Islamic, or Islamicate, civilization, but it will also try to make sense of its relationship to civilizations that both preceded it and were contemporaneous with it. It must also reckon with the dominance of Western civilization in the Technical Age.

Since material culture pervades in any reckoning of hierarchy between civilizations, scientific breakthroughs had to combine with technological mastery to create the Technical Age. These provided the necessary, albeit not the sufficient, cause for the global hegemony of Western Europe, generally, and the rise of British and French empires, in particular. The sufficient cause was the ideology of empire. It relied on civilizational discourse. It presupposed the superiority of urban elites, within as well as beyond their national boundaries. "The civilizing mission," explains Adas, "was more than just an ideology of colonization beyond Europe. It was the product of a radically new way of looking at the world and organizing human societies" (Adas 1989: 209–10). It prized time, work, and discipline. It believed that the entire world could be converted through commerce and bureaucracy, as practiced by Western science and management. It pervaded the nineteenth and early twentieth centuries, only to face challenges from abroad, as well as dissents from within, after World War I. The "Great War" undermined the civilizational superiority of Western Europe, whether etched in Duhamel's polemical *Civilization 1914–1917* or Orwell's satirical *Burmese Days* (ibid.: 386–92), at the same time that other popular writers were drawn to Asian civilizations in their search for a more long-term, metaphysical cure of the human condition.

Religion early and often became linked to culture as a crucial civilization marker. Weber charted the breakthrough of Western modernity as itself part of a complex historical dynamic that also had to account for India and China, and later the Islamic world (see especially Turner 1974). For Braudel, too, religion is the civilizational phenomenon par excellence (Braudel 1979: 2, 495). The dominant civilizations were reckoned to be Indian/Hindu, Chinese/

Confucian, Irano-Arabic/Islamic, and Western/Judeo-Christian. Yet this listing conceals as much as it reveals. Neither India nor China was marked exclusively by one religion or by a unitary cultural impulse. Islam included many racial, linguistic, and cultural trajectories that exceeded the Middle East, while the modern West included elements of both metaphysical dread (typified by Ayn Rand) and its opposite, Protestant triumphalism, both of which preclude a symbiosis of Jewish with Christian norms and values. (See the discussion below of the alternative encatchment, Islamo-Christian Civilization, proposed by Bulliet.)

Perhaps the most bewildering of all cartographic elements to fit into the Islamicate or any civilizational mold is Southeast Asia. It contains the largest number of Muslims in a single country: 195 million, or 88 percent of the population, in Indonesia (McAmis 2002: 4). Though ignored in most theoretical studies on civilization, it is prized by geographers, along with Central Asia, as one of the major interstitial zones within a world regional framework (Lewis and Wigen 1997). For K. N. Chaudhuri, the foremost historian of premodern Asia, the case of Southeast Asia belies the connective tissue, and disposition to generalize, that civilizational discourse requires:

> The technique of filtering the identity of a civilization by fixing the outer and inner limits in the conceptual image of the social structure, adopted for Islam and India, which is also relevant for China, breaks down in the case of South East Asia. There is no single dominating ideology here that creates through a dialectical process of acceptance and sanctions a single unified civilization.
>
> (Chaudhuri 1990: 59)

To paraphrase from our earlier thumbnail definition of civilization, there is no "culture writ large over space and time" that can be projected as an ideology inclusive of the myriad islands, the spatial, temporal, linguistic and material elements of what Friend calls "the Phil-Indo Archipelago" (2006: 10).

Yet civilization is more than a shibboleth for religious claims or cultural irredentism; it is also an inescapable part of the effort to forge a ranking of cultures, and even to claim the superiority of one over rival others. In this sense, civilization rests on a taxonomic contrast that pits dyadic opposites against one another. Even before the civilizing mission of British and French (and, more recently, American) missionaries in Africa and Asia, there was a distinction between civilized folk and barbarian "others," just as there was also the ternary division of time into corresponding social units. Desert tribes or agrarian communities were deemed to be "primitive" and major premodern empires "classical," while "modern" was reserved for democratic, capitalist-based nation-states (the ternary myth is exposed by Laroui 1977: 11). In political theory, "modern" means that "the achievement of a liberal state [is seen as] a precondition for the creation of a modern civilization"

(Kaviraj and Khilnani 2001: 292). So inextricably was the word "modern" linked to capitalism that "a certain relation between unrestricted commercial activity and the jurisdiction of a limited state was central to this new, higher stage of civilization." What characterized the superiority of modern (read Euro-American plus Japanese) civilization from earlier stages of social development was

> a society of civility, in the sense of social order, pacification, and restraint. It was a society of civility in the sense of gentle manners, opposed not merely to the wildness and violence of primitive or warlike peoples, but also to the great volatility caused by the passions of military aristocrats or conquering rulers.
>
> (Ibid.: 294)

In effect, the new turn to civil society, like the prior invocation of "the civilizing mission," becomes yet another transformation of civilizational discourse into a metaphysical truth. In this case, there is a mysterious, unsubstantiated link between the bourgeois middle class as agents of commercial prosperity and advocates of political openness. While A. N. Whitehead would be pleased, a more robust analysis of civilizational discourse requires not just a look at the present but a review of the past: one must explore routes not taken, meanings not explored, and also pioneers not acknowledged, especially in the realm of Islam and Muslim subjects.

Ibn Khaldun: the first proponent of civilization

In order to relate Islam to civilizational discourse, one must revisit the foundational moment for the concept of civilization. It was Islam or, rather, a major Muslim intellectual who founded civilizational discourse. 'Abd ar-Rahman ibn Muhammad ibn Khaldun (d. 1406 CE) wrote an introduction to history or *Muqaddimah* which Arnold Toynbee called "undoubtedly the greatest work of its kind that has ever yet been created by any mind in any time or place" (Toynbee 1953: 3, 322). Not only does the *Muqaddimah* chart "the emergence of the Islamic world system 1000–1500" (Irwin 1996: 35), it was also the first major work to deal with Civilization as an analytical category. Beyond assessing in brilliant strokes the peculiarities of Islamic history, Ibn Khaldun inaugurates an entirely new discipline, one he terms the science of civilization or human society (*'ilm al-'umran*). The very nature of his argument belies the effort to see West and East as irreducible opposites, with Islam as some persistent enemy or restive outlier to the dominant ethos of Western civilization. In a recent essay, "Ibn Khaldun: The Last Greek and the First *Annaliste* Historian," the Eurasian historian Stephen Dale demonstrated that Ibn Khaldun was not only a judge, a litterateur, and a sometime poet but also a rationalist, a social theorist, and, above all, a rigorous linguist searching for universal principles (Dale 2006: 432–6).

Ibn Khaldun focused on the meaning of Political Events. The full title of the larger book, *Kitab al-'ibar*, to which the *Muqaddimah* serves as an introduction, was *Kitab al-'ibar wa-diwan al-mubtada' wa-l-khabar fi ayyam al-'Arab wal-'Ajam wal-Barbar wa-man 'asarahum min dhawi as-sultan al-akbar*. In translation the title becomes *The Book of Lessons and Archive of Origins, Dealing with Political Events Concerning Arabs, Non-Arabs and Berbers, and with their Contemporary Major Rulers*. While Ibn Khaldun hopes to offer *'ibar* (instructions or lessons), their content revolves around understanding Political Events. Political Events are the bookends of history, the beginning and the end, with *khabar* having a multi-layered meaning. Each Political Event may be cause or outcome. Ibn Khaldun used linguistics in the service of a science of society or civilization. Its subject becomes the early conditions, or first instances, of social organization, namely, *badawa* or desert civilization. The very first civilization is not the city but the desert, and it is the desert which sets the stage for what follows, namely, the emergence of world civilization (*'umran*) through sedentary or urban civilization (*hadara*). *Badawa* and *hadara* contrast, and even compete, with one another, but their dyadic tension becomes the basis for *'umran*, the inhabited world connecting the parts of Islamdom but also relating them to places and perspectives beyond an Islamicate circumference.

And so, if we are to think of civilizational politics in the twenty-first century, we cannot conjure a genealogy that is traceable to the northern Mediterranean or to the Enlightenment or to European empire building from the sixteenth century on. Instead, we must go back to a North African Arab jurist who understood Aristotle and used Aristotelian logic to construct a new science, the science of world civilization. Civilizational discourse is neither an invention of nor a social construct limited to the West. It is a product of cosmopolitan, juridical Islam in the shadow of classical Greek philosophy, and its key term is Event. Because Ibn Khaldun was a jurist before he became a world historian, Event retains a juridically weighted meaning. Event is integral to Tradition scholarship – that is, trying to discern whether statements attributed to the Prophet Muhammad were in fact authentic or, as too often happened, spurious. Events were accounts from persons whose integrity was being reviewed in order to verify or disqualify what they reported as Tradition. But, for Ibn Khaldun, the grammatical and juridical meanings of Event expand into something more vital and visionary: the surplus of labor, but also of thought, that produces a model of civilization across time and space. The linchpin to transforming Event into this new conceptual domain was *mutabaqa*, or conformity. Even while eschewing the notion that all forms are external, Ibn Khaldun did believe in conformity – namely, that what one remembered as Event could, or should, conform to historical reports of what others witnessed as Event.

If this sounds familiar it is because already, in the early fifteenth century, Ibn Khaldun was pondering what later became in Western social science the distinction between categories of practice (what was remembered through oral reports) and categories of analysis (what could be confirmed through actual witnesses). Like every other Muslim jurist, he was faced with the daunting task of winnowing out true from false Traditions. By the third century after the *hijra* (exodus),[1] the tracing of *isnad* or chains of transmission had become a fixed part of Islamic legal training. One book even catalogues all the various categories of malfeasants who make up Traditions. They range from atheists and heretics to outright falsifiers of Traditions, including those who would invent Traditions in order to embellish religious stories they told in mosques and hence collect larger donations from gullible believers![2]

In order to establish his new science, Ibn Khaldun the jurist had to affirm his own practice of Tradition criticism, but through it go beyond its parameters in order to open up another way to approach human social organization, itself the basis of global or world civilization (*'umran al-'alam*). In effect, his forensic skill as a litterateur allowed him to cite Event, itself an ancillary part of Tradition scholarship, as an independent term conveying the surplus of meaning that he wanted to impart to the study of human social organization or the history of world civilization. Distinguishing Tradition from Event, while affirming both, became the pathway to his new science.

At the same time, Ibn Khaldun needed to fashion a new language, whether by using existing terms in novel ways or by inventing new words – that is, neologisms – to convey the added complexity he saw in human social relations. "*'Asabiya*," or "group feeling," is the major neologism permeating all of Ibn Khaldun's work. It is a variable pinned between religion (*din*) and the state (*dawla*), both of which demand loyalty, but of variant, even incommensurate kinds. Explains a leading Maghribi historian: "At one and the same time, 'asabiya is the cohesive force of the group, the conscience that it has of its own specificity and collective aspirations, and the tension that animates it and impels it ineluctably to seek power through conquest" (Talbi 1973: 4). This last element – the drive to power through conquest – seems to fall outside the juridical realm, unless one realizes that the law is also an instrument of power, whether through persuasion or domination. It is this fluid itinerary in Ibn Khaldun's linguistic usage that needs to be underscored: *'asabiya*, in effect, becomes "a concept of relation by sameness, opposed both to the state (*dawla*), based on relations of difference or complementarity, and to religion (*din*), which alone supersedes it" (Anderson 1984: 120).

Reliance on metaphor allows Ibn Khaldun to demonstrate how the same word, like the same event or person, can be viewed differently over time, and also from different places in the same time frame. In other words, he demonstrates from within an Islamicate worldview how civilization projects "culture writ large over space and time." Perhaps the most crucial argument that he makes on behalf of history as an Islamic science is that historians alone among Muslim scientists can explain how Islam arose out of a context of orality and nomadism/primitivism (*badawa*) to become a proponent of both writing and urban civilization (*hadara*). What had been speech and a habit became writing and a craft.[3] Yet the very lifeline of Islam depended on maintaining the connection between literacy and orality, between writing and speech, as also between civilized and nomad. In short, analogy, while it had its most immediate application in law, could, and did, apply to the understanding of the laws of history – above all, the history of Muslim civilization.

Yet analogy conceals what is the most basic aspect of Ibn Khaldun's methodology that links him to all future proponents of civilizational discourse: the propensity to rely on dyads for explaining the force of intellectual inquiry and the utility of analytical judgments. Ibn Khaldun never ceases to frame all issues in terms of competing or complementary sets of two. The most basic for history is the *badawa/hadara* dialectic, framed within the overarching concept of *'umran*. But also evident and recurrent are his references to *'arab* and *'ajam* as two linguistic resources, with *'arab* the superior but *'ajam* the more creative. Additionally, there is the accent on oral and written as two expressions of language, with oral expressing the greater claim to *'asabiya* or intrinsic solidarity, while written is the more necessary for bureaucratic activities essential to urban society, sedentary culture and statecraft.

Finally, of course, there is the dyad of *'aql* and *naql*, or reason and tradition. They are as much complementary as competitive, both belonging to a larger conception of *'ilm*. This is evident in the syllabus formation of Ghubrini, Ibn Khaldun's Maghribi predecessor and author of a seminal work in which he distinguishes between two types of knowledge: *'ilm al-diraya* and *'ilm al-riwaya*. One is the subject of discussion and debate, the other of memorization and transmission, yet in actual syllabi some topics fall within both *diraya* and *riwaya*, *'aql* and *naql* (Al-Azmeh 1981: 102) Among them are *fiqh* (jurisprudence) and *din* (religion), undercutting the too neat oppositions that often mark the dichotomous, post-Enlightenment reading of Ibn Khaldun as the advocate of reason over religion, logic over belief. All dyads need to be collapsed into a spectrum of possibilities, not into a neat either/or classificatory judgment.

The showcase for Islamicate civilization was its ability to self-replicate across the ecumene or the Afro-Eurasian oikumene. According to a recent Turkish researcher, there was a clearly identifiable Islamicate civilization with its epistemic communities interlinked across the "court societies" of Istanbul, Isfahan, Herat, Delhi, and Cairo, among others, manifested along the three related domains of cities, empires, and religion. Islamic empires depended on Islamic cities, which grew out of, even as they in turn reinforced, Islam as a religion and worldview (*Weltanschauung*). Arabic was the universal medium of religious discourse, Persian often the language of high culture, and there was a commonly shared set of canonical readings, including non-religious literary masterpieces such as the poems of Omar Khayyam as well as famous interpretations of the Qur'an. Architects made careers building palaces and tombs, fountains and bridges, from Agra in India to Sarajevo in Bosnia (Akturk 2009).

One of the most famous witnesses of a clearly identifiable Islamicate Civilization was Ibn Battuta (d. 1368), a Maghribi jurist and contemporary of

Ibn Khaldun. Ibn Battuta was able to travel from Timbuktu in Mali to the Middle Volga, from northern India to Muslim Spain. Everywhere he went he could, and often did, speak about a range of topics in Arabic with the learned men in these regions. Today we know about Ibn Battuta not only because of his travels but because of the royal attention and support they attracted. The Moroccan sultan Abu 'Inan was so impressed with the peripatetic jurist that he commissioned a belle lettrist, Ibn Juzayy, to record and embellish his countryman's twenty-nine years on the road and at sea, from 1325 to 1354 (see illustrative map in Musallam 1996: 166–7). The resulting *Rihla* tells the legendary travels of a Moroccan religious scholar who journeyed throughout the Afro-Eurasian oikumene (Dunn 1989). Patronage was not so easily obtained in every instance and, as Cornell has shown in an astute essay on Ibn Battuta, not even his generous royal patron could be fully trusted (Cornell 2005: 47–9). Yet, for many centuries throughout Islamdom, there was a fierce competition between the palaces in Istanbul (Ottoman), Isfahan (Safavid), and Herat (Timurid) over the most talented poets, architects, and musicians, each dynast offering a competitive package of benefits to the artists and intellectuals in his court or within his reach.

Two successors to Ibn Khaldun in civilizational discourse

Whether Muslim civilization, or Islamic(ate) civilization, stands by itself or in conjunction with other civilizations, it remains a focal point for exploring larger fields of inquiry. Is the largest field of inquiry world history or world systems? Both have a well-established provenance in social science literature, but which is to be preferred in thinking about Islam, Muslim nation-states, and Muslim actors, whether in macro— or micro-terms? Put bluntly, is Islam best understood as a singular civilizational construct within world history, or is it instead a mere subset of some larger world system?

I will argue below that *both* genealogies are possible, though the choice is fraught with consequences for evaluating Islamicate evidence. Islam does stand apart from other civilizations, especially in its notions of hierarchy and kingship. Yet neither of these concepts is intrinsic to Islam as religion, and so Islam in civilizational discourse must be viewed as a cultural variable, linked to but exceeding religious connotations. Just as the noun Islamdom encompasses the Muslim majority regions of Africa and Asia, so the adjective Islamicate best describes those features of cross-regional filiation that link discrete parts of Africa and Asia and form the Islamicate subset of the Afro-Eurasian oikumene. In other words, Islamicate civilization evokes a larger geocultural grid than would be defined solely by loyalty to Islam as creed, liturgy, and law. While Islamicate civilization cannot, and should not, be viewed as part of some inherent or deterministic world system, it also cannot be understood apart from the other civilizations with which it interacted, both shaping and being shaped by them, in its long historical trajectory. Functionally speaking, Islamicate civilization is the bridge from ancient to modern social systems, though the work of Western scholars and Muslim apologists alike has obscured that crucial, link function of Islamicate norms and values, actors and processes.[4]

In making this argument, and in using this vocabulary, I am following the lead of Marshall G. S. Hodgson, the premier Islamicist of his generation. Because Hodgson has been consistently ignored by most major theoreticians – even Edward Said did not deign to give him a footnote in *Orientalism*[5] – it is crucial to revisit his labor and to extrapolate his unique, compelling perspective on Islamicate civilization. The value of Hodgson's labor becomes clearer when his oeuvre is compared, and contrasted, with that of Immanual Wallerstein, the author of world systems. Unlike Hodgson, Wallerstein has enjoyed widespread recognition for his rethinking of the relationship between material and cultural elements that define large-scale social units. Indeed, Wallerstein stands out among contemporary social scientists for his adroit combination of developmental theory with historical sociology, though he stumbles onto Islamic data and remains a minor figure in civilizational discourse.

Wallerstein

The major unit in Wallerstein's scheme, the cornerstone of his theory, is the capitalist world economy (see Ragin and Chirot 1984). More than the sum total of capitalist nation-states (antecedents of the current G8 and G20), the capitalist world economy amounts to a world system because it functions as "an economic entity spanning continents and polities, [making it] a unique and encompassing social system." In effect, the world according to Wallerstein is run by economics, not by politics, with nation-states being interlinked through a dynamic socioeconomic system in which they participate but over which they have no ultimate control. Ironically, the Marxist redux becomes a capitalist promoter, at least in theory, since the absence of centralized political control means that "economic actors have greater freedom of movement, which enhances their opportunities to amass wealth and promote accumulation on a global scale" (Wallerstein 1980: 287).

Having foregrounded the world system or the capitalist world economy, Wallerstein does not ignore other units. He also compares nation-states, regions, and cities to the modern world system, but their chief value is instrumental: to demonstrate the role they play in making the world system as a whole continue to work.

The evidence for Wallerstein's theoretical corpus comes not from his own fieldwork but from the *Annales* school. He uses the work of the *Annalistes* for a bluntly political agenda, to wit, "not only to understand the history of the capitalist world system, but also to attempt to prepare the intellectual ground for the coming of a world socialist system" (Wallerstein 1980: 307). It is more than mere coincidence that the center which he has overseen and which has been the engine for his academic production is called the Fernand Braudel

Center or, in its fuller title, the Fernand Braudel Center for the Study of Economies, Historical Systems, and Civilizations.

Often criticized as reductive, Wallerstein's millenarian socialism omits two crucial features that are important for the Muslim world and especially relevant to the viability of Islamicate civilization as an analytical category: (1) sustained attention to the semi-peripheries and (2) recurrent emphasis on cultural production as a decisive element both for collective identity and for ultimate survival.

The semi-periphery remains one of the most original and ingenious of Wallerstein's units of analysis. While his crucial frame of reference is center–periphery, a familiar dyad, the semi-periphery, by straddling the center and the periphery, highlights regions/nation-states that are neither driving nor driven by the world system yet function as bridge players, aligned in some features with the center, in others with the periphery. Major examples for Wallerstein are Venice and Spain in the late sixteenth century, Sweden in the seventeenth, Prussia in the eighteenth, Russia in the nineteenth and twentieth, Japan in the late nineteenth and early twentieth, and, today, Brazil and South Africa.

What is noticeable for their absence from the above list, and from Wallerstein's work in general, is attention to the major Muslim nations of the Asian subcontinent and the archipelago. It is almost as if the canopy of colonialism, cast over this vast region principally through the second wave of modernity represented by the British and the Dutch, has occluded from Wallerstein's systemic model-building vision all the elements of middle Asia. He remains riveted to the westernmost region of Asia, now known as Europe, along with its island neighbor, Britain, and alternatively to the easternmost region of Asia, China and its neighbors, but the Muslim middle is largely missing. Because of this almost reflexive oversight, Wallerstein fails to elaborate the central function of Islam as a bridge civilization, an extended semi-periphery with resilience that affirms, even as it modifies, his originary conceptual vision.

There is one Islamic polity that does figure in Wallerstein's model building. Repeatedly he draws attention to the Ottoman empire: perhaps because of all the premodern Muslim polities, it is the Ottoman empire which seems to conform to Wallerstein's own a priori judgments. It is closest to Europe. It is part of a larger European trajectory into world history and contemporary geopolitics, so much so that in 1998 the eighth biennial conference of the Fernand Braudel Center for the Study of Economies, Historical Systems, and Civilizations highlighted the Ottoman empire and the world economy, with special attention to issues of law and legitimation. Omitted from consideration were the myriad aspects of cultural production in the most major and long-lasting Muslim empire of the premodern period (for a partial corrective, see Rogers 2000).

Crucially absent from Wallerstein's project is any deep reading of culture as intrinsic to civilization. If civilization is culture writ large over space and time, as has been argued repeatedly above, then it does not fit the Wallersteinian template of civilization as a precursor to the dawn of a world socialist system. When Wallerstein does invoke the plural "civilizations," it is largely as a polemic: only because of the supposed superiority of the West – a world-dominant civilization equated with progress, enlightenment, and universalism – are other civilizations adduced, their counter-values "limited" to identity, autonomy, and diversity (see the critique of Arnason 2003a: 7–10).

Hodgson

The central question facing Wallerstein was the same as that facing all major social scientific theorists, namely, "Why the West?" The answer he gave was the distinctive interaction of politics and economics, with almost no attention either to technical inventiveness or to cultural motives. In retelling the familiar story of the emergence of modernity, he mines the deep memory of but one strand of world history.

There is another answer given by others, Max Weber principal among them. It is to stress the interaction between cultural norms and economic or market forces. As Eisenstadt lamented, most of the opponents of Orientalism have not escaped what the Iranian critic Jalal Al-i Ahmad lamented as "Westoxification." "They have tended to see Weber as a Eurocentric author," noted Eisenstadt, "preoccupied with the analysis of the origin of modern capitalism, demonstrating the superiority of the West but neglecting the other side of his argument that emphasized the continual internal dynamics of different civilizations" (Eisenstadt and Schluchter 1998: 6).[6]

Hodgson provides the necessary corrective to crude Weberianism. He intended to slight neither the social achievements nor the cultural norms of non-Western societies; he wanted to reclaim and to underscore what they had deemed to be both creative and productive. And so in his major essay on the ambiguous character of modernity, published over forty years ago, Hodgson drew attention not to Euro-American global dominance but to the downside of this dominance for the dominated or the marginalized.

In accenting the underside of the emergent capitalist world economy, Hodgson prefigures the tone of Wallerstein's own analysis, yet he sees the road to recuperation in utterly opposite terms. "It was part of the transmutational character of the new Transformation," he argued,

> that it broke down the very historical presuppositions in terms of which gradual diffusions had maintained parity among Afro-Eurasian citied societies. In the new pace of historical change, when decades sufficed to produce what centuries had produced before, a lag of four of five centuries was no longer safe. The old gradual diffusion or adjustment was no longer possible. . . . Those untransmutated agrarianate-level societies that did not share Western cultural presuppositions had perforce to continue developing in their own traditions at their own pace, adopting

from alien traditions only what could be assimilated on that basis. Hence the Western Transmutation, once it got well under way, could neither be paralleled independently nor be borrowed wholesale. Yet it could not, in most cases, be escaped. The millennial parity of social power broke down, with results that were disastrous almost everywhere.

(Hodgson 1993: xiii, n. 8)

From this point of parallel with Wallerstein's project, Hodgson then diverges. For him, as for Antonio Gramsci, the dominance – and also hegemony – of Western Europe/North America was closely allied to imperialism and colonialism. Since cultural capital as much as economic capital is involved in propagating and resisting the myth of Western superiority, one cannot escape an analysis of religion. Religion is deeply implicated in the debate about the origin and scope of Euro-American global influence. Insofar as resistance to that influence can be theorized and traced in multiple cultural contexts, they represent voices from the Martinican psychiatrist Frantz Fanon to the American political theorist James Scott. While Fanon advocated the benefit of violence against colonial impositions in Algeria and elsewhere, Scott demonstrated how sophisticated are resistance strategies, or hidden transcripts, against post-colonial state structures in Southeast Asia but also in the American South.

In this reading, transformation becomes the rhetorical capstone of victors "inasmuch as the major historical forms of domination have presented themselves in the form of a metaphysics, a religion, a world view," yet to oppose domination others have also resorted to religion as a symbolic capital, so that the discourse of the victors has "provoked the development of more or less equally elaborate replies in the hidden transcript [of those oppressed or marginalized]" (Scott 1990: 115).

In the spirit of Hodgson, one must render problematic wholesale, unwieldy abstractions such as the West and the Third World, center/periphery, and metropolitan/local. Janet Abu-Lughod, for instance, argues that one must take seriously the local differentiation of culture and the multiple referents of the world system in each region and in each axial period of history. If one does, she goes on to assert, then it is necessary above all to look at the distinct character of regions as nodes of culture and, above all, of religious loyalty and practice, values, and norms. While each religion, including Islam, has a universal scope encompassing all races, languages, and cultures, it is still the case that each cosmopolitan/metropolitan setting frames the character and tone of religious life according to its own rhythm and resources (Abu-Lughod 1989: 24–38 and 1993: 96–102). For the Indian Ocean region, the centerpiece of Islamicate civilization, the major goal, as Sugata Bose intimated, is: "to keep in play an Indian Ocean inter-regional arena of economic *and cultural* interaction as an analytical unit while avoiding the pitfalls of assuming any uncomplicated and unsustainable thesis about continuity" (Bose 1998: 8).

I would argue, following Bose but also Chaudhuri cited earlier (Chaudhuri

1990), that it is the Indian Ocean region, rather than MENA – the Middle East and North Africa – that has given Islam its particular civilizational shape, making Islamic civilization a vital, pivotal category for historical and contemporary analysis. Through its presence in the Indian Ocean, Islam became a pan-Asian cultural agent. It influenced – and continues to influence – the beliefs and practices of millions of Asians, from Central to South to Southeast Asia. While there are other pan-Asian religions – Hinduism to the far south, Buddhism to the Far East – none spans the southern rim of the Asian continent to the extent that Islam does. (See, for example, Simpson and Kresse 2008.)

Pre-modern kingship

Civilization invokes religion and also exceeds it. Civilization requires attention to the social as well as cognitive markers for those patterned by Islamic loyalty. Warriors and traders were crucial agents of change in both South and Southeast Asia. It was Muslim invaders from the northeast who brought with them, or developed after arrival, traits that have since characterized the Islamic experience in South Asia for much of its known history. Centuries later, it was Muslim traders, coming from Arabia as well as India, who began to settle in significant numbers in the archipelago known today as Southeast Asia. They too professed and pursued Islamic loyalty, but in different circumstances, with disparate outcomes.

Much more important for their ultimate destiny, however, was the shaping of Asian Muslim polities by a model of governance known as kingship. It derives from patterns of social mobility and civic organization that typify South Asia from the pre-Axial Age (*c.* 1000 BCE on):

- a militarized society, with a standing army which requires regular use, often to invade and conquer adjacent regions;
- autocratic rule by a military leader invested with instrumental power but often claiming divine authority and patronizing scholars to further that claim;
- monuments commemorating religious heroes as well as rulers of the past, built by the military leaders to strike awe in the living.

In this sense, the prehistory of Islamic South Asia is not to be located in the life of Muslim societies further to the west but rather in the reigns, or imagined reigns and legacies, of the most illustrious kings of previous dynasties. Two stand out from the Axial Age: Alexander the Great (356–323 BCE) and Ashoka the Munificent (r. 272–236 BCE). Together they project Greek and Buddhist legacies into South Asia. Alexander was a brilliant soldier who wanted to be remembered as a wise king. Among the scholars he patronized was Aristotle. He represented the Achaemenid style of governance linked to the Persian emperors Cyrus and Darius. Ashoka founded the Mauryan dynasty. He had no courtier to rival Aristotle, but, through the monumental building inspired by his dramatic conversion to Buddhism, he continued the style of royal patronage familiar from his Persian-Greek predecessors. Even though no literary texts survived, Ashoka's monuments did persist, and they were used and reused by successive dynasties, including the later Muslim monarchs of Central Asia whom we examine below.

Persian is the crucial element. While one can identify Arabic and Turkish elements in South Asia, they matter less than the Persian. Despite the fact that Islam is often identified with the Arabic language and Arab norms, these provided merely the patina for Muslim expansion into the subcontinent. While Turks comprised the main resource for Muslim armies, neither the Turkish language nor Turkish cultural forms characterized the outlook of these newcomers to Hindustan. Beyond the Arabic patina, as also the Turkish frame, was the central image of this newly emerging social formation. The picture had its own design, and it was Persianate.

Persianate is a new term, first coined by Marshall Hodgson to offer a different explanation of Islam in the world system than that extrapolated from Wallerstein. While Persianate depicts a cultural force that is linked to the Persian language and to self-identifying Persians, Persianate is more than either a language or a people; it highlights elements that Persians share with Indo-Aryan rulers who preceded Muslims to the subcontinent. Two elements are paramount:

- *hierarchy*, which consists of top-down status markings that link all groups to each other, but in a clear order of rank that pervades all major social interactions;
- *deference*, which requires rules of comportment toward those at the top of the status scale, especially the reigning monarch or emperor.

The office of emperor depended, first of all, on military prowess, with defense of the realm, provision of public works, cultivation of land, collection of taxes, and dispensation of justice among his major administrative tasks. But equivalent to these functional aspects were the adornments of his office: magnificent palaces, expansive gardens, a lofty throne, and garments of unimagined splendor. In short, the emperor was the focal point of a court culture that included a whole set of specialists: architects and artists, craftsmen, musicians, poets, and scholars. Ibn Battuta, as noted above, had his equivalents in the courts of Istanbul, Isfahan, and Herat.

If the above profile describes the totalitarian ideal of a hermetically sealed hieratic system of governance, it omits several crucial elements that came to describe the kind of imperial rule exercised by the new Aryan elites – the Persianate Turks who came to dominate North Indian life from the tenth century on. Chief among these, as Robert Canfield (1991) has noted, were the use of the Persian language itself in a wide range of functions, administrative as well as literary, and then the development of an expanding cultural elite that saw itself expressing Persianate values, even when they were not fully allied with Islamic norms.

One might call this expansion and rearticulation of Indo-Aryan social values either Persianate, if one wants to stress the importance of Persian as a linguistic component, or Islamicate, if one wants to acknowledge the way in which Islam itself is invoked even when the connection between cultural observance and religious loyalty is very slim. Sometimes the two terms are so close that they can be used interchangeably. Crucial in each case is their expansion of connotative meaning to include more than linguistic usage (Persian) or religious commitment (Islamic) (Alam 1998; Eaton 1993). [7] By either reading, culture cannot be reduced to "mere" economics or regional patterns of socioeconomic dominance.

Decisive for civilizational analysis, in the Muslim world generally but especially in South and Southeast Asia, is the polyvalence of Islam. The paramount need is to examine Islam as more powerful symbolically than either its exponents or its detractors project it to be. Civilizations draw on the imaginary as well as the institutional power of *all* available religions, yet they do not exhaust the availability of any one religion to oppositional groups. Time and again, we find groups who resist a Muslim ruler in the name of the same God, the same Prophet, and the same community of believers as their opponents. The contest is over political authority even when it is framed as a contest over religious truth, and, as Sanjay Subrahmanyam (1998) has argued with telling force, future historians need to pay still more careful attention to social groups – their composition, their tensions, their outcomes – rather than simply to invoke the charismatic individual as an explanatory model. The lesson from both South and Southeast Asia is to recognize Islamic norms and values as transferable and persistent in multiple contexts, whoever the rulers and whatever the stake in local or regional contests for power. It is a lesson that Hodgson would applaud; it is one that Wallerstein and his disciples have yet to apply to the juggernaut of macro-economics, with scenarios that exclude culture and so occlude the actual dynamics of historical struggle and human contingency in shaping civilizational politics.

Modern correctives

In the mold of Hodgson, but with an eye to cadences of contemporary media, the Iranian historianof Iran Richard W. Bulliet has tried to expand the analytical power of civilization and to twin Islam and Christianity as cooperative members of the same civilization rather than oppositional members of competitive civilizations. In a monograph provocatively titled *The Case for Islamo-Christian Civilization*, Bulliet advances Islamo-Christian civilization as a neologism suited for the present, post-9/11 moment in world history. While many Muslims reduce the whole of the West to the USA, and while most Americans tend to see the Islamic world only in the template of Arab/ Muslim terrorists, the truth is more complex. Against Samuel Huntington's prediction of a clash of civilizations (between the West and the rest, especially Islam), and against Bernard Lewis's rhetorical query "What went wrong?" (everything, it turns out, linked to the name of Islam), Bulliet espies a future beyond the screeds of American Islamophobes but also against the hopes of Muslim extremists, whether they be religious fanatics or secular tyrants. "The past and future of the West cannot be fully comprehended without appreciation of the twinned relationship it has had with Islam over some fourteen centuries. The same is true of the Islamic world" (Bulliet 2004: 45).

If the Euro-American West and the Islamic world do, in fact, depend on each other, then neither makes sense without its sibling, which is also its rival. Each must produce leaders who espouse, embody, and embolden inclusive ideals. A historian turned prophet, Bulliet concludes that

> the next twenty to thirty years will see [Muslim] religious leaders of tolerant and peaceful conscience, in the mold of Gandhi, Martin Luther King [Jr.], and Nelson Mandela, eclipse in respect and popular following today's advocates of jihad, intolerance, and religious autocracy.
>
> (2004: 161)

Despite the hyperbole of this self-conscious manifesto, the case for reconsidering the future of humankind through the lens of civilizational analysis is secure. Dyads are never unqualified, and some of the most major cleavages rest on "small" differences that conceal larger elements of convergence and comity. The benefit of focusing on civilization, either singly or, better, in tandem, is to understand the cultural/religious framework within which identity and authority, hope, and loyalty are shared, even more than they are contested.

In the context of Afro-Eurasian Islam, Islamicate civilization becomes a bridge civilization that decenters a narrowly Western–Islamic dialogue, and instead offers the full spectrum of contemporary West–East vignettes, whether it be Afro-Islam in Senegal and other parts of post-colonial Francophone North and West Africa, or the indirect British legacy in Saudi Arabia and Iran, reflecting and also reinforcing the larger Sunni/Shi'a divergence in the Middle East, or, further to the east, the British impact in Malaysia, the Dutch in Indonesia (see Schulze 2002: 86–9). No category is mapless. Context matters, and the historical context generated by European expansion and colonial rule across the Indian Ocean cannot be ignored in thinking about either Islamic identity or Muslim subjectivity, wherever one looks in the Afro-Asian ecumene. There is no Islam without Muslim subjects, and it is the latter who project the cosmopolitan legacy of Islamicate civilization into the twenty-first century.

Those who follow a political rather than a historical model of civilization, and civilizational patterning, may demur. The favorite dyad in political scientific discourse about the Muslim world is religion versus politics. The too familiar canard is that "they" are not like "us"; Muslims, unlike post-

Enlightened Western European liberal democratic capitalists, do not separate religion from politics. Talal Asad has questioned this facile reflex in several of his writings, and Adullahi an-Na'im has now published a major study arguing that religion not only can but should be, and historically has been, separate from state machinations in the Muslim world (An-Na'im 2008).

Among political scientists there are also significant efforts to rethink, and so complicate, the nature of the religious and the political in Islam. Two efforts merit special consideration. Peter Mandaville, following the lead of Asad, has argued that defining what is religious and political depends on prior notions of the secular. While religious and secular law were never clearly distinguished in most of the Muslim world until recently, the advent of colonial rule produced dual legal systems, separating common law (regarding civil and criminal matters) from religious law (defining personal status, as in marriage, divorce, and inheritance), with the result that the religious law, or *shari'a*, came to imply the benchmark of Islamic loyalty or authenticity. Mandaville concludes that, despite Muslim protests against secularism as a godless, "material" ideology, there is a de facto institutional secularism that pervades and shapes most Muslim majority polities (Mandaville 2008: 10–15).

Another political scientist, Olivier Roy, goes still further in blurring the line between secular and religious identities, both individual and collective. For Roy, modern communications, combined with diasporic displacements, whether voluntary or (more often) involuntary, have produced a wholesale shift in contemporary Muslim identity. Muslims are at once deracinated and deterritorialized as never before. Civilization is itself simply part of the outdated vocabulary that no longer reflects the ground-level reality of Muslim self-expression and group desire. Change, not continuity, is the harbinger for the future.

> At a time when the territorial borders between the great civilizations are fading away, mental borders are being reinvented to give a second life to the ghost of lost civilizations: multiculturalism, minority groups, clash or dialogue of civilizations, etc. Ethnicity and religion are being marshaled to draw new borders between groups whose identity relies on a performative definition: we are who we say we are, or what others say we are. *These new ethnic and religious borders do not correspond to any geographical territory or area.* They work in minds, attitudes and discourses. They are more vocal than territorial, but all the more eagerly endorsed and defended because they have to be invented, and because they remain fragile and transitory. Deterritorialization of Islam leads to a quest for definition, because Islam is no longer embedded in territorial cultures.
>
> (Roy 2004: 20)

Roy has been quoted at length because his views repeatedly surface in discussions about Islam, especially among non-experts.[8] The difficulty is that most

Muslims, like most non-Muslims, carry passports. That is to say, the globalized citizen is still the member of some territory. She or he is marked by that territorial, political location, as distinct from others who are denied the privilege, as also the burden, of a particular nation-state identity. While politics is not limited to the state, and while civil society insures, or should insure, the plurality of group identities apart from the surveillant gaze of the state and its guardians, it is still majority Muslim nation-states that embrace the notion of a collective, homogeneous identity. It is they who advance themselves as the carriers of a distinctive Islamicate civilization. We do not have to share, or approve, their commitment to its content, yet we cannot dismiss boundaries and censuses, flags and armies, as merely "secular" symbols of a modern nation-state. They also convey a Muslim identity: while it has many parts, as also disparate interpretations and divergent outcomes, it has been projected over space and time through a single, continuous vehicle: Islamicate civilization.

Notes

1 *Hijra* is the exodus of the Prophet Muhammad from Mecca to Medina, on account of the threats on his life, and those of his followers, from hostile Quraysh. It occurred in 622 CE, and became the baseline for measuring years and centuries in the lunar or Islamic calendar. The relation of Ibn Khaldun to the technical sciences of Islamic scholarship has been further developed in my introduction to Ibn Khaldun (2005).

2 Farhat J. Ziadeh, "Integrity (*'Adalah*) in Classical Islamic Law," quoting al-Busti, *Kitab al-majruhin*, in Heer (1990: 89).

3 It may be confusing to speak of writing as a craft when the sciences include the sciences linked to the Arabic language – grammar, lexicography, syntax, style, and criticism as well as literature, but Ibn Khaldun's unwavering criterion is manual labor, so that both the art of writing and book production are listed as crafts (Chapter 5: 29, 30), while not only medieval Arabic language but also Qur'anic Arabic (Mudar) and South Arabian Arabic (Himyarite) and Spanish Arabic – all are treated, along with poetry and the distinction between poetry and prose, in Chapter 6 as instances of scientific production.

4 Among the many analytical efforts to locate Islam/Islamicate civilization in the cluster of great, global, or world civilizations is Arnason (2003a). After a review of the entire literature on the subject, Arnason concludes by advocating two kinds of civilization as important to the history of the West: those from the past and those from the contemporary world (or, better, contemporary phase in world history). He cites the Indian and Chinese cases as primary examples of otherness, and then depicts Islamic(ate), along with Byzantine, civilization as "intermediary cases between the two poles of otherness" (ibid.: 327). I demur from this analysis, because it constructs an implicit hierarchy of civilizations, one that Hodgson had lamented in Volume 3 of *The Venture of Islam* (1974). Conscious and unconscious invocations of hierarchy in civilizational analyses are inevitable, but they also need to be problematized. In my view, while hierarchy – both internal and external – is crucial to understanding formative elements in the emergence and development of civilizational profiles, the Islamicate evidence is far more complex than Arnason and like-minded macro-sociologists allow.

5 B. S. Turner, while critiquing Hodgson's notions of piety and conscience, still argues that he uniquely proposed an alternative to Orientalism:

> a discourse of sameness which would emphasise the continuities between various cultures rather than their antagonism . . . In the case of Islam, it is clear that we may regard Islamic cultures as part of a wider cultural complex which would embrace both Judaism and Christianity.
>
> (Turner 1994: 53–66)

"We need therefore a new form of secular ecumenicalism," one that reflects "the historical and moral sensitivity [which] clearly underlined the work of Marshall G. S. Hodgson" (ibid.: 102). One of the major efforts to see Occidentalism as itself a reflex, a kind of mirror opposite, of Orientalism, is provided in Buruma and Margalit (2004). Yet Islam is treated merely as a Middle Eastern cultural force. There is no mention of Islam or Islamicate civilization in South and Southeast Asia, apart from the work of the Pakistani ideologue Abu'l-Ala Maududi and his high-minded opposite, the poet-philosopher Muhammad Iqbal (ibid.: 121–5).

6 Others besides Eisenstadt have noted the benefit of a civilizational rather than world system episteme or paradigm for cross-cultural analysis. Among them is Yitzhak Sternberg, who argues that for both macro— and micro-analysis "it seems to me that the concept 'historical civilization' is more appropriate than the concept 'historical system', suggested by Wallerstein" (Sternberg 2001: 90). Yet neither Sternberg nor any of the other contributors to the volume he co-edited include reference to either Islamicate civilization or the contribution of Marshall Hodgson. Similarly, Arnason critiques many of the narrowly Westocentric views of civilization, yet himself discusses Hodgson only briefly as a corrective to the crudest form of Weberianism, which projects Islam as "a regressive version of monotheism" (Arnason 2003a: 245–6). Later, he does commend Hodgson for proposing "a distinction between Islamic religion and Islamicate civilization" (ibid.: 292), but he does not elaborate on the implications of such a distinction.

7 In Alam's essay both the contingent and ideological elements of Indo-Persianate culture are addressed, with principal attention to distinctive aspects of the Mughal period and its polity. The same point is picked up and elaborated, with documentary concision and analytical agility, by Eaton in reference to the Islamization of Bengal during the Mughal period.

8 Appiah, for example, cites Roy as the paramount authority for his own argument regarding the ahistorical disposition of Muslim fundamentalists or, as Roy terms them, neo-fundamentalists. See Appiah (2006: 138–9).

8 How to think about civilizations[1]

Patrick Thaddeus Jackson

Any reader of the preceding chapters will certainly have noted a series of persistent themes animating the ongoing scholarly conversation, including the complexity of the efforts to identify a civilization or to demarcate its boundaries precisely. It is quite challenging to determine where any one civilization ends and another begins, even though every kind of analysis of what a civilization is or does depends, at least implicitly, on some sort of boundary-demarcation exercise. Whether civilizations are "real" or not is, as Matthew Melko (1969: 4) once observed, quite beside the point – what matters is whether "we can find value in the concept of civilizations," value expressed in terms of the kinds of social dynamics and relations that the concept highlights and to which it calls attention. But, in order to unlock this value, it is first necessary to determine what a given civilization consists of and where its boundaries are. However, whether we are speaking geographically, historically, or even conceptually, any concrete specification of where a particular civilization starts or stops seems to be quite contestable, calling the ensuing analysis into question.

There are an impressively large number of scholarly solutions to this problem, a variety of which are on display in this volume. It would therefore be easy for me to spend my time in this concluding chapter criticizing those boundary-demarcation exercises that do not conform to my own preferred way of dealing with the issue. Indeed, that might be the expected thing to do in a situation such as this. In international relations, Susan Strange's famous contribution to Stephen Krasner's edited volume on regimes serves as exemplary of this approach: launch a critique of the preceding contributions, pose some "more fundamental questions about the questions" asked in those chapters, and suggest an alternative not previously on offer in the volume (Strange 1983: 337–8). Perhaps I could even come up with a characterization of civilizational analysis as memorable as Strange's condemnation of regime analysis as "woolly." But I am not going to take that tack, in part because I've already come out in print elsewhere (Jackson 2004, 2006) in defense of taking civilizations seriously in the analysis of world politics, so it would be highly unusual for me now to declare civilizational analysis suspect. That said, I do have a perspective on *how* to take civilizations seriously that is somewhat at variance from that of many of the other authors represented in this volume, as I am – as Peter Katzenstein pointed out in his introductory chapter – more interested in civilizational discourse than in the putatively dispositional properties of civilizations. So I could simply set up camp here and defend my position against the rest of the scholarly community, hoping to cause sufficient damage to my opponents that I win some converts among the volume's readers.

I could, but I'm not going to. Instead, I have a somewhat different agenda in this chapter. Rather than impose an answer to the question of how we ought to think about civilizations in world politics, I am going to spend some time ordering and formalizing the various options available to us. In this way, I aim to ideal-typify the positions involved in this scholarly conversation, not for the purpose of selecting one over another, but instead for the purpose of clarifying the issues at stake in the selection of any of these avenues of inquiry. In so doing, I am not looking for points of agreement either conceptual or empirical; if anything, my bias is in the opposite direction, toward points of *dis*agreement. I do not think that there is an implicit consensus position on civilizations lurking somewhere behind the contributions of the various authors gathered in this volume, and I would strenuously resist efforts to impose one. Rather, the only thing that unifies the various chapters – beyond their vague assent to the proposition that civilizations and their dynamics are important to the study of contemporary world politics – is that they disagree about roughly the same things.

This is an important point, so let me unpack it a bit. We spend altogether too much time in our scholarly lives either looking for points of agreement between ourselves and others, or regarding points of disagreement as occasions for a zero-sum game in which we score points by dismantling the claims advanced by others. Lurking not too far behind both of these scholarly practices, and implicit within them, is the presumption that the goal of scholarship is *consensus*, and that the best way to build reliable knowledge is through the steady accumulation of broader and broader consensuses. The philosophical poverty of this brand of neo-positivism – "neo" because it embraces the post-Popperian methodology of falsification as an avenue to constructing consensus by weeding out possible contenders, and "positivist" because it continues to posit the production of globally unified knowledge as its goal – does not seem to have affected everyday scholarly practice all that much, at least not in our field. We still treat disagreements as something to *adjudicate* or *resolve*; we remain uncomfortable with the notion that the world might be qualitatively more complicated than our analytical tools for interrogating it, and more complicated in such a way that the world might support different, even divergent, ways of making sense of it.

And with good reason: "in fulfilling our responsibilities as competent and professional academics, we must write *systematic texts*; we run the risk of being accounted incompetent if we do not" (Shotter 1993a: 25). Hence it is difficult for us even to *raise* the question of whether systematicity and global logical coherence – and, ultimately, agreement among fellow scholars on important points of fact and theory – is the proper way to construct knowledge. There is something almost heretical about raising the suggestion that maybe the exercise of constructing knowledge should *not* be thought of as a drive toward consensus, but should instead be thought of as something quite different: a play of discourses, maybe, or an opportunity for the contentious clarification of basic and unresolvable assumptions – perhaps an occasion to forge and refine useful conceptual tools for the investigation of future, as-yet-unknown situations. This last suggestion owes a lot to the pragmatist sensibilities of John Dewey (1920: 126–7, 149), who argued that the role of the sciences, including the social sciences, was to do just that, and that scholars should take advantage of the relative isolation of the scholarly world from the world of application in order to design conceptual instruments that are subtle and refined enough to be used to make sense of a variety of situations. John Shotter refers to this as "critical tool-making" and highlights the often overlooked fact that the most significant of such tools are not sharply delineated recipes or programmatic ideologies, but rather more ambiguous.

> The meaning of many important distinctions within Western life . . . are not in any sense fully predetermined, already decided distinctions. They are expressed or formulated in different ways in different, concrete circumstances, by the use of a certain set of historically developed . . . "topological" *resources* within the Western tradition. Thus, what might be called a "living tradition" does not give rise to a completely determined form of life, but to dilemmas, to different possibilities for living, among which one must choose.
>
> (Shotter 1993b: 170–71)

These topological resources – which we might call *commonplaces* (see Jackson 2006: 27–32) – and their availability or non-availability (in the first instance) and their specific deployment so as to entail a specific outcome (in the second instance) can be used to construct explanations of social and political action. But an analysis of commonplaces can also be used to make sense of scholarly conversations: "'Topics,' already in existence in the background common sense of arguers, are what can hold an argument together as an intelligible social enterprise and give it its style" (Shotter 1993b: 156). Such an analysis can be conducted on a fairly broad scale, as when Andrew Abbott (2001) argues that the dynamics of whole academic disciplines, and the divisions between them, can be neatly parsed as the self-similar synchronic and diachronic repetition and interaction of a few basic distinctions (such as positivism and interpretivism, or social determinism and individual freedom). In Abbott's conception, what holds an academic discipline together intellectually is the ready availability of a set of distinctions and debates the various sides of which are easily *recognizable* to others socialized in the discipline; one need not invent one's argument out of whole cloth, but can instead simply begin working *in media res*, intervening into an already ongoing set of contentious conversations and exploring a novel combination of commitments or a unique place within the overall disciplinary landscape.

I would like to suggest that the same kind of analysis of the ongoing conversation about civilizations in world politics would be useful in at least two ways. First, by identifying the commonplaces over which we contend and the distinctions that unite us in a single conversation by giving us all places to stand relative to one another, it may be possible better characterize the whole discussion better as something of a group effort – Shotter would call it "joint action" (1993b: 3–4) – to make plain the implications of adopting different combinations of analytical orientations toward social action. Indeed, I will illustrate that the commonplaces over which we are wrestling in this book are not really unique to the study of civilizations, or of civilizational states, but are instead much broader considerations pertinent to the analysis of social life as a whole, and in particular to the analysis of community and communities. Civilizations have certain empirical peculiarities that exacerbate some issues, but there is nothing like a "civilizational theory" on offer here or, for that matter, in the writings of many of the authors on whom the contributors to this conversation draw.

Second, if Dewey is right that the value of social science lies in its refining of conceptual tools, then the lack of consensus on offer here is a *positive* development, since the conversation as a whole then offers a plethora of options from which the reader may choose. Each has its characteristic strengths and weaknesses, and none perfectly captures everything of interest in a complex and ambiguous world – but that is only to be expected, once we abandon the rather naïve belief in some kind of "prediscursive providence which predisposes the world in our favor" (Foucault 1981: 67). A scholarly conversation can at least offer the reader an *informed* choice between equally imperfect alternatives.

Two debates

In looking for a way to characterize the discussion of civilizations in world politics, I have been guided by two striking facts. First, it has become quite common to see near the beginning of any scholarly article on civilizations a ritualistic denunciation of Samuel Huntington's *The Clash of Civilizations and the Remaking of World Order* (1996) – almost as common as it once was to see near the beginning of any scholarly article on the international system ritualistic denunciations of Kenneth Waltz's *Theory of International Politics* (1979). Virtually no scholar of cultures and civilizations, with the possible exception of Lawrence Harrison (2006), self-identifies as a "Huntingtonian," and virtually every contemporary scholar distances their work from that of Huntington by critiquing the latter's conception of civilizations for being too static, too fixed, too *essentialist*. Civilizations for Huntington might as well be big states, except for the fact that they are states without central governments or authorized representatives; civilizations have pretty firm borders, and relations between civilizations look uncannily like the relations that structural realists expect to see between states in a multipolar system. Intercivilizational anarchy doesn't appear to be much different from interstate anarchy.

Basically, everyone rejects this analytical ensemble. Instead, most analysts embrace the notion that "Civilizations are complex and heterogeneous entities that are capable of developing in a variety of directions . . . Civilizations are not closed systems like billiard balls but porous and open to outside influences" (Melleuish 2000: 118). Far from the Huntingtonian formula of mono-culturalism at home plus multiculturalism abroad (1996: 318), contemporary civilizational analysis embraces the notion that civilizations are internally diverse, and that the lines dividing them from one another are rarely as sharp as they appear in Huntington's maps. We thus end up with notions such as "civilizational constellation" as a way of discussing how a specific group of people make sense of the world, or a rethinking of a civilization as designating a not entirely consistent set of habits and commonsensical practices that a group of people has historically evolved over time for dealing with a plethora of political-economic issues (Cox 2002b: 157). Different authors deploy different analytical vocabularies, but they virtually all begin their scholarship on civilizations with a rejection of strong Huntingtonian essentialism.

The second striking fact is that there are a variety of different ways to reject Huntingtonian essentialism. Roughly speaking, two emphases obtain in the contemporary literature: one pathway emphasizes the temporal variability of a civilization, concentrating on how a variety of historical practices and processes came together to generate a certain characteristic ensemble, while the other looks more closely at the internal debates and conversations among self-identified members of a civilization about what their civilization entails, and concentrates on the nuances of those conversations as well as their contentious character. This suggests that Huntingtonian essentialism might itself be composed of the conjoining of two analytically distinct commitments – commitments that could be accepted or rejected individually as well as jointly. And that, in turn, suggests a simple categorization of ways of studying civilizations, a categorization animated by two analytical distinctions: one involving a turn from static civilizational *attributes* to dynamic civilizational *processes*, and one involving a turn from the identification of a civilization's key features by *scholars* to an identification of a civilization's key features by the *participants* in that civilization.

I will discuss each of these distinctions in turn before assembling them into a coherent matrix of scholarly positions.[2]

Attributes versus processes

The distinction between attributes and processes is a well-established feature of discussions within scientific ontology. By "scientific ontology" I mean the catalogue of basic objects with which a theory or a research agenda operates;

this is distinct from a theory's *philosophical* ontology, which pertains to the "hook-up" between the scientific research and the world that is being investigated (Patomäki and Wight 2000: 215). Every theory presumes, even if only implicitly, both a philosophical and a scientific ontology, and these presumptions act as world-disclosing grounds for subsequent empirical claims (Habermas 1990: 321). Such preconditions for sensible thought and action within a given research community, which are often part of what John Searle (1995) calls the "background" of our dealings with the world, express the shared presuppositions that members of the research community hold in common – and precisely because they are shared and presupposed, they don't have to be discussed under normal circumstances. But philosophers, and by implication philosophically inclined social scientists, aren't operating in normal circumstances; the very artificiality of a philosophical discussion allows the explicit consideration of what might otherwise remain merely tacit. Ontology, both philosophical and scientific, can thus be *foregrounded* in such discussions (Jackson 2008).

"Attributes" and "processes" are aspects of scientific ontology and set the parameters for how objects appear in a theory. An attribute-ontology treats objects as collections of properties, held together at their core by some bare and propertyless substantial existence, a dispositional "being-that" around which the object's different qualities are arranged. Properties that are essential to the object's existence as the kind of object that it is – properties close to its core – might be thought of as the object's "primary" properties, while other more contingent qualities might be thought of as "secondary" properties (Rescher 1996: 47). For example, in modern natural science one might think of the primary properties of a substance such as "gold" as involving its atomic structure; the secondary properties of gold, such as its solidity or liquidity, are a consequence of those primary properties interacting with a particular environment and its temperature, and as such are less essential to the "goldness" of gold than is gold's atomic structure (Sylvan and Majeski 1998: 88–9). And back behind both secondary and primary properties, inferred rather than directly experienced, is the simple existence of the object *qua* object – an existence that, as René Descartes argued when first establishing this kind of scientific ontology, is grasped by the mind rather than by the senses, and establishes the continuous persistence of an object even when it undergoes a myriad of changes (Descartes 1993: 67–9).

The relevance of these rather abstract considerations becomes readily apparent when we apply them to the existence and dynamics of social objects such as individuals or states – or civilizations. Within an attribute-ontology, the claim that something exists depends on the identification of some relatively stable set of primary properties that persists over time; this relatively stable set, in turn, serves as the point of departure for a judgment of existence. Hence we equip ourselves with a definition of an object and go out into the world looking for things that fit the definition: states, for example, might be defined in the Weberian manner as successfully upholding the monopoly of the legitimate use of force within a given territory, and with that as a guide to the primary properties of a state we might proceed to identify a number of existing states in the contemporary world. Of course, if we were to modify the definition, perhaps by supplementing the Weberian definition with additional primary properties such as "sovereignty" and "having a society" (Wendt 1999: 201–2), we would generate a different catalogue of existing states. But the point is that the grounds for saying that a state *exists* involve the empirical identification of certain properties, which might or might not be possessed by the potential state under investigation.

Attribute-ontology is quite prominently on display in the scholarly conversation about civilizations in world politics. Huntington's own civilizational essentialism is a potent instance of this scientific ontology, as he proposes a definition of a civilization as involving commonalities in the spheres of "blood, language, religion, [and] way of life" (Huntington 1996: 42–3) and then proceeds to identify on that basis a number of actually existing civilizations. But a similar gesture can be found whenever an analyst asks a question about whether a particular civilization exists and then proceeds to adduce empirical evidence either supporting or refuting a conjectured answer to the question. This is perhaps most powerfully illustrated when the candidate civilization is not widely acknowledged to *be* a civilization, as when Oswald Spengler devotes a substantial portion of his magnum opus *The Decline of the West* to establishing the existence of a "Magian" or "Arabian" Culture[3] that lives historically between the decline of the Classical and the rise of the Western. For Spengler, the central property of a Culture is its "prime symbol" – "a common world-feeling and a common world-form derived from it" (1926: 174) – and wherever he can discern such a commonality of world-feeling (especially in art, music, and architecture) he concludes that a separate Culture exists. In this volume, Bruce Lawrence's discussion of an "Islamicate" civilization and James Kurth's analysis of a US-led "Western" civilization illustrate this gesture most clearly, seeking to identify a civilization through the empirical enumeration of its core components.

Attribute-ontology is also implicated, perhaps even more clearly, when analysts turn from the identification of existing civilizations to an explanation of their activities. Again, the analytical parallels with explanations involving other social objects help to make the logic clear: as when applied to the explanation of state or individual action, an attribute-ontology reasons from a set of properties possessed by an entity to that entity's activities. Thus, to pick a fairly prominent example from international relations scholarship, we have the claim that democracies are less prone to go to war with one another than non-democracies (for example, Russett 1993); the logic here runs from a property of an entity (democracy) to an outcome (a democratic state not going to war with other states sharing that property). Note that the basic logic is not at all affected if we make the causal property "fuzzy" rather than "crisp" (Ragin 2000) and allow entities to differ in their degrees of democracy-ness; we just get a more finely grained association of a property and an outcome. Along these lines, we have claims about what a state's relative endowment of assorted power resources inclines it to do internationally, what kinds of strategies an ethnic group's internal organizational structure disposes it to undertake, and what sorts of decisions are more or less necessitated by a particular set of beliefs or pattern of information. In all cases, what matters here is a kind of reasoning that Andrew Abbott (1988) refers to as "general linear reality": the presence or absence, and perhaps the degree of intensity, of some property of an object leads more or less inevitably to an observed outcome.

This aspect of attribute-ontology is also clearly present in the scholarly conversation about civilizations. The logic of properties need not take the form of Huntington's bold claim that "Islam has bloody borders" (1996: 258), a stark example of essentialist reasoning inasmuch as responsibility for conflict is transferred to a deep dispositional characteristic of Islam per se. Instead, what we most commonly see is a form of reasoning from properties to outcomes that, much like a great deal of constructivist scholarship in international relations, emphasizes how ideas and meanings and beliefs held by actors lead to particular courses of action. In this volume, the clearest example is Emanuel Adler's identification of a new self-identity for European countries – "normative power Europe" – that informs a variety of decisions and strategies. The shift of empirical attention from "material" characteristics to "ideational" self-identification does not affect the explanatory logic in any significant way, whatever implications it might have for the mutability of the property causing the outcome (Tilly 1998). To say that how the members of a civilization understand themselves *as* a civilization leads to their doing certain things rather than others is not, at least not necessarily, to step outside of an attribute-ontology.

The alternative to an attribute-ontology would be a *process-ontology* (Emirbayer 1997; Jackson and Nexon 1999). Such a scientific ontology would not regard objects as collections of properties, but would instead analytically embed the existence of objects in an unfolding set of transactional mechanisms and relations that have the effect of reproducing the object from moment to moment. Instead of starting with substances in isolation, we begin with concrete connections and interactions:

> The fact is that all we can ever detect about "things" relates to how they act upon and interact with one another – a substance has no discernible, and thus no justifiably attributable, properties save those that represent responses elicited from its interaction with others.
>
> (Rescher 1996: 48–9)

So, for example, instead of states with varying degrees of power and wealth, we would have a pattern of political and economic relations that is denser in some places (the "core") and more diffuse in others (the "periphery"). State sovereignty, in such a conception, goes from being a stable property of a state to an ongoing practice of differentiation, whereby states and their boundaries are perpetually shored up and reinscribed (Mitchell 1991; Bartelson 1998). The emphasis moves from solid objects with discernible and stable qualities to constellations and arrangements of fluctuating practices and historical patterns.

The application of a process-ontology to civilizations is arguably the "mainstream" of contemporary civilization scholarship, at least outside of international relations. As Peter Katzenstein's opening chapter makes clear, the innovations introduced by Shmuel Eisenstadt and Norbert Elias clearly turn in a processual direction, emphasizing the extent to which a civilization is a complex arrangement of habits, principles, and historic traditions of action on which people may draw in a variety of ways. The notion that civilizations are internally pluralistic is more than a simple empirical observation; it is a mutation in scientific ontology, one that allows analysts to get past the quest to identify a civilization's "core" or essence and to focus instead on the concrete implications of particular political and economic and cultural arrangements. In this volume, a clear example of that kind of analysis is David Kang's careful tracing of how various "Chinese" practices diffused into regions surrounding China proper, making possible a set of actions that might not otherwise have been possible. Other examples of this kind of analysis dominate the essays that Martin Hall and I collected for our recent volume on civilizations in world politics (Hall and Jackson 2007b). The key feature here is the emphasis not on a fully formed social entity with dispositional properties, but instead on the contingent historical emergence and reproduction of those entities in practice.

Obviously, the kind of "general linear reality" explanatory logic associated with an attribute-ontology will not work particularly well in an approach more centrally focused on processes. If properties don't produce outcomes, the only viable alternative is to look to practices themselves – and in particular to look to practices that intend to shift the contours of an actor's social environment, since action in a process-ontology emerges not from "inside" of an actor but from the concrete and specific ways that an actor is connected to her or his environment (Joas 1997: 161–2). So we could investigate those kinds of historical endowments that a particular pattern of diffusion has made available to a group of actors, and thus treat a civilization as a kind of structural context for action – much as Kang does. Alternatively, we could focus our attention on those moments where explicit discussions about the nature and boundaries of a civilization are taking place, since the contingent resolution of those discussions actively shapes what the participants in those discussions do subsequently; this is the strategy undertaken in this volume by Susanne Rudolph, whose empirical field of investigation even extends to the scholars of Indian civilization themselves and makes them and their work part of the explanatory account. Similarly, David Leheny's discursive approach examines the ways in which a variety of voices are actively contesting the meaning of "Japan," contending over the precise specification of key symbols and historical events. The object of investigation here is the production and reproduction of civilizational boundaries – an object of investigation that only occurs within a process-ontology.

Who specifies?

A second, cross-cutting analytical distinction that we can see within the scholarly conversation about civilizations involves the question of who gets to make the determination about what constitutes a civilization. Whether an analyst is committed to an attribute-ontology or a process-ontology, the question of delineation still remains. Does the analyst look at the historical data and try to derive her or his own account of what constitutes a given civilization? Or does she or he follow the actors themselves as they seek to make sense out of their situations in civilizational terms? In the former case, scholarly analysts are in a sense empowered to determine the most appropriate descriptive and explanatory categories for a particular set of social actions without paying much attention to the ways in which the actors themselves understand their situation; analysts can cut through what actors think that they are doing, replacing the operative terminology of the actors with a conceptual vocabulary that corresponds more to academic concerns and debates than it does to the actors' own self-understandings. In the latter case, scholarly analysts are in a sense constrained to limit their academic speculations by referring their descriptions and explanations back to the ways in which social actors themselves engage the world, and in particular to take very seriously the meaning-laden accounts of action with which social actors themselves generate and operate – not as secondary-source descriptions or explanations of what those actors are doing, but as inextricably involved with the situation under investigation.

The distinction I am drawing here is by no means a novel one. It picks up some of what linguistic anthropologist Kenneth Pike (1967) was getting at by distinguishing between "emic" and "etic" perspectives on a culture: an emic perspective adopts an "insider's" point of view and tries to explicate how participants in that culture make sense of their own activities, while an etic perspective adopts an "outsider's" point of view and brings a detached scholarly vocabulary to bear on a culture. Similarly, the "interpretive turn" in the human sciences (Alker 1996; Yanow 2006), which emphasizes the need to use the self-understandings of social actors as a point of departure for both description and explanation, thematizes something like the distinction with which I am concerned in contrasting interpretive ways of producing knowledge with "positive" alternatives.

But these ways of talking about the distinction between a scholarly account that deploys an abstract conceptual vocabulary, thus making its own determinations about what actors are doing, and a scholarly account that follows actors' self-determinations of what they are doing, this remaining more firmly grounded in the actors' lived experiences, reach too quickly for issues in philosophical ontology. Emic/etic, like positive/interpretive, invoke overall perspectives on how scholarly analysts are plugged into the world – whether they are necessarily internal to their objects of study or whether they stand sufficiently apart from those objects to produce generally valid knowledge of them (Adcock 2006) – rather than concerning themselves with the character of the objects under investigation. As such, these philosophical distinctions are more like what I have elsewhere (Jackson 2008) termed "monism" and "dualism," with the latter designating a firm differentiation between the knowing subject and the known world and the former designating a fundamental continuity between knower and known. These distinctions don't specifically pertain to the analysis of social objects.[4]

Instead, what I have in mind here is something more like Benedict Anderson's famous declaration that national "communities are to be distinguished, not by their falsity/genuineness, but by the style in which they are imagined" (1991: 6). Anderson suggests that scholars should put aside any pretense of determining whether a given group of people belong together according to some abstract criteria, and should instead look at the ways that people organize themselves into groups. For Anderson, this is less a general statement about knowledge of the world and more a specific claim about the character of human community and human social action. The dynamics associated with a national community or nation, in Anderson's perspective, depend on the participation of a number of individuals in a set of meaningful practices, and cannot be reduced to or explained in terms of pre-social or non-meaningful factors. As for Rogers Brubaker (1996, 2006), "nation" for Anderson is a category of practice, not a category of analysis; what matters is how people speak and act so as to reproduce, or to challenge, their membership in the nation and the implications that such membership carries.

Traditional scholarship on nations and nationalism often conflates this distinction with the attribute/process distinction, as though scholarly delineation went hand in hand with an attribute-ontology and attentiveness to participant narratives necessarily entailed a process-ontology. But there is no logical reason why a scholar couldn't adopt a process-ontology together with a commitment to deploying an abstract scholarly vocabulary rather than grounding an analysis firmly in the lived experience of one's informants; this would mean not advancing the kind of explanatory claims based on categorical membership that are characteristic of a "general linear reality" approach to explanation, but instead turning to some other explanatory logic to interrogate the effects of mechanisms and processes that were abstractly delineated by the scholar. Fortunately for such a scholar, there is a long-standing tradition of structural analysis in the social sciences that does precisely this, utilizing notions such as "function" and "feedback" to clarify how processes – such as the circulation of capital (Poulantzas 2008), the maintenance of hegemony (Jessop 1990), and the reinforcement of organizational changes (Pierson 2004) – exert their effects without necessarily having to manifest themselves in the consciousness or experience of the actors involved.

Similarly, there is no logical reason why a scholar couldn't combine an attribute-ontology with a commitment to ground an analysis in lived experience; the central statement of one version of constructivist international relations theory – "people act toward objects, including other actors, on the basis of the meanings that objects have for them" (Wendt 1992: 396–7) – inclines in precisely this direction, and a similar commitment has given rise to a number of empirical efforts to map and assess the consequences of various ways that social actors in world politics have understood themselves at different points in time (Finnemore 1996; Hall 1999; Crawford 2002).

Therefore I would like to draw a distinction between a scholarly delineation of a social object (such as a civilization) and a scholarly effort to trace and explain how actors themselves delineate that social object. This is a matter of scientific ontology, in the terms that I have used here, because – much like attribute-ontology versus process-ontology – it speaks to the general parameters for how objects appear in a particular scholarly analysis. Do we regard a civilization to be the kind of thing that is best identified by a detached scholarly analyst as a part of an academic explanation, or do we on the contrary regard a civilization to be a social and cultural resource that manifests primarily in the discourse in which actors engage as they seek to act creatively in and interact with their social environment? If 'civilization' is a tool or instrument for making sense of social dynamics, *whose tool is it*: does it belong to us or to the people whom we are investigating?

This distinction neatly divides the authors in this volume as well as does the distinction between attribute-ontology and process-ontology, but in an orthogonal way: the volume's contributors are grouped differently if we take this distinction as an organizational principle. On the "scholarly delineation" side of the ledger, we find Kang, Lawrence, and Kurth; all three are concerned to identify the civilization in which they are interested by sifting through a pile of empirical data in order to come up with a scholarly account of the civilization that they are studying. Kang operates with a set of Chinese practices that are identified as such based on his research experience and scholarly gaze, not on the identification of those practices as Chinese either by the Chinese themselves or by those who import or adapt them. Lawrence does something quite similar in establishing the existence and dynamics of Islamicate civilization. Kurth goes one step further, drawing from his historical sketch of components of Western Civilization a series of goals and prescriptions for the members of that civilization – goals and prescriptions that follow from his scholarly delineation of the core elements of Western Civilization.

On the other side of the ledger, we find Adler, Leheny, and Rudolph, all of whom seek to ground their analyses more directly in the discourse and experience of those that they are studying. Adler cites speeches and statements to demonstrate that "normative power Europe" is not a scholarly abstraction but a concrete political strategy being undertaken by various actors in the European political space. Leheny documents the ways in which different

Japanese actors seek to frame both Japan's cultural distinctiveness and its continuity with those of other "civilized" countries, and does not limit his field of evidence to the traditional material of "high politics" – hence we get to listen in on discussions of Japanese baseball and *manga/anime*, in order to see what that tells us about Japanese notions about their own civilization. Rudolph ranges the furthest in her adducing of evidence, even to the point of pursuing the discussion and debate about indigenous Indian society into a California courtroom.

This last is a particularly telling example of what is at stake in allowing the self-identified participants in a given civilization to delineate their own sense of what is involved, since a consistent determination to follow those debates can sometimes necessitate setting aside even the most rudimentary notions of where a civilization stops and starts: in this case, Indian civilization and the efforts to bound it extend halfway around the world. A scholar operating with an *ex ante* specification of what a civilization consists of – regardless of whether that specification consists of attributes or processes – would likely never appreciate the relevance of those California conversations. A scholar proceeding more inductively, casting her or his net widely in order to see what people are talking about and where they are talking about it, might see the California conversations as telling us something particularly important about the practice of civilizational identity: the reproduction of a civilization over time seems to be crucially dependent on the passing down of certain origin stories to the next generation, *irrespective of who does the passing down.* The claim in the California case was not that the state of California was part of Indian civilization and obligated to act in the best interests of Indian civilization. Instead, it was the rather different claim that, by passing down an account of Indian history that did not support the claim that Indian culture and religion were entirely indigenous to the subcontinent, the state of California was undermining Indian civilization (by sanctioning a view of Indian civilization as not being entirely self-contained) both for those Indians living in the United States and for those non-Indians who would receive the non-indigenous account of Indian history. This intriguing push for certification of an origin narrative by outsiders adds a different dimension to the study of civilizations, suggesting that the kind of dynamics of recognition some scholars have explored in the national state context (for example, Ringmar 1996) might also be in evidence in intercivilizational relations.[5]

Four combinations

The two distinctions that I have been outlining here can be easily plotted so as to create a rudimentary two-by-two matrix of available combinations of commitments on either side of these distinctions. Combining a commitment to a scholarly specification of a social object with an attribute-ontology gives us a concern with the *interests* of that object; a commitment to letting participants specify the social object of concern, combined with an attribute-ontology, yields a concern with the *identity* of that object; scholarly specification plus process-ontology leads to a concern with *structural context* within which the object exists; and participant specification plus process-ontology gives rise to the *boundary practices* that establish and reestablish that object from moment to moment. The names I have given to each of these combinations indicate both the primary descriptive concern of each scholarly approach and the central explanatory factor that each upholds in its explanations.

	Scholarly specification	*Participant specification*
Attribute-ontology	Interests	Identity
Process-ontology	Structural context	Boundary practices

Applied to the study of civilizations in particular, this matrix foregrounds particular aspects of civilizational analysis propounded by different scholars. Huntington, along with David Gress (1998) and other unreconstructed civilizational essentialists, is centrally concerned with identifying the core principles of various civilizations (especially Western Civilization) so that he can urge retrenchment and defense of those principles; in that way, civilizational essentialists are investigating and proclaiming the interests both of Western Civilization and of all those who consider themselves participants in it. That gesture, in turn, depends both on considering a civilization to be a collection of attributes and on allowing scholars to specify what a civilization consists of. This is almost exactly the same way in which interest-based arguments about other social objects (states and individuals spring to mind here) rely on a scholarly determination of essential attributes over which the social object, and those actors representing or otherwise responsible for the object, has little or no direct influence. Rational economic consumers, or states in a self-help environment, cannot endogenously change their preferences over outcomes; neither, in this conceptualization, can civilizations endogenously change their basic beliefs and values, and in all three cases the only viable option is to act in accordance with those exogenously determined and authoritatively specified interests.

The other three cells of the matrix represent various ways of taking issue with the civilizational essentialist account. Relaxing the demand for essential attributes of a civilization, along the lines recommended by analysts such as Eisenstadt and Cox and Elias, yields a greater appreciation for the historically variable structural context of action, such that a civilization shows itself less in a set of core values and more in a relatively homogeneous pattern of activities on the part of its members. Relaxing the demand for an *ex ante* scholarly specification of a civilization yields a greater concern with what might be called "civilizational identity" – in which self-conception, either of a civilization as a whole or of various representatives of that civilization, leads to actions and outcomes, in much the same way that personal or state identity is taken to lead to actions and outcomes in social-psychological and constructivist scholarship. And relaxing both demands simultaneously yields a focus on practices of civilizational boundary-drawing in assorted practical contexts; a civilization *itself* ceases to mean much, analytically speaking, as the emphasis here is on how appeals to and efforts to reinscribe civilizational boundary-lines work to promote various aims. Taking a cue from David Campbell (1992), we might call this fourth approach "writing civilizations."[6]

As is usual in such exercises – indeed, as is usual in the ideal-typical elaboration of distinctions in general – I have upheld the polite fiction that there is no middle ground between the commitments on each of the axes of my matrix. The whole point of drawing sharp analytical distinctions is to clarify the abstract logic of each side of the distinction in the kind of splendid conceptual isolation that one never finds in the messy world of actual entities and actions. Once drawn, one could treat the matrix as a map and use it to place cases in relation to one another by assigning them to their proper quadrant; this can disclose hitherto unacknowledged points of similarity and dissimilarity between the cases, whether those cases are empirical research sites or, as they are in this instance, scholarly positions. But these insights come at a significant cost, inasmuch as a map is a relatively static representation of an actual empirical situation – useful for finding your way around, perhaps, but only inasmuch as the landscape remains relatively unchanging. And static maps also have problems dealing with ambiguous cases, cases that seem to fall someplace near the lines dividing the regions of the map from one another – cases that display elements of more than one commitment.[7]

There is, however, another option. Instead of treating the four quadrants of my matrix as absolute locations, we might embrace what Andrew Abbott (2001: 12) calls the "indexicality" of social life, including academic life: the notion that our most important commitments are made meaningful only by their opposition and contrast to other commitments in the local environment. For example, Abbott points out that, despite all the ink spilled within the social sciences distinguishing between social determinism and individual freedom, all social scientists are basically on the same side of this issue when contrasted to others outside of the social sciences:

> Social scientists, broadly speaking, think of human social behavior as determined, indeed determined enough, irrespective of human volition, to be worth thinking about rigorously and comprehensively. Hence, they are determinists by comparison with those who believe that people are completely free to act as they please and that they are therefore only loosely scientizable.
>
> (Ibid.: 202)

Freedom/determinism, then, is not an absolute or categorical distinction between two firm and abstract positions. It is instead a distinction that replicates itself in a self-similar, or fractal, way: first we have the division between social scientists (determinism) and others (freedom), and then we have the repetition of the division *within* the camp of social scientists (structure versus agency, in contemporary parlance). But this also means that a commitment to one or another side of a distinction such as this is less of an absolute planting of a flag in a piece of conceptual territory and more of a gesture in a certain direction: a way of contrasting oneself to a set of local interlocutors.

So I suggest that we should treat attribute-ontology/process-ontology and scholarly specification/participant specification as indexical, fractally repeating distinctions, rather than as the absolute boundaries of a fixed conceptual territory. To identify a given piece of scholarship as supervening on an attribute-ontology and the scholarly specification of social objects is, in this rendering, implicitly to contrast the piece of scholarship with others *by comparison with which* it engages in the scholarly specification of essential attributes and conducts its explanations in terms of interests. I have placed Huntington in the upper left-hand corner of my matrix; my doing so is a reflection of my judgment that, in *any* comparative context involving civilizational scholarship and scholars, Huntington will occupy the relatively interest-based position. And since my starting point for this analysis – indeed, the conceptual starting point for the volume as a whole – was a rejection of Huntingtonian essentialism, treating Huntington as the relatively fixed point of reference against which to define alternatives is simply a reflection of the empirical character of the scholarly discussion itself.

Graphically, we might imagine my two-by-two matrix replicating itself *within* each cell of the original matrix, which would yield $4 \times 4 = 16$ different positions that civilizational scholarship might in principle occupy. As a first benefit, this allows much more fine-grained specifications of where scholars fall in relation to one another. For example, consider a further internal division of the "structural context" quadrant:

	Scholarly specification	
Process-ontology	Kurth Lawrence	Kang

I place Kurth's chapter in this volume in the upper-left-hand portion of the quadrant because his position on Western Civilization, while certainly more accepting of historical change than Huntington, is still concerned with roughly the same things that Huntington is concerned with: identifying the essential principles of Western Civilization for the purpose of identifying its core interests. But because Kurth is *first* located in the "structural context" quadrant of the original matrix, his work plays out differently than does Huntington's, even though it is relatively essentialist when contrasted to Kang's discussion of elites attempting to impose "Chinese" solutions on their populations (an attempt that triggers some dynamics best located in the realm of identity, as they involve the implications of self-conceptions) or Lawrence's analysis of how Islamicate civilization is fundamentally shaped by its geographical context. But, despite these differences, all three authors are more processual and less attribute-oriented in comparison with Huntington. Such fine-grained distinctions help us to get a firmer grasp on precisely where people stand relative to one another in this debate.[8]

Furthering the conversation

But, beyond the drawing of finer-grained maps, the real payoff of this fractal-izing of analytical distinctions is to suggest ways in which the scholarly conversation might proceed. If I am right about the importance of these distinctions, then it follows that further rounds in the debate should unfold along the lines envisioned by various combinations of attribute- and process-ontologies on one hand with scholarly and participant specification on the other. In this way the ideal-typical matrix I have constructed stops being merely a static map and becomes instead a dynamic generator of potential future conversations.

That said, there are a number of logical combinations that might poten-tially be explored – but not all of them are likely to be particularly productive or illuminating. In order to clarify what I see as the most fruitful intellectual avenues, I need briefly to advance two separate lines of argument. The first involves a dynamic endogenous to the distinctions that I have offered as a way of characterizing the debate, a dynamic that presses scholars and schol-arship toward two of the four quadrants at any given level of the matrix and renders the other two quadrants somewhat unstable. The second involves the fact that different combinations of commitments offer different resources and lessons for scholars in international relations, and the future course of the debate about civilizations that we might have within the field will, I think, be decisively influenced by how civilizational analysis intersects with the tradi-tional concerns of international relations – especially the question of the political interactions between states. Here, again, certain quadrants are privi-leged over others, but in this case three quadrants are privileged (again, at any given level of the matrix) while the fourth quadrant – the upper-left-hand "civilizational essentialist" quadrant – has the least to offer to our field.

Conceptual attractors

Although I have been operating with two different axes of differentiation throughout this discussion of the scholarly conversation about civilizations, there is an important sense in which the two axes are conceptually similar to one another. For the purpose of clarifying the debate about civilizations, the division between the axes is useful because it illustrates available combinato-rial possibilities which are, I have argued, actually realized in the existing discussion: scholars and scholarship do occupy these different combinations of commitments with respect to one another. But the two axes are also unified by a sensibility involving the perennial contrast between explanations based on determinism or freedom, or structure versus agency, or – as I prefer to think of the contrast – necessity versus contingency.

A necessity-explanation explains outcomes by subsuming them under some sort of general principle, such that the outcome becomes something "to be expected" in the light of various antecedent conditions. A contingency-explanation, by contrast, explains an outcome in terms of a case-specific concatenation of factors that gives rise to that outcome in an individual instance; the outcome is not quite "to be expected," but instead becomes comprehensible by being rooted in a particular circumstance.[9] Necessity/contingency is a potent fractal distinction, with an election for either side of the contrast almost immediately falling into a further subdivision along similar lines; in large part this has to do with the fact that *both* necessity *and* contingency are value-commitments firmly established in contemporary liberal society, often in the guises of "law" and "liberty" respectively. This in turn means that there is virtually never any shortage of defenders of either pole of the contrast, and hence always a possibility of further fractalization.

Necessity/contingency informs both of the axes I used to construct my matrix insofar as each axis has a "necessity" pole and a "contingency" pole. Scholarly specification, for example, is the "necessity" pole of its axis in that actions and outcomes are explained by subsuming them under an *ex ante* delineation of what a civilization involves; observed patterns of action are made comprehensible by integrating them into a conceptual whole of which the actors themselves might be entirely ignorant. Participant specification, on the other hand, is the "contingency" pole in that there is no way to predict what associations and oppositions the participants in a particular civilization will draw; scholarly analysis follows participant activity and explicates it, but cannot render it "to be expected" in the light of anything that precedes or governs that activity. Similarly, attribute-ontology is the "necessity" pole of its axis in that explanation means linking core civilizational attributes to outcomes; process-ontology is the "contingency" pole, in that explanation is about tracing assorted civilizational processes and seeing how they play out.

The fact that each of my axes has a necessity and a contingency pole makes the whole matrix susceptible to a mechanism that Abbott calls "fractionation" (2001: 84–6). In any single fractal distinction, there are a series of advantages to taking up an extreme position in which one always selects the same side of the distinction at any given point in the discussion – always necessity, for example, or always contingency. The advantages of an extreme position include the prestige accorded to rigorous consistency in many academic settings, the "pleasures of unconventionality" associated with standing someplace both outside of the messy middle of a debate and in opposition to a widely held alternative value-commitment (and selecting *either* necessity *or* contingency permits one to stand in opposition to a widely held alternative value-commitment, further enhancing the appeal of the extreme position), and the greater ease with which one can critically engage other scholars from a position of meticulous logical coherence. These advantages of extremism provide something of an internal motor for the discussion over time, as partisans of either extreme critique their interlocutors for their mix of commitments, provoke reactions, and drive the debate into a further round.

Applied to my matrix, fractionation works to drive the upper-left and bottom-right quadrants further apart, since the upper-left "interests" quadrant represents the conjoining of both "necessity" poles, while the bottom-left "boundary practices" quadrant represents the conjoining of both "contingency" poles. Civilizational essentialism is opposed by what we might call civilizational post-essentialism: *post*-essentialist rather than *anti*-essentialist because it is concerned not simply to reject civilizational essentialism but to account for the power that essentialist claims about civilizations have in social and political practice. Essentialism suggests that essences generate outcomes; post-essentialists retort that it is the practical attribution of essences that generates those outcomes. And, while they clash, these partisans of each extreme also criticize other scholars for combining what the partisans see as incompatible commitments. Out of the responses, and the empirical work that is generated by all parties, different areas of the conceptual landscape are explored, and the practical value of different combinations of commitments is put to the test.

Consider, in this respect, various depictions of the relations between and among civilizations. Huntington's position, most famously, is that a clash between civilizations is more or less inevitable; because civilizations are essentially different from one another, and because they "are the biggest 'we' within which we feel culturally at home as distinguished from all the other 'thems' out there" (1996: 42), there is no overarching community strong enough to prevent civilizations from engaging in conflict with one another from time to time. The post-essentialist position, by contrast, would argue that clashes of civilizations are a consequence not of deep civilizational essences but of a set of ways of inscribing civilizational boundaries in practice; change the writing-style, so to speak, and the clash vanishes, along with the putative constitutively autonomous civilizations themselves. That said, post-essentialists do argue that, so long as civilizations are inscribed in the Huntingtonian way, the Huntingtonian consequences follow – an argument that parallels the post-structural critique of state sovereignty in international relations (Ashley 1984; Walker 1993) in arguing that practices, not essences, give rise to conflictual dynamics.

Caught between these extremes are the various claims that conflict between civilizations can be ameliorated by some kind of "dialogue among civilizations." Scholars working on civilizational identity might highlight the possibility of an "other-regarding" identity for a group of civilizations, one that might serve to cement peaceful relations between them. Scholars working on structural context might highlight the interplay of similarities and differences across civilizations, such as the extent to which they are all variations of modern social arrangements in a manner that produces (in Eisenstadt's language) "multiple modernities" that are simultaneously different from and similar to one another in ways that might make for interesting exchange and mutual exploration. Or, inhabiting an even more conceptually blended space, consider Naeem Inayatullah and David Blaney's (1996, 2004) ongoing effort to foreground the discovery of the Self in its relations with the Other by pointing to the necessary incompleteness of any given articulation of civilizational identity and the consequent need of any civilization – in particular, Western Civilization – to travel conceptually if not physically in order to encounter reflections of itself in the world it helped to make through colonial domination. Civilizations in these conceptualizations remain separate from one another, but conflictual consequences do not inevitably follow.

"Dialogue among civilizations" arguments, however, are susceptible to two different avenues of critique. Civilizational essentialists criticize dialogue in much the same way that international relations realists have been known to criticize liberal and constructivist strategies for promoting peaceful relations among states: as long as civilizations remain essentially separate from one another, the possibility of conflict remains eternally present, and a prudent civilization (or its prudent representatives) needs to take this into account . . . which basically vitiates any effort permanently to escape a clash of civilizations. Post-essentialist scholars would call attention to the fact that the very idea of a dialogue implies separate parties to that dialogue, and that separation makes calls for dialogue collapse into a hopelessly optimistic view of what separate civilizations would do in relation to one another; their prescription, of course, if one actually wants to avoid a clash of civilizations, would be to move even further away from essentialism and focus on boundary practices. But where civilizational essentialists might claim that no cross-civilizational interaction can do much to alter the underlying dynamics of inter-civilizational relations, post-essentialist scholars might argue that a series of dialogues and debates might have an effect if – and only if – they resulted in the production of novel conceptual tools for making sense of global diversity, and if those tools were subsequently disseminated far and wide enough to affect the conditions of possibility for action of public officials and ordinary people alike.

The point here is that advocates of a dialogue among civilizations have to establish the efficacy of their proposals and accounts against both civilizational essentialism and the kind of post-essentialist view of civilizations upheld by some of the most recent work on civilizations in world politics (Hall and Jackson 2007a). In the effort to do so both theoretically and empirically, novel positions are adopted, novel combinations of commitments are forged, and the discussion proceeds in new directions. And perhaps, along the way, clashes of civilizations are avoided – but only time will tell.

Substantive overlaps

The attraction of extreme positions within the civilizations debate helps to provide an "internal" explanation for the future course of the discussion – internal, in this case, to the debate itself. But discussions and debates do not simply unfold in splendid isolation; "external" factors always intervene and shape the course of conceptual refinement and academic research in important ways. There are many such factors, ranging from the distribution of research funding to the organization of the contemporary academy itself, but for the moment I want to focus on one context in particular: the context of academic international relations scholarship, which claims for itself the right and the capacity to focus on global issues in a way that other academic fields and disciplines often do not. Hence, the future course of the academic debate about civilizations will be shaped, at least in part, by the interaction of civilization scholarship with the traditional concerns and considerations of academic international relations.

Arguably, the most important of these concerns is, and remains, the (sovereign, territorial) state. The field of international relations has been grappling with sovereign states and the anarchy that they produce in relation to one another since its earliest beginnings in international law, history, and political science (Schmidt 1998). Despite numerous attempts to broaden its focus and efforts to introduce different actors (firms, transnational social movements, global classes) onto the world stage, the field's concerns remain stubbornly intertwined with what states do and how other actors influence state action. Whether this reflects an empirical acknowledgment of the continued importance of states (Wendt 1999: 8–10) or some kind of collective failure or repression of theoretical innovation (Zehfuss 2002) is somewhat beside the point. What matters is that international relations is defined largely as a separate field of academic inquiry by its concerns with sovereignty, territoriality, and the relations between units constituted on such principles, whatever else might affect those relations.

Indeed, Huntington's initial call for renewed attention to civilizations explicitly made space for this state-centrism. "Civilizations are cultural not political entities," he declared; this means that "they do not, as such, maintain order, establish justice, collect taxes, fight wars, negotiate treaties, or do any of the other things *which governments do*" (1996: 44, emphasis added). In other words, for Huntington, civilizations are not *actors* in their own right, but are instead elements of a global political environment within which states remain "the primary actors in world affairs" (ibid.: 34–5). It was therefore relatively easy for mainstream international relations scholarship to absorb civilizational essentialism as one among other sources of state interest, adding civilizational membership to the list of potential factors affecting state action. Unfortunately, once scholars did this and began comparatively to evaluate the relative importance of civilizational ties versus other factors, such as religious affiliation (Fox 2001) and traditional state concerns with power and wealth (Russett, Oneal, and Cox 2000), civilizational considerations started to drop out of the equations, and these days Huntington's famous thesis receives little sustained scholarly attention in most of the field of international relations.

Civilizational essentialism, then, had little to offer to academic international relations scholarship after a brief flurry of excitement in the late 1990s (and, in point of fact, most of that excitement was played out in policy journals such as *Foreign Affairs* and the *National Interest* rather than in social-scientific journals – good for the circulation of some essentialist commonplaces, perhaps, but less good as a vehicle for shaping the field). In fact, even if one wanted to persist with the state-centrism of academic international relations, other quadrants of the conversation might prove more fruitful. A focus on civilizational processes and constellations as part of the structural context within which states act might provide a more nuanced way to analyze patterns of alliance and enmity between states than a search for dispositional essences in the sphere of basic values; in this volume, Lawrence and Kang incline most clearly in this direction. A focus on civilizational identity might attack that problem from the opposite angle, updating classic work on "security communities" by looking more closely at the terms on which states and their representatives consider one another to be part of a larger whole; Adler's chapter, along with some of his earlier work on the subject, inclines most clearly in this direction.

Finally, a post-essentialist "writing civilizations" approach to the subject would highlight the kinds of civilizational strategies that states undertake in their efforts to relate to one another; elements of this approach can be glimpsed in the chapters by Rudolph and Leheny. Much as Rodney Bruce Hall (1997) does with moral authority, civilizational post-essentialism converts civilizational notions into power resources that states and their representatives can deploy more or less strategically. Among other things, this would provides a less Huntingtonian way of reading the kind of civilizational leadership that Kurth identifies as constitutive of American global political action – it would shift the focus from the (likely unanswerable) question of whether or not the secularized Protestantism of the American Creed and the global civilization that Kurth identifies as emanating from it actually is a kind of pre-Axial Age paganism, and instead focus attention on the *claims* about "Western" or "global" civilization and the efficacy of those claims in bringing about distinct outcomes. Where Kurth's analysis suggests that the success or failure of American global leadership depends on dispositional qualities out of the control of any political actor – in short, that a clash between the pre- or post-Axial Age social arrangement exemplified by the United States, and the various Axial Age social arrangements on offer in the rest of the world, is more or less inevitable – a post-essentialist perspective suggests, to the contrary, that what happens in the relations between civilizations depends on how those civilizations are bounded in practice. Therefore, the future of American global leadership as the core state of a civilization depends both on whether state officials elect to deploy civilizational resources at all and whether those deployments work to bound discrete civilizations in a way that gives rise to irreconcilable conflicts.

Civilizational essentialism, therefore, has little to offer a state-centric international relations field. Civilizational membership does not seem to be the most significant attribute affecting interstate relations, and attention to the various ways in which states engage and deploy civilizational difference is more clearly entailed by the other quadrants of the matrix. Indeed, if the claims of civilizational essentialism were taken seriously, state-centrism itself would have to evaporate in the face of irreconcilable civilizational differences; Huntington's protestations to the contrary, I can see little point in continuing to focus on states if one truly believed that broader cultural communities were the really important factors in world politics, and the implication might be to follow Fernand Braudel (1994) into the *longue durée* where civilizations rise and fall and stop worrying about states at all. That's a tough enough sell for academic international relations – witness the marginalization of world systems theory and world system history in mainstream scholarship – but the real irony here is that replacing sovereign, territorial states with essentially delimited civilizations wouldn't change the most basic presumptions about global political actors. Recall the ways in which Huntingtonian civilizations confront one another like states in anarchy, and subsist on core properties that are very bit as essential as the constitutive properties thought to be possessed by states. A shift to a conception of world politics dominated by essential civilizations might get rid of state-centrism, but essential actors would remain.

In that way, the most important potential contribution that the debate about civilizations might make to academic international relations would be to *dissolve* essentialism along the lines that contemporary scholars of civilization have critiqued Huntington. Loosening the theoretical definition of an actor to incorporate self-conceptions more centrally would be a first step, since that would make room for the emergence of actors such as "Europe" out of collective identifications. Tracing the diffusion of characteristic practices would be a second step, since that might show us how different social arrangements that we might associate with actors such as "China" or "the Islamic world" need not always occur together. And a turn to post-essentialism, finally, would unpack actorhood more or less completely, allowing international relations scholarship to focus on how various attributions of actorhood become commonsensical: how it comes to make sense to say that "the Islamic world" did something, or that "the West" reacted in a particular way. This is a phenomenon akin to the way in which it has become commonsensical to say that "France" or "the United States" did something – a commonsensical assumption that is normally passed over in most international relations scholarship. Opening up this line of inquiry – paving the way for *post-essentialist scholarship* in the scholarly field of international relations

– might be the ultimate academic consequence of continuing the conversation about civilizations in world politics.

Notes

1 Obliquely, conversations with Alex Wendt, Nick Onuf, Dan Nexon, and Naeem Inayatullah have shaped this chapter. Directly, comments by Peter Katzenstein and Will Schlickenmaier helped to sharpen the argument.
2 I would be remiss if I did not also admit that these distinctions stem, in part, from my own scholarly work and the value-commitments that drive it. Perhaps someone else looking at the same academic conversation about civilizations would extract alternative axes along which to compare and contrast positions taken up by various participants in that conversation. They are of course welcome to do so, but I'm not going to get into the endless exercise of trying to anticipate all possible ways of dividing up the conversation – nor am I going to try to offer any transcendental grounding for the two analytical distinctions that I am proposing. As fascinating as that can be – see Onuf (1989) for a sustained example – my tastes run more to allowing an ideal-typical matrix to demonstrate its worth on pragmatic grounds.
3 Spengler's terminology is somewhat unique among civilizational scholars. For Spengler, the entities that others call "civilizations" are known as "the higher Cultures," and what he calls "civilization" represents a distinct phase in the life history of one of the higher Cultures. David Leheny touches on this particularly Germanic paring of "culture" and "civilization" in his chapter above; see also Bowden (2004a) and Jackson (2006: 84–6).
4 There are costs in moving too quickly to the level of philosophical ontology, not the least of which is that questions of philosophical ontology are somewhat more fundamental than questions of scientific ontology. This is not to say that questions of scientific ontology are any easier to resolve in practice; rather, the main difference is that such questions are less likely directly to implement commitments about the basic character of knowledge – commitments that are, in many cases, almost theological in character. So differences of scientific ontology might lead to some fierce scholarly debates but probably won't spill over into scorched-earth scholarly wars. And separating scientific and philosophical ontology in the way that I have throughout this chapter opens the possibility that scholars with divergent commitments about the nature of knowledge might find some shared ground in a conceptualization of their common object of study: a dualist and a monist might both agree, for example, that the self-conceptions of actors are critical to the empirical investigation of social action, and that those self-conceptions should be treated as provisionally fixed attributes of relatively stable social entities, but then disagree on precisely *how* to study those social entities. Separating scientific and philosophical ontology, then, provides more elaborate combinatorial possibilities – and that may be the most important academic effect of a good ideal-typification of scholarly debates.
5 Of course, those inclined to *ex ante* specifications of a civilization might reply by arguing that the California case illustrates the extent to which civilizations have become detached from their geographical bases, and then formulate something like a globalized definition of a civilization that takes this trans-locality into account. My point here is only that operating without the *ex ante* specification can let one see what actors are saying and doing in ways that an *ex ante* specification might preclude.
6 This was, in point of fact, the original working title of Hall and Jackson (2007b). Unfortunately, given the matrix I've been developing here, the published title of

that edited volume associates it with a quadrant that many of the authors in the book spend much of their time critiquing and criticizing.

7   One obvious solution is to convert the discrete divisions of the matrix into continuous axes of variation, but that in turn means abandoning much of the logical clarity that was achieved by treating the distinctions as logically pure in the first place!

8   Of course, there is no need to stop with one level of self-similar replication of the original matrix. There is no logical reason why the matrix couldn't replicate a second time within each of the sixteen cells of the fractalized matrix; that would give us 16 x 4 = 64 possible scholarly positions. But the practical utility of such a 64-cell matrix as a way of locating scholars and scholarship would depend, in turn, on whether scholars were in fact occupying most of the logically possible cells. Otherwise, the matrix would be largely empty, and we would need to provide some kind of a compelling explanation for why scholarly work on civilizations occurred only in certain conceptual locations but not in others.

9   Note that contingency-explanations often – but not always – feature a configurational notion of causality emphasizing the elucidation of causal mechanisms, as opposed to the notion of causality emphasizing cross-case covariations that is often found in necessity-explanations. But this is not a global correspondence, as it is quite possible to have a contingency-explanation that uses a covariation notion of causality (as in, for example, Gourevitch 1986 and Hall 1986), as well as a necessity-explanation that uses a mechanistic notion of causality (as in many forms of social network theory, for example, Wellman 1997). Here, again, separating philosophical ontology (which informs conceptions of causality) and scientific ontology (which informs styles of explanation) increases combinatorial possibilities.

References

Abbott, Andrew (1988) "Transcending General Linear Reality," *Sociological Theory*, 6: 169–86.

—— (2001) *Chaos of Disciplines*, Chicago: University of Chicago Press.

Abe, Shinzō (2006) *Utsukushii kuni e* [*Toward a Beautiful Country*], Tokyo: Bungei shinsho.

Abramson, Marc S. (2008) *Ethnic Identity in Tang China*, Philadelphia: University of Pennsylvania Press.

Abu-Lughod, Janet L. (1989) *Before European Hegemony: The World System A.D. 1250–1350*, Oxford: Oxford University Press.

—— (1993) "The World System in the Thirteenth Century," in Michael Adas (ed.), *Islamic and European Expansion: The Forging of a Global Order*, Philadelphia: Temple University Press.

Adamson, Fiona B. (2005) "Global Liberalism versus Political Islam: Competing Ideological Frames in International Politics," *International Studies Review*, 7: 547–69.

Adas, Michael (1989) *Machines as the Measure of Men: Science, Technology, and Ideologies of Western Dominance*, Ithaca, NY, and London: Cornell University Press.

Adcock, Robert (2006) "Generalization in Comparative and Historical Social Science," in Dvora Yanow and Peri Schwartz-Shea (eds), *Interpretation and Method: Empirical Research Methods and the Interpretive Turn*, Armonk, NY: M. E. Sharpe, pp. 50–66.

Adler, Emanuel (2005) *Communitarian International Relations: The Epistemic Foundations of International Relations*, New York: Routledge.

—— (2008) "The Spread of Security Communities: Communities of Practice, Self-Restraint, and NATO's Post Cold War Transformation," *European Journal of International Relations*, 14(2): 195–230.

Adler, Emanuel, and Barnett, Michael (1998a) "A Framework for the Study of Security Communities," in Emanuel Adler and Michael Barnett (eds), *Security Communities*, Cambridge: Cambridge University Press, pp. 29–65.

—— (eds) (1998b) *Security Communities*, Cambridge: Cambridge University Press.

Adler, Emanuel, and Crawford, Beverly (2006) "Normative Power: The European Practice of Region-Building and the Case of the Euro-Mediterranean Partnership," in Emanuel Adler, Federica Bicchi, Beverly Crawford, and Raffaella A. Del Sarto (eds), *The Convergence of Civilizations: Constructing a Mediterranean Region*, Toronto: University of Toronto Press, pp. 3–47.

Adler, Emanuel, and Greve, Patricia (2009) "When Security Community Meets Balance of Power: Overlapping Regional Mechanisms of Security Governance," *Review of International Studies*, 35: 53–84.

Adler, Emanuel, and Pouliot, Vincent (2008) "The Practice Turn in International Relations: Introduction and Framework," draft.

Ahmed, Imtiaz (1966) "Ashraf–Ajlaf Dichotomy in Muslim Social Structure in India," *Indian Economic and Social History Review*, 3(3): 268–78.

Ajami, Fouad (1993) "The Summoning," *Foreign Affairs*, 72(4): 2–9.

Akturk, Sener (2007) "What Is a Civilization? From Huntington to Elias: The Varying Uses of the Term 'Civilization,'" seminar paper, Department of Political Science, University of California at Berkeley.

—— (2009) "What Is a Civilization: From Huntington to Elias: The Varying Uses of the Term 'Civilization,'" in S. Unay and M. Senel (eds), *Global Orders and Civilizations: Perspectives from History, Philosophy and International Relations*, New York: Nova Science Publishers.

Alam, Muzaffar (1998) "The Pursuit of Persian: Language in Mughal Politics," *Modern Asian Studies*, 32(2): 317–49.

Al-Azmeh, Aziz (1981) *Ibn Khaldun in Modern Scholarship: A Study in Orientalism*, London: Third World Centre.

Albert, Mathias, Brock, Lothar, and Wolf, Klaus Dieter (eds) (2000) *Civilizing World Politics: Society and Community beyond the State*, Lanham, MD: Rowman & Littlefield.

Alker, Hayward (1996) *Rediscoveries and Reformulations: Humanistic Methodologies for International Studies*, Cambridge: Cambridge University Press.

—— (2007) "Discussion: On the Discursive Turn in Civilizational Analysis," in Martin Hall and Patrick Thaddeus Jackson (eds), *Civilizational Identity*, New York: Palgrave, pp. 51–8.

Allchin, F. R. (1995) *The Archaeology of Early Historic South Asia: The Emergence of Cities and States*, Cambridge: Cambridge University Press.

Anderson, Benedict (1983) *Imagined Communities: Reflections on the Origins and Spread of Nationalism*, London: Verso.

—— (1991) *Imagined Communities: Reflections on the Origins and Spread of Nationalism*, rev. edn, London: Verso.

Anderson, James (2007) *The Rebel Den of Nung Tri Cao: Loyalty and Identity along the Sino-Vietnamese Border*, Seattle: University of Washington Press.

Anderson, Jon (1984) "Conjuring with Ibn Khaldun," in Bruce B. Lawrence (ed.), *Ibn Khaldun and Islamic Ideology*, Leiden: E. J. Brill.

Anderson, Perry (1977) *Lineages of the Absolutist State*, London: New Left Books.

Andrews, Bruce (1975) "Social Rules and the State as a Social Actor," *World Politics*, 27(4): 521–40.

An-Na'im, Abdullahi (2008) *Islam and the Secular State*, Cambridge, MA: Harvard University Press.

Aoki, Tamotsu (1999) *Ajia direma* [*Asian Dilemma*], Tokyo: Chūō kōron shinsha.

—— (2001) "'Miwaku suru chikara' to Bunka seisaku" ['The Power to Fascinate' and Cultural Policy], in Takenaka Heizō, Sedakawa Yoshiyuki, and the Fujita Institute of Future Management (eds), *Posuto IT kakumei 'sofuto pawā' Nihon fukken e no michi* [*Soft Power after the Information Technology Revolution: The Road to Japan's Rehabilitation*],Tokyo: Jitsugyō no nihonsha, pp. 146–76.

Appiah, Kwame Anthony (2006) *Cosmopolitanism: Ethics in a World of Strangers*, New York: W. W. Norton.

Arjomand, Saïd Amir, and Tiryakian, Edward A. (2004a) "Introduction," in Saïd Amir Arjomand and Edward A. Tiryakian (eds), *Rethinking Civilizational Analysis*, London and Thousand Oaks, CA: Sage, pp. 1–13.

—— (eds) (2004b) *Rethinking Civilizational Analysis*, London and Thousand Oaks, CA: Sage.

Arnason, Johann P. (1997) *Social Theory and Japanese Experience: The Dual Civilization*, London: Kegan Paul International.

—— (2003a) *Civilizations in Dispute: Historical Questions and Theoretical Traditions*, Leiden: E. J. Brill.

—— (2003b) "East and West: From Invidious Dichotomy to Incomplete Deconstruction," in Gerard Delanty and Engin F. Isin (eds), *Handbook of Historical Sociology*, Thousand Oaks, CA: Sage, pp. 220–34.

—— (2004) "Civilizational Patterns and Civilizing Processes," in Saïd Amir Arjomand and Edward A. Tiryakian (eds), *Rethinking Civilizational Analysis*, London and Thousand Oaks, CA: Sage, pp. 103–18.

Arnason, Johann P., Eisenstadt, S. N., and Wittrock, Björn (eds) (2005) *Axial Civilizations and World History*, Leiden: E. J. Brill.

Arrighi, Giovanni, Hui, Po-keung, Hung, Ho-fung, and Selden, Mark (2003) "Historical Capitalism, East and West," in Giovanni Arrighi, Takeshi Hamashita, and Mark Selden (eds), *The Resurgence of East Asia, 500, 150, and 50 Year Perspectives*, London: Routledge, pp. 259–333.

Ashcroft, Bill, Griffiths, Gareth, and Tiffin, Helen (1998) *Key Concepts in Post Colonial Studies*, New York: Routledge.

Asō, Tarō (2007) *Totetsumonai Nihon* [*Japan the Tremendous*], Tokyo: Shinchōsha.

Aydin, Cemil (2007) *The Politics of Anti-Westernism in Asia: Visions of World Order in Pan-Islamic and Pan-Asian Thought*, New York: Columbia University Press.

Aysha, Emad El-Din (2003) "Samuel Huntington and the Geopolitics of American Identity: The Function of Foreign Policy in America's Domestic Clash of Civilizations," *International Studies Perspectives*, 4: 113–32.

Barani, Luca (2006) "Hard and Soft Law in the European Union: The Case of Social Policy and the Open Method of Coordination," Webpapers on Constitutionalism & Governance beyond the State, 2; available at: http://www.bath.ac.uk/esml/conWEB/ConWeb%20papers-filestore.conweb2–2006.pdf (accessed 29 December 2008).

Barfield, Thomas (1989) *The Perilous Frontier: Nomadic Empires and China, 221 BC to AD 1757*, Oxford: Blackwell.

Bartelson, Jens (1998) "Second Natures: What Makes the State Identical with Itself?" *European Journal of International Relations*, 4: 295–326.

Barth, Boris, and Osterhammel, Jürgen (eds) (2005) *Zivilisierungsmissionen: Imperiale Weltverbesserung seit dem 18. Jahrhundert*, Konstanz: UVK Verlagsgesellschaft.

Batten, Bruce (2003) *To the Ends of Japan: Premodern Frontiers, Boundaries, and Interactions*, Honolulu: University of Hawai'i Press.

Bellah, Robert (2003) *Imagining Japan: The Japanese Tradition and its Modern Interpretation*, Berkeley: University of California Press.

Ben-Yehuda, Hemda (2003) "The 'Clash of Civilizations' Thesis: Findings from International Crises, 1918–94," *Comparative Civilizations Review*, 49: 28–42.

Bernard, Mitchell, and Ravenhill, John (1995) "Beyond Product Cycles and Flying Geese: Regionalization, Hierarchy, and the Industrialization of East Asia," *World Politics*, 47(2): 171–209.

Berry, Mary Elizabeth (1982) *Hideyoshi*, Cambridge, MA: Harvard University Press.

Bhabha, Homi (1983) "The Other Question: 'The Stereotype and Colonial Discourse,'" *Screen*, 24(6): 18–36.

Bially Mattern, Janice (2005) "Why 'Soft Power' Isn't So Soft: Representational Force and the Sociolinguistic Construction of Attraction in World Politics," *Millennium*, 33(3): 583–612.

Bicchi, Federica (2006) "'Our Size Fits All': Normative Power Europe and the Mediterranean," *Journal of European Public Policy*, 13(2): 286–303.

Blavatsky, H. P. (1972) *Key to Theosophy*, Pasadena, CA: Theosophical University Press.

Borovoy, Amy (2008) "*Nihonjinron* and the Problem of Communalism in Postwar Japan," Princeton University, Department of East Asian Studies.

Bose, Sugata (1998) "Space and Time on the Indian Ocean Rim: Theory and History," unpublished paper given at an international workshop, "Oceans Connect: Mapping a New Global Scholarship," Duke University.

Botsman, Daniel (2004/2005) "Review" [of Johann Arnason, *The Peripheral Centre*], *Pacific Affairs*, 77(4): 761–2.

Bowden, Brett (2004a) "The Ideal of Civilisation: Its Origin and Socio-Political Character," *Critical Review of International Social and Political Philosophy*, 7(1): 25–50.

—— (2004b) "In the Name of Progress and Peace: The 'Standard of Civilization' and the Universalizing Project," *Alternatives*, 29: 43–68.

—— (2005) "The Colonial Origins of International Law: European Expansion and the Classical Standard of Civilization," *Journal of the History of International Law*, 7: 1–23.

—— (2007) "The River of Inter-Civilisational Relations: The Ebb and Flow of Peoples, Ideas and Innovations," *Third World Quarterly*, 28(7): 1359–74.

—— (ed.) (2009) *Civilization: Critical Concepts in Political Science*, 4 vols, New York: Routledge.

Bowden, Brett, and Seabrooke, Leonard (eds) (2006) *Global Standards of Market Civilization*, New York: Routledge.

Bowen, Ezra (1986) "Nakasone's World-Class Blunder," *Time* (6 October), available at: http://www.time.com/time/magazine/article/0,9171,962472,00.html (accessed 25 July 2008).

Bozeman, Adda B. (1960) *Politics and Culture in International History*, Princeton, NJ: Princeton University Press.

Braudel, Fernand (1972) *The Mediterranean and the Mediterranean World in the Age of Philip II*, Vol. I, New York: Harper & Row.

—— (1979) *Civilisation & Capitalism, 15th–18th Century*, trans. Sian Reynolds, 3 vols, New York: Harper & Row.

—— (1994) *A History of Civilizations*, trans. Richard Mayne, New York: Penguin.

Brindley, Erica (2003) "Barbarians or Not? Ethnicity and Changing Conceptions of the Ancient Yue (Viet) Peoples, ca 400–450 BC," *Asia Major*, 16(1): 1–32.

Brubaker, Rogers (1996) *Nationalism Reframed: Nationhood and the National Question in the New Europe*, Cambridge: Cambridge University Press.

—— (2006) *Ethnicity without Groups*, new edn, Cambridge, MA: Harvard University Press.

Bulliet, Richard W. (2004) *The Case for Islamo-Christian Civilization*, New York: Columbia University Press.

Burleigh, Michael (2005) *Earthly Powers: The Clash of Religion and Politics in Europe, from the French Revolution to the Great War*, New York: Harper Collins.

—— (2007) *Sacred Causes: The Clash of Religion and Politics, from the Great War to the War on Terror*, New York: Harper Collins.

Buruma, Ian, and Margalit, Avishai (2004) *Occidentalism: A Short History of Anti-Westernism*, London: Atlantic Books.

"California Textbook Issue Has Its First Day in Court" (2006) *Hinduism Today*, available at: http://www.hinduismtoday.com/archives/2006/7–9/36_education.shtml (accessed 1 January 2009).

Campbell, David (1992) *Writing Security*, Minneapolis, MN: University of Minnesota Press.

Canfield, Robert L. (ed.) (1991) *Turko-Persia in Historical Perspective*, Cambridge: Cambridge University Press.

Chaudhuri, Kirti N. (1990) *Asia before Europe: Economy and Civilisation of the Indian Ocean from the Rise of Islam to 1750*, Cambridge: Cambridge University Press.

Chiozza, Giacomo (2002) "Is there a Clash of Civilizations? Evidence from Patterns of International Conflict Involvement, 1946–97," *Journal of Peace Research*, 39(6): 711–34.

Cho, Young-mee Yu (2002) "Diglossia in Korean Language and Literature: A Historical Perspective," *East Asia: An International Quarterly*, 20(1): 3–23.

Choi, So-ja (1997) *Myŏngchong sidae chunghan kwanggyesa yŏngu* [*Study on Sino-Korean Relations during Ming-Qing Periods*], Seoul: Ewha Womans University Press.

Chua, Amy (2007) *Day of Empire: How Hyperpowers Rise to Global Dominance – and Why They Fail*, New York: Doubleday.

Clive, John, and Pinney, Thomas (eds) (1972) *Thomas Babington Macaulay: Selected Writings*, Chicago and London: University of Chicago Press.

Cohen, Mark R. (1995) *Under Crescent and Cross: The Jews in the Middle Ages*, Princeton, NJ: Princeton University Press.

Collins, Randall (1998) *The Sociology of Philosophies: A Global Theory of Intellectual Change*, Cambridge, MA: Harvard University Press.

—— (1999) *Macro-History: Essays in Sociology of the Long Run*, Stanford, CA: Stanford University Press.

—— (2000) "The Sociology of Philosophies: A Précis," *Philosophy of the Social Sciences*, 30: 157–201.

—— (2004) "Civilizations as Zones of Prestige and Social Contact," in Saïd Amir Arjomand and Edward A. Tiryakian (eds), *Rethinking Civilizational Analysis*, London and Thousand Oaks, CA: Sage, pp. 132–47.

Commission to the European Communities (2003) *Wider Europe – Neighborhood: A New Framework for Relations with our Southern Neighbors*, 104 Final, Brussels.

—— (2007) "Stepping up the Fight against Terrorism," 6 November, COM(2007) 649 final [not published in the Official Journal], available at: http://eur-lex.europa.eu/LexUriServ/LexUriServ.do?uri=COM:2007:0649:FIN:EN:PDF (accessed 18 January 2008).

Cornell, Vincent J. (2005) "Ibn Battuta's Opportunism: The Networks and Loyalties of a Medieval Muslim Scholar," in miriam cooke and Bruce B. Lawrence (eds), *Muslim Networks from Hajj to Hip Hop*, Chapel Hill, NC: University of North Carolina Press.

Council of the European Union (2003) *A Secure Europe in a Better World: European Security Strategy*, Brussels, 12 December, available at: http://www.consilium. europa.eu/uedocs/cmsUpload/78367.pdf (accessed 17 August 2008).

—— (2005) *The European Union Counter-Terrorism Strategy*, Brussels, 30 November, available at: http://register.consilium.eu.int/pdf/en/05/st14/st14469-re04.en05.pdf (accessed 17 August 2008).

Cox, Michael (2003) "Commentary: Martians and Venutians in the New World Order," *International Affairs*, 79(3): 523–32.

Cox, Robert W. (2000) "Thinking about Civilizations," *Review of International Studies*, 26: 217–34.

—— (2001) "Civilizations and the Twenty-First Century: Some Theoretical Considerations," *International Relations of the Asia-Pacific*, 1: 105–30.

—— (2002a) "Civilization in the Twenty-First Century: Some Theoretical Considerations," in Mehdi Mozaffari (ed.), *Globalization and Civilizations*, London: Routledge, pp. 1–23.

—— (2002b) *The Political Economy of a Plural World*, London: Routledge.

Craig, Campbell (2004) "American Realism versus American Imperialism," *World Politics*, 57(1): 143–71.

Crawford, Neta C. (2002) *Argument and Change in World Politics*, Cambridge: Cambridge University Press.

—— (2008) "'Man in the Mirror: Human Nature and World Politics," unpublished paper, Boston University, Department of Political Science.

Crossley, Pamela (1997) *The Manchus*, Oxford: Blackwell.

—— (2008) "China as a Strategic Idea: An Overview," unpublished manuscript, Dartmouth College, Hanover, NH.

Cumings, Bruce (1984) "The Origins and Development of the Northeast Asian Political Economy: Industrial Sectors, Product Cycles, and Political Consequences," *International Organization*, 38(1): 1–40.

Dabashi, Hamid (2004) "For the Last Time; Civilizations," in Saïd Amir Arjomond and Edward Tiryakian, *Civilizational Analysis*, London and Thousand Oaks, CA: Sage, pp. 245–50.

Dale, Stephen F. (2006) "Ibn Khaldun: The Last Greek and the First *Annaliste* Historian," *International Journal of Middle East Studies*, 38: 431–51.

Dallmayr, Fred (2004) "Beyond Monologue: For a Comparative Political Theory," *Perspectives on Politics*, 2(2): 249–57.

—— (2005) "Empire or Cosmopolis? Civilization at the Crossroads," *Globalization*, 2(1): 14–30.

Dallmayr, Fred, and Manoochehri, Abbas (eds) (2007) *Civilizational Dialogue and Political Thought: Tehran Papers*, Lanham, MD: Rowman & Littlefield.

Deitelhoff, Nicole (2009) "The Discursive Process of Legalization: Charting Islands of Persuasion in the ICC Case," *International Organization*, 63(1): 33–66.

Delanty, Gerard (1995) *Inventing Europe: Idea, Identity, Reality*, London: Macmillan.

—— (2002) "Models of European Identity: Reconciling Universalism and Particularism," *Perspectives on European Politics and Society*, 3(3): 345–59.

—— (2003) "The Making of a Post-Western Europe: A Civilizational Analysis," *Thesis Eleven*, 72: 8–25.

—— (2006) "Civilizational Constellations and European Modernity Reconsidered," in Gerard Delanty (ed.), *Europe and Asia beyond East and West*, New York: Routledge, pp. 45–60.

—— (2007a) "European Citizenship: A Critical Assessment," *Citizenship Studies*, 11(1): 63–72.

—— (2007b) "Peripheries and Borders in Post-Western Europe," available at: http://www.eurozine.com/articles/2007-08-29-delanty-en.html (accessed 17 August 2008).

Delorme, Jesco (2007) "Multiculturalism is Not Relativism!," available at: http://www.signandsight.com/features/1240.html (accessed 17 August 2008).

Deng, Gang (1997) "The Foreign Staple Trade of China in the Pre-Modern Era," *International History Review*, 19(2): 253–83.

Descartes, René (1993) *Discourse on Method and Meditations on First Philosophy*, 3rd edn, Indianapolis, IN: Hackett.

Deuchler, Martina (1992) *The Confucian Transformation of Korea: A Study of Society and Ideology*, Cambridge, MA: Harvard University Press.

Deudney, Daniel H. (2007) *Bounding Power: Republican Security Theory from the Polis to the Global Village*, Princeton, NJ: Princeton University Press.

Deutsch, Karl W., *et al.* (1957) *Political Community and the North Atlantic Area*, Princeton, NJ: Princeton University Press.

Dewey, John (1920) *Reconstruction in Philosophy*, Kessinger.

Di Cosmo, Nicola (2002) *Ancient China and its Enemies: The Rise of Nomadic Power in East Asian History*, Cambridge: Cambridge University Press.

Diez, Thomas (2005) "Constructing the Self and Changing Others: Reconsidering 'Normative Power Europe,'" *Millennium: Journal of International Studies*, 33(3): 613–36.

Diez, Thomas, and Manners, Ian (2007) "Reflecting on Normative Power Europe," in F. Berenskoetter and M. J. Williams (eds), *Power in World Politics*, London: Routledge, pp. 173–88.

Diez, Thomas, and Pace, Michelle (2007) "Normative Power Europe and Conflict Transformation," paper presented at the EUSA conference, Montreal, 17–19 May.

Dower, John W. (2002) "After Saddam," *The Guardian*, 20 November, available at: http://www.guardian.co.uk/world/2002/nov/20/iraq.guardiananalysispage (accessed 23 July 2008).

Doyle, Michael W. (1986) *Empires*, Ithaca, NY: Cornell University Press.

Duchêne, François (1973) "The European Community and the Uncertainties of Interdependence," in Max Kohnstamm and Wolfgang Hager (eds), *A Nation Writ Large? Foreign Policy Problems before the European Community*, London: Macmillan.

Duerr, Hans-Peter (1988) *Der Mythos vom Zivilisationsprozess*, Vol. 1: *Nacktheit und Scham*, Frankfurt am Main: Suhrkamp.

—— (1990) *Der Mythos vom Zivilisationsprozess*, Vol. 2: *Intimität*, Frankfurt am Main: Suhrkamp.

—— (1993) *Der Mythos vom Zivilisationsprozess*, Vol. 3: *Obszönität und Gewalt*, Frankfurt am Main: Suhrkamp.

—— (1997) *Der Mythos vom Zivilisationsprozess*, Vol. 4: *Der Erotische Leib*, Frankfurt am Main: Suhrkamp.

Dunn, Ross (1989) *The Adventures of Ibn Battuta: a Muslim Traveler of the 14th Century*, Berkeley, CA: University of California Press.

Durkheim, Émile, and Mauss, Marcel (1971) "Note on the Notion of Civilization," trans. Benjamin Nelson, *Social Research*, 38(4): 808–13.

Eaton, Richard M. (1993) *The Rise of Islam and the Bengal Frontier, 1204–1760*, Berkeley, CA: University of California Press.

—— (ed.) (2000) *Essays on Islam and Indian History*, Oxford: Oxford University Press.

Eisenstadt, S. N. (1963) *The Political Systems of Empires: The Rise and Fall of Historical Bureaucratic Societies*, New York: Free Press.

—— (1982) "The Axial Age: The Emergence of Transcendental Visions and the Rise of Clerics," *European Journal of Sociology*, 23(2): 294–314.

—— (ed.) (1986) *The Origins and Diversity of Axial-Age Civilizations*, Albany, NY: SUNY Press.

—— (1987) *European Civilization in a Comparative Perspective*, Oslo: Norwegian University Press.

—— (1992a) *Jewish Civilization: The Jewish Historical Experience in Comparative Perspective*, New York: SUNY Press.

—— (1992b) "Frameworks of the Great Revolutions: Culture, Social Structure, History and Human Agency," *International Social Science Journal*, 133: 385–401.

—— (1996) *Japanese Civilization: A Comparative View*, Chicago: University of Chicago Press.

—— (1998a) *Die Antinomien der Moderne: Die jakobinischen Grundzüge der Moderne und des Fundamentalismus, Heterodoxien, Utopismus und Jakobinismus in der Konstitution fundamentalistischer Bewegungen*, Frankfurt am Main: Suhrkamp.

—— (1998b) "Axial and Non-Axial Civilizations – The Japanese Experience in Comparative Perspective – The Construction of Generalized Particularistic Trust," in Hidehiro Sonoda and S. N. Eisenstadt (eds), *Japan in a Comparative Perspective*, Kyoto: International Research Center for Japanese Studies, pp. 1–17.

—— (1999a) *Fundamentalism, Sectarianism, and Revolution: The Jacobin Dimension of Modernity*, Cambridge: Cambridge University Press.

—— (1999b) *Paradoxes of Democracy, Fragility, Continuity, and Change*, Baltimore, MD: Johns Hopkins University Press.

—— (2000a) "The Civilizational Dimension in Sociological Analysis," *Thesis Eleven*, 62(1): 1–21.

—— (2000b) "Multiple Modernities," *Dædalus*, 129: 1–29.

—— (2000c) "The Reconstruction of Religious Arenas in the Framework of 'Multiple Modernities,'" *Millennium*, 29(3): 591–612.

—— (2000d) *Die Vielfalt der Moderne*, Weilerswist: Velbrück Wissenschaft.

—— (2001) "The Civilizational Dimension of Modernity: Modernity as a Distinct Civilization," *International Sociology*, 16(3): 320–40.

—— (2003) *Comparative Civilizations and Multiple Modernities*, 2 vols, Leiden: E. J. Brill.

—— (2004a) "The Civilizational Dimension of Modernity," in Säid Amir Arjomand and Edward A. Tiryakian (eds), *Rethinking Civilizational Analysis*, London and Thousand Oaks, CA: Sage, pp. 48–66.

—— (2004b) *Explorations in Jewish Historical Experience: The Civilizational Dimension*, Leiden: E. J. Brill.

Eisenstadt, S. N., and Schluchter, Wolfgang (1998) "Introduction: Paths to Early Modernities – A Comparative View," *Dædalus*, 127(3): 1–18.

El Desouky, Mohamed Ibrahim (2005) "Two Suns in the East," *Al-Ahram Weekly*, no. 771, 1–7 December, available at: http://weekly.ahram.org.eg/2005/771/in3.htm (accessed 14 July 2008).

Elias, Norbert (1978a) *The History of Manners*, Oxford: Blackwell.

—— (1978b) "On Transformation of Aggressiveness," *Theory and Society*, 5(2): 229–42.

—— (1982) *State Formation and Civilization*, Oxford: Blackwell.

—— (1994) "Introduction: A Theoretical Essay on Established and Outsiders," in Norbert Elias and J. L. Scotson, *The Established and the Outsider: A Sociological Enquiry into Community Problems*, London: Sage, pp. xi–lii.

—— (1997) "Toward a Theory of Social Processes: A Translation," *British Journal of Sociology*, 48(3): 355–83.

—— (2000) *The Civilizing Process: Sociogenetic and Psychogenetic Investigations*, rev. edn, Oxford: Blackwell.

Emirbayer, Mustafa (1997) "Manifesto for a Relational Sociology," *American Journal of Sociology*, 103(2): 281–317.

Euro-Mediterranean Partnership (2005) *Regional Co-operation: An Overview of Programmes and Projects*, Brussels: European Commission.

Farrenkopf, John (2000) "Spengler's Theory of Civilization," *Thesis Eleven*, 62: 23–38.

Farris, William Wayne (1998) "Trade, Money, and Merchants in Nara Japan," *Monumenta Nipponica*, 53(3): 303–34.

Ferguson, Niall (2002) *Empire: The Rise and Demise of the British World Order and the Lessons for Global Power*, New York: Basic Books.

Ferguson, Yale H. (2007a) "Pathways to Civilization," in Martin Hall and Patrick Thaddeus Jackson (eds), *Civilizational Identity*, New York: Palgrave, pp. 191–7.

—— (2007b) "Along the Imperial Continuum: Varieties of Empire," paper prepared for the 103rd annual meeting of the American Political Science Association, Chicago, 30 August –2 September.

Ferguson, Yale H., and Mansbach, Richard W. (1996) *Polities: Authority, Identities, and Change*, Columbia, SC: University of South Carolina Press.

Ferguson, Yale H., Mansbach, Richard W., *et al.* (2000) "What is a Polity? A Roundtable," *International Studies Review*, 2(1): 3–31.

Finnemore, Martha (1996) *National Interests in International Society*, Ithaca, NY: Cornell University Press.

Fiskesjo, Magnus ((1999) "On the 'Raw' and 'Cooked' Barbarians of Imperial China," *Inner Asia*, 1: 139–68.

Foucault, Michel (1981) "The Order of Discourse," in R. Young (ed.), *Untying the Text: A Poststructuralist Reader*, London: Routledge.

Fox, Jonathan (2001) "Clash of Civilizations or Clash of Religions: Which is a More Important Determinant of Ethnic Conflict?" *Ethnicities*, 1: 295–320.

—— (2004) *Religion, Civilization, and Civil War: 1945 through the Millennium*, Lanham, MD: Lexington Books.

Fraga, Luis, and Segura, Gary M. (2006) "Culture Clash? Contesting Notions of American Identity and the Effects of Latin American Immigration," *Perspectives on Politics*, 4(2): 279–87.

Friend, Theodore (ed.) (2006) *Religion and Religiosity in the Philippines and Indonesia*, Washington, DC: Brookings Institution.

Fujiwara, Masahiko (2005) *Kokka no hinkaku* [*The Dignity of a Nation*], Tokyo: Shinchōsha.

Fukuyama, Francis (2006) *The End of History and the Last Man*, 2nd edn, New York: Free Press.

Fukuzawa, Yukichi (1973) *An Outline of a Theory of Civilization*, trans. David A. Dilworth and G. Cameron Hurst, Tokyo: Sophia University Press.

Geertz, Clifford (1973) *The Interpretation of Cultures*, New York: Basic Books.

Giersch, Charles (2001) "'A Motley Throng': Social Change on Southwest China's Early Modern Frontier, 1700–1880," *Journal of Asian Studies*, 60(1): 67–94.

Gilpin, Robert (1981) *War and Change in World Politics*, New York: Cambridge University Press.

Gluck, Carol (1991) "The 'Long Postwar': Japan and Germany in Common and in Contrast," in Ernestine Schlant and J. Thomas Rimer (eds), *Legacies and Ambiguities: Postwar Fiction and Culture in West Germany and Japan*, Washington, DC: Woodrow Wilson Center, pp. 63–80.

Göle, Nilüfer (2007) "Islam, European Public Space and Civility," available at: http://www.eurozine.com/search.html (accessed 17 August 2008).

Gong, Gerrit W. (1984a) *The Standard of "Civilization" in International Society*, Oxford: Clarendon Press.

—— (1984b) "China's Entry into International Society," in Hedley Bull and Adam Watson (eds), *The Expansion of International Society*, Oxford: Oxford University Press, pp. 171–83.

Goudsblom, Johan, Jones, Eric L., and Mennell, Stephen (eds) (1996) *The Course of Human History: Economic Growth, Social Process and Civilization*, London: M. E. Sharpe.

Gourevitch, Peter (1986) *Politics in Hard Times: Comparative Responses to International Economic Crises*, Ithaca, NY: Cornell University Press.

Gowalkar, M. S. (1939) *We, or Our Nationhood Defined*, Nagpur: Bharat.

—— (1966) *Bunch of Thoughts*, Bangalore: Vikrama Prakashan.

Gress, David (1998) *From Plato to NATO: The Idea of the West and its Opponents*, New York: Free Press.

Grossberg, Kenneth (1976a) "Bakufu Bugyonoin: The Size of the Lower Bureaucracy in Muromachi Japan," *Journal of Asiatic Studies*, 35(4): 651–4.

—— (1976b) "From Feudal Chieftans to Secular Monarch: The Development of Shogunal Power in Early Muromachi Japan," *Monumenta Nipponica*, 31(1): 29–49.

Ha, U-bong (1994) "Chosŏn chŏngiui taeil kwangye" [Early Choson's Foreign Policy toward Japan], in Jo Hang-rae, Ha U-bong, and Son Seung-Chol (eds), *Kangjwa hanil kwangyesa* [*Lectures on Korea–Japan Relations*], Seoul: Hyonumsa.

Haas, Ernst B. (1997) *Nationalism, Liberalism and Progress*, Vol. 1: *The Rise and Decline of Nationalism*, Ithaca, NY: Cornell University Press.

—— (2000) *Nationalism, Liberalism, and Progress*, Vol. 2: *The Dismal Fate of New Nations*, Ithaca, NY: Cornell University Press.

Habermas, Jürgen (1990) *The Philosophical Discourse of Modernity: Twelve Lectures*, Cambridge, MA: MIT Press.

Habermas, Jürgen, and Derrida, Jacques (2005) "February 15, or, What Binds Europeans Together: Plea for a Common European Policy, Beginning in Core Europe," in Daniel Levy, Max Pensky, and John Torpey (eds), *Old Europe, New Europe, Core Europe: Transatlantic Relations after the Iraq War*, London and New York: Verso, pp. 3–13.

Hall, Martin, and Jackson, Patrick Thaddeus (2007a) "Introduction: Civilizations and International Relations Theory," in Martin Hall and Patrick Thaddeus Jackson (eds), *Civilizational Identity: The Production and Reproduction of "Civilizations" in International Relations*, New York: Palgrave, pp. 1–12.

—— (eds) (2007b) *Civilizational Identity: The Production and Reproduction of "Civilizations" in International Relations*, New York: Palgrave.

Hall, Peter A. (1986) *Governing the Economy: The Politics of State Intervention in Britain and France (Europe and the International Order)*, New York: Oxford University Press.

Hall, Rodney Bruce (1997) "Moral Authority as a Power Resource," *International Organization*, 51: 591–622.

—— (1999) *National Collective Identity: Social Constructs and International Systems*, New York: Columbia University Press.

Hamashita, Takeshi (2008) *China, East Asia, and the Global Economy: Regional and Historical Perspectives*, ed. Linda Grove and Mark Selden, London: Routledge.

Harootunian, Harry (2006) "Japan's Long Postwar: The Trick of Memory and the Ruse of History," in Tomiko Yoda and Harry Harootunian (eds), *Japan after Japan: Social and Cultural Life from the Recessionary 1990s to the Present*, Durham, NC: Duke University Press, pp. 98–121.

Harrison, Lawrence E. (2006) *The Central Liberal Truth: How Politics Can Change a Culture and Save it from Itself*, Oxford and New York: Oxford University Press.

Harrison, Lawrence E., and Huntington, Samuel (eds) (2000) *Culture Matters: How Human Values Shape Human Progress*, New York: Basic Books.

Hart, D. G., and Muether, John R. (2007) *Seeking a Better Country: 300 Years of American Presbyterianism*, Phillipsburg, NJ: P&R.

Hartz, Louis (1955) *The Liberal Tradition in America*, New York: Harcourt, Brace.

Hatch, Walter, and Yamamura, Kozo (1996) *Asia in Japan's Embrace: Building a Regional Production Alliance*, Cambridge: Cambridge University Press.

Hawley, Samuel (2005) *The Imjin War*, Berkeley, CA: University of California Press.

Heer, Nicholas (ed.) (1990) *Islamic Law and Jurisprudence: Studies in Honor of Farhat J. Ziadeh*, Seattle, WA: University of Washington Press.

Hellyer, Robert W. (2002) "Historical and Contemporary Perspectives on the Sakoku Theme in Japanese Foreign Relations: 1600–2000," *Social Science Japan Journal*, 5(2): 255–9.

Hemming, Ann (1999) "Civilization as Rhetoric," *Comparative Civilizations Review*, 40: 76–89.

Henderson, Errol A., and Tucker, Richard (2001) "Clear and Present Strangers: The Clash of Civilizations and International Conflict," *International Studies Quarterly*, 45: 317–38.

Herzog, Roman (1999) *Preventing the Clash of Civilizations: A Peace Strategy for the Twenty-First Century*, New York: St Martin's Press.

Hevia, James (1995) *Cherishing Men from Afar: Qing Guest Ritual and the Macartney Embassy of 1793*, Durham, NC: Duke University Press.

Hirschman, Albert O. (1970) *Exit, Voice, and Loyalty: Responses to Decline in Firms, Organizations, and States*, Cambridge, MA: Harvard University Press.

Ho, Ping-ti (1998) "In Defense of Sinicization: A Rebuttal of Evelyn Rawski's 'Reenvisioning the Quing,'" *Journal of Asian Studies*, 57(1): 123–55.

Hobson, John M. (2004) *The Eastern Origins of Western Civilisation*, New York: Cambridge University Press.

—— (2007) "Deconstructing the Eurocentric Clash of Civilization: De-westernizing the West by Acknowledging the Dialogue of Civilizations," in Martin Hall and Patrick Thaddeus Jackson (eds), *Civilizational Identity*, New York: Palgrave, pp. 149–66.

Hobson, John M., and Sharman, J. C. (2005) "The Enduring Place of Hierarchy in World Politics: Tracing the Social Logics of Hierarchy and Political Change," *European Journal of International Relations*, 11(1): 63–98.

Hodgson, Marshall G. S. (1974) *The Venture of Islam: Conscience and History in a World Civilization*, 3 vols, Chicago: University of Chicago Press.

—— (1993) *Rethinking World History: Essays on Europe, Islam and World History* (ed. Edmund Burke IV), Cambridge: Cambridge University Press.

Hogan, Michael J. (ed.) (1999) *The Ambiguous Legacy: U.S. Foreign Relations in the "American Century,"* New York: Cambridge University Press.

Hollister, J. N. (1979) *The Shia of India*, Delhi: Munshiram Manoharlal.

Holzner, Burkart (1982) "The Civilization Analytic Frame of Reference: Benjamin Nelson and the Foundations of Cultural Sociology," *Comparative Civilizations Review*, 8: 15–30.

Huntington, Samuel P. (1968) *Political Order in Changing Societies*, New Haven, CT: Yale University Press.

—— (1993) "The Clash of Civilizations?" *Foreign Affairs*, 72(3): 22–49.

—— (1996) *The Clash of Civilizations and the Remaking of World Order*, New York: Simon & Schuster.

—— (2004a) "The Hispanic Challenge," *Foreign Policy* (March–April): 31–45.

—— (2004b) *Who Are We? The Challenges to America's National Identity*, New York: Simon & Schuster.

Hutchins, Francis G. (1967) *The Illusion of Permanence: British Imperialism in India*, Princeton, NJ: Princeton University Press.

Ibn Khaldun (2005) *The Muqaddimah: An Introduction to History*, trans. Franz Rosenthal, abridged N. J. Dawood, intro. Bruce B. Lawrence, Princeton, NJ: Princeton University Press.

Ifversen, Jan (2002) "The Crisis of European Civilization after 1918," in Menno Spiering and Michael Wintle (eds), *Ideas of Europe since 1914: The Legacy of the First World War*, New York: Palgrave MacMillan, pp. 14–31.

Ikegami, Eiko (1997) *The Taming of the Samurai: Honorific Individualism and the Making of Modern Japan*, Cambridge, MA: Harvard University Press.

Inayatullah, Naeem, and Blaney, David L. (1996) "Knowing Encounters: Beyond Parochialism in International Relations Theory," in Yosef Lapid and Friedrich Kratochwil (eds), *The Return of Culture and Identity in IR Theory*, Boulder, CO: Lynne Rienner, pp. 65–84.

—— (2004) *International Relations and the Problem of Difference*, London: Routledge.

Irwin, Robert (1996) "The Emergence of the Islamic World System 1000–1500," in Frances Robinson (ed.), *The Cambridge Illustrated History of the Islamic World*, Cambridge: Cambridge University Press.

Ishida, Hiroshi (1993) *Social Mobility in Contemporary Japan*, Stanford, CA: Stanford University Press.

Islam, Shafiqul (1993) "Foreign Aid and Burdensharing: Is Japan Freeriding to a Coprosperity Sphere in Pacific Asia?" in Jeffrey A. Frankel and Miles Kahler (eds), *Regionalism and Rivalry: Japan and the United States in Pacific Asia*, Chicago: University of Chicago Press, pp. 321–90.

Ivy, Marilyn (1995) *Discourses of the Vanishing: Modernity, Phantasm, Japan*, Chicago: University of Chicago Press.

Iwabuchi, Koichi (2002) *Recentering Globalization: Popular Culture and Japanese Transnationalism*, Durham, NC: Duke University Press.

Jackson, Patrick Thaddeus (2004) "Whose Identity? Rhetorical Commonplaces of American Wartime Foreign Policy," in Patricia M. Goff and Kevin C. Dunn (eds), *Identity and Global Politics: Empirical and Theoretical Elaborations*, New York: Palgrave, pp. 169–89.

—— (2006) *Civilizing the Enemy: German Reconstruction and the Invention of the West*, Ann Arbor, MI: University of Michigan Press.

—— (2007) "Civilizations as Actors: A Transactional Account," in Martin Hall and Patrick Thaddeus Jackson (eds), *Civilizational Identity*, New York: Palgrave, pp. 33–49.

—— (2008) "Foregrounding Ontology: Dualism, Monism, and IR Theory," *Review of International Studies*, 34: 129–53.

Jackson, Patrick Thaddeus, and Nexon, Daniel H. (1999) "Relations before States: Substance, Process, and the Study of World Politics," *European Journal of International Relations*, 5: 291–332.

Jagchid, Sechin, and Symons, Van Jay (1989) *Peace, War, and Trade along the Great Wall: Nomadic–Chinese Interaction through Two Millennia*, Bloomington: Indiana University Press.

James, Harold (2006) *The Roman Predicament: How the Rules of International Order Create the Politics of Empire*, Princeton, NJ: Princeton University Press.

Jansen, Marius (1992) *China in the Tokugawa World*, Cambridge, MA: Harvard University Press.

Jaspers, Karl (1953) *The Origin and the Goal of History*, London: Routledge & Kegan Paul.

Jenco, Leigh Kathryn (2005) "'What Does Heaven Ever Say?' The Challenge of Chinese Classicism to the Western Model of Cross-Cultural Dialogue," paper delivered at the annual meeting of the American Political Science Association, 1–4 September.

Jessop, Bob (1990) *State Theory: Putting Capitalist States in their Place*, University Park, PA: Pennsylvania State University Press.

Jha, N. and Rajaram, N. S. (2000) *The Deciphered Indus Scripts: Methodology, Readings, Interpretations*, New Delhi: Aditya Prakashan.

Joas, Hans (1997) *The Creativity of Action*, Chicago: University of Chicago Press.

Johnston, Alastair Iain (1995) *Cultural Realism: Strategic Culture and Grand Strategy in Chinese History*, Princeton, NJ: Princeton University Press.

Judt, Tony (2005) *Postwar: A History of Europe since 1945*, New York: Penguin.

Kagan, Robert (2003) *Of Paradise and Power: America and Europe in the New World Order*, New York: Knopf.

Kang, David C. (2007) *China Rising: Peace, Power, and Order in East Asia*, New York: Columbia University Press.

Kang, Etsuko (1997) *Diplomacy and Ideology in Japanese–Korean Relations: From the Fifteenth to the Eighteenth Century*, New York: St Martin's Press.

Kasahara, Shigehisa (2004) "The Flying Geese Paradigm: A Critical Study of its Application to East Asian Regional Development," discussion paper, United Nations Conference on Trade and Development, available at: http://www.unctad.org/en/docs/osgdp20043_en.pdf (accessed 22 July 2008).

Katzenstein, Peter J. (2005) *A World of Regions: Asia and Europe in the American Imperium*, Ithaca, NY: Cornell University Press.

Kaviraj, Sudipta, and Khilnani, Sunil (eds) (2001), *Civil Society: History and Possibilities*, Cambridge: Cambridge University Press.

Kavolis, Vytautas (1982) "Social Movements and Civilizational Processes," *Comparative Civilizations Review*, 8: 31–58.

Kawazoe, Noboru (1994) *Rettō bunmei: umi to mori no seikatsushi* [*Civilization of the Archipelago: Lifestyle Records of the Ocean and Forest*], Tokyo: Heibonsha.

Keal, Paul (2003) *European Conquest and the Rights of Indigenous Peoples: The Moral Backwardness of International Society*, Cambridge: Cambridge University Press.

Keay, John (2001) *India Discovered: The Recovery of a Lost Civilization*, London: Harper Collins.

Keene, Donald (1974) "Literature," in Arthur E. Tiedemann (ed.), *An Introduction to Japanese Civilization*, New York: Columbia University Press.

Keene, Edward (2002) *Beyond the Anarchical Society: Grotius, Colonialism and Order in World Politics*, Cambridge: Cambridge University Press.

Kejariwal, O. P. (1988) *The Asiatic Society of Bengal and the Discovery of India's Past, 1784 to 1838*, New Delhi and New York: Oxford University Press.

Keyes, Charles (2002) "The Peoples of Asia: Science and Politics in the Classification of Ethnic Groups in Thailand, China, and Vietnam," *Journal of Asian Studies*, 61(4): 1163–203.

Khan, Dominique-sila (1995) "Ramdeo Pir and the Kamadiya Panth," in N. K. Singhi and Rajendra Joshi (eds), *Folk, Faith and Feudalism*, Jaipur and New Delhi: Rawat, pp. 295–327.

Khanna, Parag (2008) *The Second World: Empires and Influence in the New Global Order*, New York: Random House.

Khazanov, Anatoli M. (1984) *Nomads and the Outside World*, Cambridge: Cambridge University Press.

Kim, Young-soo (2006) *Kŏngukui chŏngch'i: yŏmal sŏncho, hyŏkmyŏnggwa munmyŏng jonhwa* [*The Politics of Founding the Nation: Revolution and Transition of Civilization during the late Koryŏ and early Choson*], Seoul: Yeehaksa.

Kocka, Jürgen (2001) "Multiple Modernities and Negotiated Universals," paper prepared for the conference on Multiple Modernities, Social Science Research Center (WZB), Berlin, 5–7 May.

Kondo, Seiichi (2008) "Wielding Soft Power: The Key Stages of Transmission and Reception," in Watanabe Yasushi and David L. McConnell (eds), *Soft Power Superpowers: Cultural and National Assets of Japan and the United States*, Armonk, NY: M. E. Sharpe, pp. 191–206.

Koschmann, J. Victor (1997) "Asianism's Ambivalent Legacy," in Peter J. Katzenstein and Takashi Shiraishi (eds), *Network Power: Japan in Asia*, Ithaca, NY: Cornell University Press, pp. 83–110.

—— (2006) "National Subjectivity and the Uses of Atonement in the Age of Recession," in Tomiko Yoda and Harry Harootunian (eds), *Japan after Japan*, Durham, NC: Duke University Press, pp. 122–41.

Krasner, Stephen (2001) "Organized Hypocrisy in Nineteenth-Century East Asia," *International Relations of the Asia-Pacific*, 1: 173–97.

Krebs, Ronald R., and Jackson, Patrick Thaddeus (2007) "Twisting Tongues and Twisting Arms: The Power of Political Rhetoric," *European Journal of International Relations*, 13(1): 35–66.

Kumar, Krishan (2008) "The Question of European Identity: Europe in the American Mirror," *European Journal of Social Theory*, 11(1): 87–105.

Kupchan, Charles (2002) *The End of the American Era: U.S. Foreign Policy and the Geopolitics of the Twenty-First Century*, New York: Knopf.

Kurth, James (1998) "The Protestant Deformation and American Foreign Policy," *Orbis*, 42(2): 221–39.

—— (2001a) "America and the West: Global Triumph or Western Twilight," *Orbis*, 45(3): 333–41.

—— (2001b) "Religion and Ethnic Conflict – In Theory," *Orbis*, 45(2): 281–94.

—— (2003) "Western Civilization, Our Tradition," *Intercollegiate Review*, 39(1): 5–13.

—— (2004) "The Late American Nation," *National Interest*, 77 (Fall): 117–26.

—— (2005) "The Protestant Deformation," *American Interest*, 1(2): 4–16.

Laitin, David D. (2008) "American Immigration through Comparativists' Eyes," *Comparative Politics*, 41(1): 103–20.

Lake, David (2009) *Hierarchy in International Relations*, Ithaca, NY: Cornell University Press.

Lam, Peng-er (2007) "Japan's Quest for 'Soft Power': Attraction and Limitation," *East Asia*, 24(4): 349–63.

Laroui, Abdullah (1977) *The History of the Maghrib*, trans. R. Manheim, Princeton, NJ: Princeton University Press.

Ledyard, Gari (2006) Posting on the Korea Web, 22 March, available at: http://korea web.ws.

Lee, Chong-sin (2004) *Koryŏ sidaeui chŏngch'i pyŏndonggwa daeoejŏngch'aek* [*Political Changes and Foreign Policy of Goryo*], Seoul: Gyongin Munwhasa.

Lee, Jang-hee (1999) *Imjin waeransa yŏngu* [*Research on the History of the Imjin War*], Seoul: Asea Munwhasa.

Leheny, David (2003) *The Rules of Play: National Identity and the Shaping of Japanese Leisure*, Ithaca, NY: Cornell University Press.

—— (2006a) "A Narrow Place to Cross Swords: Soft Power and the Politics of Japanese Popular Culture in Asia," in Peter J. Katzenstein and Takashi Shiraishi (eds), *Beyond Japan: The Dynamics of East Asian Regionalism*, Ithaca, NY: Cornell University Press, pp. 211–33.

—— (2006b) *Think Global, Fear Local: Sex, Violence, and Anxiety in Contemporary Japan*, Ithaca, NY: Cornell University Press.

Levine, Donald N. (1995) *Visions of the Sociological Tradition*, Chicago: University of Chicago Press.

—— (2004) "Note on the Concept of an Axial Turning in Human History," in Saïd Amir Arjomand and Edward A. Tiryakian (eds), *Rethinking Civilizational Analysis*, London and Thousand Oaks, CA: Sage, pp. 67–70.

Lewis, Bernard (1987) *The Jews of Islam*, Princeton, NJ: Princeton University Press.

—— (2002) *What Went Wrong? Western Impact and Middle Eastern Response*, Oxford: Oxford University Press.

Lewis, Mark Edward (2007) *The Early Chinese Empires: Qin and Han*, Cambridge, MA: Harvard University Press.

Lewis, Martin W., and Wigen, Kären E. (1997) *The Myth of Continents: A Critique of Metageography*, Berkeley, CA: University of California Press.

Lieberman, Victor (1993) "Local Integration and Eurasian Analogies: Structuring Southeast Asian History, c. 1350–c. 1830," *Modern Asian Studies*, 27(3): 475–572.

—— (2003) *Strange Parallels: Southeast Asia in Global Context, c. 800–1830*, Vol. 1: *Integration on the Mainland*, Cambridge: Cambridge University Press.

Limbach, Jutta (2005) "Making Multiculturalism Work," 17 August, available at: http://www.signandsight.com/features/313.html (accessed 16 August 2008).

Linklater, Andrew (2004) "Norbert Elias, the 'Civilizing Process' and the Sociology of International Relations," *International Politics*, 41: 3–35.

Liska, George (1967) *Imperial America: The International Politics of Primacy*, Baltimore, MD: Johns Hopkins University Press.

Luce, Henry R. (1941) *The American Century*, New York: Farrar & Reinhart.

McAmis, Robert D. (2002) *Malay Muslims: The History and Challenge of Resurgent Islam in Southeast Asia*, Grand Rapids, MI: William B. Eerdmans.

MacDonald, Paul K. (2007) "Networks of Domination: Social Ties and Imperial Governance in International Politics," unpublished paper, American Academy of Arts and Sciences, 1 September.

McGray, Douglas (2002) "Japan's Gross National Cool," *Foreign Policy* (May/June): 44–54, available at: http://www.douglasmcgray.com/grossnationalcool.pdf (accessed 28 January 2009).

McNeill, William H. (1963) *The Rise of the West: A History of the Human Community*, Chicago: University of Chicago Press.

—— (1990) "*The Rise of the West* after Twenty-Five Years," *Journal of World History*, 1: 1–21.

—— (1992) *The Global Condition: Conquerors, Catastrophes, and Community*, Princeton, NJ: Princeton University Press.

Majumdar, R. C., Raychaudhuri, H. C., and Datta, Kalikinkar (1953) *An Advanced History of India*, London: Macmillan.

Mandalios, John (2003) "Civilizational Complexes and Processes: Elias, Nelson and Eisenstadt," in Gerard Delanty and Engin F. Isin (eds), *Handbook of Historical Sociology*, Thousand Oaks, CA: Sage, pp. 65–79.

Mandaville, Peter (2007) "The Heterarchic *Umma*: Reading Islamic Civilization from Within," in Martin Hall and Patrick Thaddeus Jackson (eds), *Civilizational Identity*, New York: Palgrave, pp. 135–48.

—— (2008) *Global Political Islam*, London and New York: Routledge.

Mandelbaum, Michael (2002) *The Ideas that Conquered the World: Peace, Democracy, and Free Markets in the Twenty-First Century*, New York: Public Affairs.

Mann, Michael (1986) *The Sources of Social Power*, Vol. 1: *From the Beginning to 1760 AD*, New York: Cambridge University Press.

—— (1993) *The Sources of Social Power*, Vol. 2: *The Rise of Classes and Nation-States, 1760–1914*, New York: Cambridge University Press.

Manners, Ian (2002) "Normative Power Europe: A Contradiction in Terms?" *Journal of Common Market Studies*, 40(2): 235–58.

—— (2006a) "The European Union as a Normative Power: A Response to Thomas Diez," *Millennium*, 35(1): 167–80.

—— (2006b) "Normative Power Europe Reconsidered: Beyond the Crossroads," *Journal of European Public Policy*, 13(2): 182–99.

Markovits, Andrei S. (2007) Book Review of Jackson (2006), *Perspectives on Politics*, 5(3): 662–3.

Mayaram, Shail (1997) *Resisting Regimes: Myth, Memory and the Shaping of a Muslim Identity*, New York: Oxford University Press.

Mazlish, Bruce (2001) "Civilization in Historical and Global Perspective," *International Sociology*, 16(3): 293–300.

—— (2004a) *Civilization and its Contents*, Stanford, CA: Stanford University Press.

—— (2004b) "Civilization in a Historical and Global Perspective," in Saïd Amir Arjomand and Edward A. Tiryakian (eds), *Rethinking Civilizational Analysis*, London and Thousand Oaks, CA: Sage, pp. 14–19.

Mead, Walter Russell (2007) *God and Gold: Britain, America, and the Making of the Modern World*, New York: Knopf.

Mehta, Uday Singh (1999) *Liberalism and Empire: A Study in Nineteenth-Century British Liberal Thought*, Chicago: University of Chicago Press.

Melko, Matthew (1969) *The Nature of Civilizations*, Boston: F. Porter Sargent.

Melleuish, Gregory (2000) "The Clash of Civilizations: A Model of Historical Development?" *Thesis Eleven*, 62: 109–20.

Mennell, Stephen (1992) "Norbert Elias," in Peter Beilharz (ed.), *Social Theory: A Guide to Central Thinkers*, Sydney: Allen & Unwin, pp. 76–83.

—— (1996) "Civilizing and Decivilizing Processes," in Johan Goudsblom, Eric L. Jones, and Stephen Mennell (eds), *The Course of Human History: Economic Growth, Social Process and Civilization*, London: M. E. Sharpe, pp. 101–16.

—— (2007) *The American Civilizing Process*, Cambridge: Polity.

Mennell, Stephen, and Goudsblom, Johan (1997) "Civilizing Processes: Myth or Reality? A Comment on Duerr's Critique of Elias," *Comparative Studies in Society and History*, 39(4): 729–33.

Menocal, Maria R. (2002) *The Ornament of the World: How Muslims, Jews and Christians Created a Culture of Tolerance in Medieval Spain*, Boston: Little, Brown.

Meyer, John W. (1994) "The Changing Cultural Content of the Nation-State: A World Society Perspective," unpublished paper, Stanford University, Palo Alto, CA (January).

Meyer, John W., Boli, John, Thomas, George M., and Ramirez, Francisco (1997) "World Society and the Nation-State," *American Journal of Sociology*, 103(1): 144–81.

Miliband, David (2007) "Europe 2030: Model Power Not Superpower," speech at the College of Europe, Bruges, 15 November, available at: http://www.brugesgroup.com/MilibandBrugesSpeech.pdf (accessed 29 December 2008).

Mill, James (1968) *A History of British India*, 6 vols, New York: Chelsea House Publishers.

Mill, John Stuart (1985) "Considerations on Representative Government," in *Three Essays*, Oxford: Oxford University Press.

Mitchell, Timothy (1991) "The Limits of the State: Beyond Statist Approaches and their Critics," *American Political Science Review*, 85: 77–96.

Mitter, Partha (1992) *Much Maligned Monsters*, Chicago: University of Chicago Press.

Mitzen, Jennifer (2006) "Anchoring Europe's Civilizing Identity: Habits, Capabilities and Ontological Security," *Journal of European Public Policy*, 13(2): 270–85.

MOFA (Ministry of Foreign Affairs) (2004) "Dai-ni-kai chūtō bunka kōryū/taiwa misshon: hōkoku to teigen" [Second Middle East Cultural Exchange and Dialogue Mission: Report and Recommendations], Tokyo: MOFA, November, available at: http://www.mofa.go.jp/mofaj/gaiko/culture/topics/pdfs/houkokuteigen2.pdf (accessed 14 July 2008).

Moravcsik, Andrew (2002) "The Quiet Superpower," *Newsweek*, 17 June.

—— (2003) "How Europe Can Win without an Army," *Financial Times*, 3 April, available at: http://www.princeton.edu/~amoravcs/library/FT_4-3-03.pdf (accessed 9 August 2008).

Moreau, Joseph (2003) *Schoolbook Nation: Conflicts over American History Textbooks from the Civil War to the Present*, Ann Arbor, MI: University of Michigan Press.

Mote, Frederick (ed.) (1988) *The Cambridge History of China*, Vol. 7: *The Ming Dynasty, 1368–1644, Part 1*, Cambridge: Cambridge University Press.

Motyl, Alexander J. (1999) *Revolutions, Nations, Empires: Conceptual Limits and Theoretical Possibilities*, New York: Columbia University Press.

—— (2001) *Imperial Ends: The Decay, Collapse, and Revival of Empires*, New York: Columbia University Press.

—— (2006) "Is Everything Empire? Is Empire Everything?" *Comparative Politics*, 39: 226–49.

Mozaffari, Mehdi (2001) "The Transformationalist Perspective and the Rise of a Global Standard of Civilization," *International Relations of the Asia-Pacific*, 1: 247–61.

—— (ed.) (2002) *Globalization and Civilizations*, New York: Routledge.

Muller, Friedrich Max (1855) *The Languages of the Seat of War in the East, with a Survey of the Three Families of Language, Semitic, Arian, and Turanian*, 2nd edn, London: Williams & Norgate.

Münkler, Herfried (2007) *Empires*, trans. Patrick Camiller, Cambridge: Polity.

Musallam, Bassam (1996) "The Ordering of Muslim Societies," in Frances Robinson (ed.), *The Cambridge Illustrated History of the Islamic World*, Cambridge: Cambridge University Press.

Nandy, Ashis (1989) "Reconstructing Childhood: A Critique of the Ideology of Adulthood," in Ashis Nandy, *Traditions, Tyranny and Utopias: Essays in the Politics of Awareness*, Delhi: Oxford University Press, pp. 56–76.

Nelson, Benjamin (1973) "Civilizational Complexes and Intercivilizational Encounters," *Sociological Analysis*, 34(2): 79–105.

Nettl, J. P. (1968) "The State as a Conceptual Variable," *World Politics*, 20(4): 559–92.

Nexon, Daniel (2007a) "Discussion: American Empire and Civilizational Practice," in Martin Hall and Patrick Thaddeus Jackson (eds), *Civilizational Identity*, New York: Palgrave, pp. 109–16.

—— (2007b) "What's This, Then? 'Romanes Eunt Domus'?," paper presented at the annual meeting of the American Political Science Association, Chicago, 30 August–2 September.

Nexon, Daniel, and Wright, Thomas (2007) "What's at Stake in the American Empire Debate?" *American Political Science Review*, 101(2): 253–72.

Nicolaïdis, Kalypso (2003) "Greek EU Presidency. Contribution on the Issue of EU–USA Relations to the Informal General Affairs and External Relations Council," 2–3 May.

Nicolaïdis, Kalypso, and Howse, Robert (2002) "'This is My EUtopia . . .': Narrative as Power," *Journal of Common Market Studies*, 40(4): 767–92.

Nicolaïdis, Kalypso, and Nicolaïdis, Dimitri (2006) "The EuroMed beyond Civilizational Paradigms," in Emanuel Adler, Federica Bicchi, Beverly Crawford, and Raffaella A. Del Sarto (eds), *The Convergence of Civilizations: Constructing a Mediterranean Region*, Toronto: University of Toronto Press, pp. 337–78.

Nishikawa, Shunsaku ([1993] 2000) "Fukuzawa Yukichi," *Prospects: The Quarterly Review of Comparative Education*, 23(3/4): 493–506; repr. UNESCO International Bureau of Education, 2000, available at: http://www.ibe.unesco.org/fileadmin/user_upload/archive/publications/ThinkersPdf/fukuzawe.pdf (accessed 23 July 2008).

Nolan, Janne E. (ed.) (1994) *Global Engagement: Cooperation and Security in the 21st Century*, Washington, DC: Brookings Institution.

Nye, Joseph S., Jr. (1990a) *Bound to Lead: The Changing Nature of American Power*, New York: Basic Books.

—— (1990b) "Soft Power," *Foreign Policy*, 80: 153–71.

—— (2004) *Soft Power: The Means to Success in World Politics*, New York: Public Affairs.

—— (2006) "Interview with Joseph S. Nye, Jr., July 2006," USAPC Washington Report, available at: http://www.eastwestcenter.org/fileadmin/resources/washington/nye.pdf (accessed 13 July 2008).

Oguma, Eiji (1995) *Tan'itsu minzoku shinwa no kigen: 'nihonjin' no jigazō no keifu* [*The Myth of the Homogeneous Nation: A Genealogy of the Meaning of Japaneseness*], Tokyo: Shin'yōsha.

Onuf, Nicholas G. (1989) *World of our Making: Rules and Rule in Social Theory and International Relations*, Columbia, SC: University of South Carolina Press.

Oros, Andrew (2008) *Normalizing Japan: Politics, Identity, and the Evolution of Security Practice*, Stanford, CA: Stanford University Press.

Osamu, Oba (1980) *Sino-Japanese Relations in the Edo Period*, trans. Joshua A. Fogel, Tokyo: Toho Shoten, available at: http://chinajapan.org/archive.html.

Osterhammel, Jürgen (1995) "Jenseits der Orthodoxie: Imperium, Raum, Herrschaft und Kultur als Dimensionen von Imperialismustheorie," *Periplus 1995: Jahrbuch für aussereuropäische Geschichte*, 5: 119–31.

—— (1998) *Die Entzauberung Asiens: Europa und die asiatischen Reiche im 18. Jahrhundert*, Munich: C. H. Beck.

—— (2001) *Geschichtswissenschaft jenseits des Nationalstaats: Studien zu Beziehungsgeschichte und Zivilisationsvergleich*, Göttingen: Vandenhoeck & Ruprecht.

—— (2005) "'The Great Work of Uplifting Mankind': Zivilisierungsmission und Moderne," in Boris Barth and Jürgen Osterhammel (eds), *Zivilisierungsmissionen*, Konstanz: UVK Verlagsgesellschaft, pp. 363–425.

Otmazgin, Nissim Kadosh (2007) "Regionalizing Culture: The Political Economy of Japanese Culture in East and Southeast Asia, 1988–2005," PhD dissertation, Graduate School of Asian and African Area Studies, Kyoto University.

—— (2008) "Contesting Soft Power: Japanese Popular Culture in East and Southeast Asia," *International Relations of the Asia-Pacific*, 8: 73–101.

Ottolenghi, Emanuele (2005) "Can Europe Do Away with Nationalism," *American Enterprise Institute for Public Policy Research, New Atlantic Initiative*, May–June.

Park, Eugene (2006) "War and Peace in Premodern Korea: Institutional and Ideological Dimensions," in Young-Key Kim-Renaud, R. Richard Grinker, and Kirk

W. Larsen (eds), *The Military and Korean Society*, Sigur Center Asia Papers, no. 26, Washington, DC: George Washington University, pp. 1–14.

Pasha, Mustapha Kamal (2007) "Civilizations, Postorientalism and Islam," in Martin Hall and Patrick Thaddeus Jackson (eds), *Civilizational Identity*, New York: Palgrave, pp. 61–79.

Patomäki, Heikki, and Wight, Colin (2000) "After Postpositivism? The Promises of Critical Realism," *International Studies Quarterly*, 44: 213–37.

Patten, Chris (2003) "Wider Europe-Neighborhood: Proposed New Framework for Relations with the EU's Eastern and Southern Neighbors," European Union, Directorate General of External Relations, 11 March.

Perdue, Peter (2005) *China Marches West: The Qing Conquest of Central Eurasia*, Cambridge, MA: Harvard University Press.

Petersson, Niels P. (2005) "Markt, Zivilisierungsmission und Imperialismus," in Boris Barth and Jürgen Osterhammel (eds), *Zivilisierungsmissionen*, Konstanz: UVK Verlagsgesellschaft, pp. 33–54.

Phillips, Andrew B. (2008) "Soldiers of God: War, Faith, Empire and the Transformation of International Orders from Calvin to Al Qaeda," PhD dissertation, Cornell University.

Pierson, Paul (2004) *Politics in Time: History, Institutions, and Social Analysis*, Princeton, NJ: Princeton University Press.

Pike, Kenneth L. (1967) *Language in Relation to a Unified Theory of the Structure of Human Behavior*, 2nd edn, The Hague: Mouton De Gruyter.

Polanyi, Karl (1957) *The Great Transformation: The Political and Economic Origins of our Time*, Boston: Beacon Press.

Pollack, David (1986) *The Fracture of Meaning: Japan's Synthesis of China from the Eighth through the Eighteenth Centuries*, Princeton, NJ: Princeton University Press.

Pollock, Sheldon (1996) "The Sanskrit Cosmopolis, 300–1300: Transculturation, Vernacularization, and the Question of Ideology," in Jan E. M. Houben (ed.), *Ideology and Status of Sanskrit: Contributions to the History of the Sanskrit Language*, Leiden and New York: E. J. Brill.

—— (2006) *The Language of the Gods in the World of Men: Sanskrit, Culture, and Power in Premodern India*, Berkeley, CA: University of California Press.

Poulantzas, Nicos (2008) *The Poulantzas Reader: Marxism, Law and the State*, London: Verso.

Pouliot, Vincent (2008) "The Logic of Practicality: A Theory of Practice of Security Communities," *International Organization*, 62(2): 257–88.

Prasad, Bimal (ed.) (1994) *Swami Vivekananda: An Anthology*, New Delhi: Vikas.

Puchala, Donald J. (1997) "International Encounters of Another Kind," *Global Society*, 11(1): 5–29.

—— (2003) *Theory and History in International Relations*, New York: Routledge.

Pye, Lucian W. (1990) "China: Erratic State, Frustrated Society," *Foreign Affairs*, 69(4): 56–74.

Ragin, Charles C. (2000) *Fuzzy-Set Social Science*, Chicago: University of Chicago Press.

Ragin, Charles, and Chirot, Daniel (1984) "The World System of Immanuel Wallerstein: Sociology and Politics as History," in Theda Skocpol (ed.), *Vision and Method in Historical Sociology*, Cambridge: Cambridge University Press.

Reckwitz, Andreas (2002) "Toward a Theory of Social Practices: A Development in Culturalist Theorizing," *European Journal of Social Theory*, 5(2): 243–63.

Rescher, Nicholas (1996) *Process Metaphysics*, Albany: SUNY Press.

Reus-Smit, Christopher (1997) "The Constitutional Structure of International Society and the Nature of Fundamental Institutions," *International Organization*, 51(4): 555–89.

Ribeiro, Darcy (1968) *The Civilizational Process*, Washington, DC: Smithsonian Institution Press.

Richardson, J. S. (1991) "Imperium Romanum: Empire and the Language of Power," *Journal of Roman Studies*, 81: 1–9.

Rifkin, Jeremy (2004) *The European Dream*, New York: Tarcher/Penguin.

Ringmar, Erik (1996) *Identity, Interest and Action*, Cambridge: Cambridge University Press.

—— (2007) "Empowerment among Nations: A Sociological Perspective," in Felix Berenskoetter and M. J. Williams (eds), *Power in World Politics*, London and New York: Routledge, pp. 189–203.

Risse, Thomas (2004) "Beyond Iraq: The Crisis of the Transatlantic Security Community," in David Held and Mathias Koenig-Archibugi (eds), *American Power in the Twenty-First Century*, Cambridge: Polity, pp. 214–40.

Robertson, Jennifer (1988) "Furusato Japan: The Culture and Politics of Nostalgia," *International Journal of Politics, Culture, and Society*, 1(4): 494–518.

Robinson, Kenneth (2000) "Centering the King of Choson: Aspects of Korean Maritime Diplomacy, 1392–1592," *Journal of Asian Studies*, 59(1): 109–25.

Rogers, John M. (2000) *Empire of the Sultans: Ottoman Art from the Khalili Collection*, London: Nour Foundation.

Roh, Gye-hyun (1993) *Yŏmong oegyosa* [*Diplomatic History of Koryŏ-Mongol Relations*], Seoul: Gapin Press.

Roland, Alex (2005) "Review of Kenneth Chase, *Firearms: A Global History to 1700*," *Journal of Interdisciplinary History*, 35(4): 617–19.

Rorty, Richard (1993) "Human Rights, Rationality, and Sentimentality," in Stephen Shute and Susan Hurley (eds), *On Human Rights: The Oxford Amnesty Lectures 1993*, New York: Basic Books, pp. 111–34.

Rossabi, Morris (1983) *China among Equals*, Berkeley, CA: University of California Press.

Roy, Olivier (2004) *Globalized Islam: The Search for a New Ummah*, New York: Columbia University Press.

Rudolph, Lloyd I. (2007) "Tod v. Mill: Clashing Perspectives on British Rule in India: An Analysis Based on James Tod's and James Mill's 32 Parliamentary Testimony," in Giles Tillotson (ed.), *Tod's Rajasthan*, Mumbai: Marg.

Rudolph, Lloyd I., and Rudolph, Susanne Hoeber (1983) "Rethinking Secularism: Genesis and Implications of the Textbook Controversy, 1977–79," *Pacific Affairs*, 56(1): 15–37.

—— (1985), "The Subcontinental Empire and the Regional Kingdoms in Indian State Formation," in Paul Wallace (ed.), *Region and Nation in India*, New Delhi: Oxford & IBH.

—— (1997) "Occidentalism and Orientalism: Perspectives on Legal Pluralism," in Sally Humphreys (ed.), *Cultures of Scholarship*, Ann Arbor, MI: University of Michigan Press, pp. 219–51.

—— (2007) *Post-Modern Gandhi and Other Essays: Gandhi in the World and at Home*, Chicago: University of Chicago Press; New Delhi: Oxford University Press.

Ruggie, John G. (1993) "Territoriality and Beyond: Problematizing Modernity in International Relations," *International Organization*, 47(1): 139–74.

Russett, Bruce (1993) *Grasping the Democratic Peace*, Princeton, NJ: Princeton University Press.

Russett, Bruce, Oneal, John R., and Cox, Michaelene (2000) "Clash of Civilizations, or Realism and Liberalism Déjà Vu? Some Evidence," *Journal of Peace Research*, 37(5): 583–608.

Said, Edward W. (1979) *Orientalism*, New York: Vintage.

Samuels, Richard J. (2007) *Securing Japan*, Ithaca, NY: Cornell University Press.

Savarkar, V. D. (1938) *Hindutva*, New Delhi: Central Hindu Yuvak Sabha.

Scheipers, Sibylle, and Sicurelli, Daniela (2007) "Normative Power Europe: A Credible Utopia?" *Journal of Common Market Studies*, 45(2): 435–57.

Schlesinger, Arthur M., Jr. (1998) *The Disuniting of America: Reflections on a Multicultural Society*, rev. and expanded edn, New York: W. W. Norton.

Schmidt, Brian C. (1998) *The Political Discourse of Anarchy: A Disciplinary History of International Relations*, Albany, NY: SUNY Press.

Schulze, Reinhardt (2002) *A Modern History of the Islamic World*, London: I. B. Tauris.

Scott, James (1990) *Domination and the Arts of Resistance*, New Haven, CT: Yale University Press.

—— (2003) "Hill and Valley in Southeast Asia, or . . . Why Civilizations Can't Climb Hills," unpublished paper, revised for the "Beyond Borders" workshop sponsored by the Centre d'Etudes et de Recherches Internationales and the Social Science Research Council.

Searle, John (1995) *The Construction of Social Reality*, New York: Free Press.

Seddon, David (2005) "Japanese and British Overseas Aid Compared," in David M. Arase (ed.), *Japan's Foreign Aid: Old Continuities and New Directions*, London: Routledge, pp. 41–80.

Sen, Amartya (2005) *The Argumentative Indian*, New York: Farrar, Strauss.

—— (2006) *Identity and Violence: The Illusion of Destiny*, New York: W. W. Norton.

Senghaas, Dieter (1998) *The Clash within Civilizations: Coming to Terms with Cultural Conflicts*, New York: Routledge.

Shah, A. M., and Shroff, R. G. (1972) "The Vahivanca Barots of Gujarat," in Milton Singer, *When a Great Tradition Modernizes*, Boulder, CO: Praeger.

Shiraishi, Takashi (2006) "The Third Wave: Southeast Asia and Middle-Class Formation in the Making of a Region," in Peter J. Katzenstein and Takashi Shiraishi (eds), *Beyond Japan: The Dynamics of East Asian Regionalism*, Ithaca, NY: Cornell University Press, pp. 237–71.

Shively, Donald H., and McCullough, William H. (eds) (1999) *The Cambridge History of Japan*, Vol. 2: *Heian Japan*, Cambridge: Cambridge University Press.

Shotter, John (1993a) *Conversational Realities: Constructing Life through Language*, Thousand Oaks, CA: Sage.

—— (1993b) *Cultural Politics of Everyday Life*, Toronto: University of Toronto Press.

Simpson, Edward, and Kresse, Kai (eds) (2008) *Struggling with History: Islam and Cosmopolitanism in the Western Indian Ocean*, New York: Columbia University Press.

Singhal, D. P. (1993) *India and Western Civilization*, 2 vols, East Lansing, MI: Michigan State University Press.

Sircar, D. C. (1975) *Inscriptions of Asoka*, New Delhi: Ministry of Information and Broadcasting.

Sjursen, Helene (2006) "The EU as a 'Normative' Power: How Can This Be?" *Journal of European Public Policy*, 13(2): 235–51.

Smits, Gregory (1999) *Visions of Ryukyu: Identity and Ideology in Early-Modern Thought and Politics*, Honolulu, HI: University of Hawai'i Press.

Solana, Javier (2005) "Working for Peace, Security and Stability," in *The European Union in the World*, Luxembourg: European Communities.

Son, Seung-chol (1994) *Chosŏn sidae hanil gwangywe yonku* [*Korea–Japan Relations during the Chosun period*], Seoul: Jisungui Sam.

Sonoda, Hidehiro, and Eisenstadt, S. N. (eds) (1999) *Japan in a Comparative Perspective*, Kyoto: International Research Center for Japanese Studies.

Spengler, Oswald (1926) *The Decline of the West*, Vol. 1: *Form and Actuality*, New York: Knopf.

—— (1939) *The Decline of the West*, New York: Knopf.

Spohn, Willfried (2001) "Eisenstadt on Civilizations and Multiple Modernity," *European Journal of Social Theory*, 4(4): 499–508.

Standen, Naomi (2007) *Unbounded Loyalty: Frontier Crossing in Liao China*, Honolulu, HI: University of Hawai'i Press.

Steenstrup, Carl (1991) "The Middle Ages Survey'd," *Monumenta Nipponica*, 46(2): 237–52.

Sternberg, Yitzak (2001) "Modernity, Civilization and Globalization," in Eliezer Ben-Rafael with Yitzak Sternberg (eds), *Identity, Culture and Globalization*, Leiden: E. J. Brill, pp. 75–92.

Stivachtis, Yannis A. (1998) *The Enlargement of International Society: Culture versus Anarchy and Greece's Entry into International Society*, New York: St Martin's Press.

Stokes, Eric (1959) *English Utilitarians in India*, Oxford: Clarendon Press.

Strange, Mark (2007) "An Eleventh-Century View of Chinese Ethnic Policy: Sima Guang on the Fall of Western Jin," *Journal of Historical Sociology*, 20(3): 235–58.

Strange, Susan (1983) "Cave! Hic Dracones: A Critique of Regime Analysis," in Stephen D. Krasner (ed.), *International Regimes*, Ithaca, NY: Cornell University Press, pp. 337–54.

Subrahmanyam, Sanjay (1998) "Hearing Voices: Vignettes of Early Modernity in South Asia, 1400–1750," *Dædalus*, 127 (73): 90–112.

Suzuki, Shogo (2005) "Japan's Socialization into Janus-Faced European International Society," *European Journal of International Relations*, 11(1): 137–64.

—— (2009) *Civilisation and Empire: East Asia's Encounter with the European International Society*, New York: Routledge.

Swedberg, Richard (2008) "A Note on Civilizations and Economies," unpublished paper, Cornell University, Department of Sociology.

Swope, Kenneth M. (2002) "Deceit, Disguise, and Dependence: China, Japan, and the Future of the Tributary System, 1592–96," *International History Review*, 24(4): 757–82.

—— (2005) "Crouching Tigers, Secret Weapons: Military Technology Employed during the Sino-Japanese-Korean War, 1592–98," *Journal of Military History*, 69: 11–42.

Sylvan, David, and Majeski, Stephen (1998) "A Methodology for the Study of Historical Counterfactuals," *International Studies Quarterly*, 42: 79–108.

Talbi, Mohamed (1973) *Ibn Khaldun: sa vie – son oeuvre*, Tunis: Université de Tunis.

Tanaka, Stefan (1993) *Japan's Orient: Rendering Pasts into History*, Berkeley, CA: University of California Press.

Taylor, Ann (1992) *Annie Besant: An Autobiography*, New York: Oxford University Press.

Taylor, Keith (1983) *The Birth of Vietnam*, Berkeley, CA: University of California Press.

—— (1987) "The Literati Revival in Seventeenth-Century Vietnam," *Journal of Southeast Asian Studies*, 18(1): 1–23.

Tehranian, Majid (2007) *Rethinking Civilization: Resolving Conflict in the Human Family*, New York: Routledge.

Thapar, Romila (1961) *Ashoka and the Decline of the Mauryas*, London: Oxford University Press.

—— (2000) "Hindutva and History," *Frontline*, 13 October.

Tibi, Bassam (2007) "Europeanization, not Islamization," 22 March, available at: http://www.signandsight.com/features/1258.html (accessed 17 August 2008).

Tilly, Charles (ed.) (1975) *The Formation of National States in Western Europe*, Princeton, NJ: Princeton University Press.

—— (1989) *Big Structures, Large Processes, Huge Comparisons*, New York: Russell Sage.

—— (1998) "International Communities, Secure or Otherwise," in Emanuel Adler and Michael Barnett (eds), *Security Communities*, Cambridge: Cambridge University Press, pp. 397–412.

Toby, Ronald (2001) "Rescuing the Nation from History: The State of the State in Early Modern Japan," *Monumenta Nipponica*, 56(2): 197–237.

Toynbee, Arnold J. (1953) *A Study of History*, 10 vols, New York and London: Oxford University Press.

—— (1988) *A Study of History*, abridged rev. edn, New York: Portland House.

Trautman, Thomas R. (1997) *Aryans and British India*, Berkeley, CA: University of California Press.

Turnbull, Stephen (2002) *Samurai Invasion: Japan's Korean War, 1592–1598*, London: Cassell.

Turner, Bryan S. (1974) *Weber and Islam*, London: Routledge & Kegan Paul.

—— (1994) *Orientalism, Postmodernism, and Globalism*, London and New York: Routledge & Kegan Paul.

Ueyama, Shunpei (1999) "The Originality of the Japanese Civilization," in Sonoda Hidehiro and S. N. Eisenstadt (eds), *Japan in a Comparative Perspective*, Kyoto: International Research Center for Japanese Studies, pp. 19–29.

Umesao, Tadao (1984) "Kindai sekai ni okeru nihon bunmei" [Japanese Civilization in the Modern World], in Umesao Tadao and Ishige Naomichi (eds), *Kindai nihon no bunmeigaku* [*Civilizational Analysis of Modern Japan*], Tokyo: Chūō Kōronsha, pp. 7–39.

van Wolferen, Karel (1990) *The Enigma of Japanese Power: People and Politics in a Stateless Nation*, New York: Vintage.

Verhofstadt, Guy (2006) *The United States of Europe*, London: Federal Trust for Education and Research.

von Herzfeld, Marianne, and Sym, C. Melvil (1957) *Letters from Goethe*, available at: http://www.hinduwisdom.info/quotes61_80.htm (accessed 16 July 2008).

Vuving, Alexander (2001) "The References of Vietnamese States and the Mechanism of World Formation," *Asien*, 79: 62–86.

Wade, Robert (1996) "Japan, the World Bank, and the Art of Paradigm Maintenance: *The East Asian Miracle* in Political Perspective," *New Left Review*, 217 (May/June): 3–37.

Walker, R. B. J. (1993) *Inside/Outside: International Relations as Political Theory*, Cambridge: Cambridge University Press.

Wallerstein, Immanuel (1980) *The Modern World-System II: Mercantilism and the Consolidation of the European World-Economy 1600–1750*, New York: Academic Press.

Waltz, Kenneth N. (1979) *Theory of International Politics*, New York: McGraw-Hill.

Watanabe, Yasushi, and McConnell, David L. (eds) (2008) *Soft Power Superpowers: Cultural and National Assets of Japan and the United States*, Armonk, NY: M. E. Sharpe.

Wellman, Barry (1997) "Structural Analysis: From Method and Metaphor to Theory and Substance," in Barry Wellman and S. D. Berkowitz (eds), *Social Structures: A Network Approach*, Greenwich, CT: JAI Press, pp. 19–61.

Wendt, Alexander (1992) "Anarchy is What States Make of It: The Social Construction of Power Politics," *International Organization*, 46: 391–425.

—— (1996) "Identity and Structural Change in International Politics," in Yosef Lapid and Friedrich Kratochwil (eds), *The Return of Culture and Identity in IR Theory*, Boulder, CO: Lynne Rienner, pp. 47–64.

—— (1999) *Social Theory of International Politics*, Cambridge: Cambridge University Press.

Wenger, Etienne (1998a) "Communities of Practice: Learning as a Social System," *System Thinker*, June.

—— (1998b) *Communities of Practice: Learning, Meaning and Identity*, New York: Cambridge University Press.

Wenger, Etienne, McDermott, Richard, and Snyder, William M. (2002) *Cultivating Communities of Practice: A Guide to Managing Knowledge*, Cambridge, MA: Harvard Business School Press.

White House (2002) *The National Security Strategy of the U.S.A.*, Washington, DC, September, available at: http://www.whitehouse.gov/nsc/nss.pdf (accessed 16 August 2008).

Whitman, Richard (n.d.) "The Fall and Rise of Civilian Power Europe?," available at: http://dspace-dev.anu.edu.au/bitstream/1030.58/12428/2/whitman.pdf (accessed 9 August 2008).

Whitmore, John K. (1997) "Literati Culture and Integration in Dai Viet, c. 1430–c. 1840," *Modern Asian Studies*, 31(3): 665–87.

—— (2005) "Vietnamese Embassies and Literati Contacts," paper presented at the annual meeting of the Association of Asian Studies.

—— (2006) "The Rise of the Coast: Trade, State, and Culture in Early Dai Viet," *Journal of Southeast Asian Studies*, 37(1): 103–22.

Wigen, Kären (1999) "Culture, Power, and Place: The New Landscape of East Asian Regionalism," *American Historical Review*, 104(4): 1183–201.

Wilkinson, David (1994) "Civilizations are World Systems!," *Comparative Civilizations Review*, 30: 59–71.

—— (1995) "Twelve Articles in Blue Covers," unpublished manuscript, University of California, Los Angeles.

—— (1996) "Sixteen Papers in Gray Covers," unpublished manuscript, University of California, Los Angeles.

—— (1999) "Power Polarity in the Far Eastern World System 1025 BC–1850 AD: Narrative and 25-Year Interval Data," *Journal of World-Systems Research*, 5(3): 501–617.

—— (2004) "The Power Configuration Sequence of the Central World System, 1500–1700 BC," *Journal of World-Systems Research*, 10(3): 655–720.

Wilkinson, David, and Tsirel, Sergey V. (2006) "Analysis of Power-Structure Fluctuations in the 'Longue Durée' of the South Asian World System," *Structure and Dynamics: eJournal of Anthropological and Related Sciences*, 1(2) (Article 2).

Wills, John E., Jr. (n.d.) "Great Qing and its Southern Neighbors, 1760–1820: Secular Trends and Recovery from Crisis," unpublished manuscript, University of Southern California, available at: http://www.historycooperative.org/proceedings/interactions/wills.html (accessed 25 January 2009).

Witzel, Michael, and Farmer, Steve (2000) "Horseplay in Harappa; the Indus Valley Decipherment Hoax," *Frontline*, 13 October.

Wolfe, Alan (2004) "Native Son: Samuel Huntington Defends the Homeland," *Foreign Affairs*, 83(3): 120–25.

Wolfers, Arnold (1962) *Discord and Collaboration: Essays on International Politics*, Baltimore, MD: Johns Hopkins University Press.

Wolters, O. W. (1976) "Le Van Huu's Treatment of Ly Than Ton's Reign (1127–37)," in C. D. Cowan and O. W. Wolters (eds), *Southeast Asian History and Historiography*, Ithaca, NY: Cornell University Press, pp. 203–26.

Womack, Brantly (2006) *China and Vietnam: The Politics of Asymmetry*, New York: Cambridge University Press.

Wong, R. Bin (1997) *China Transformed: Historical Change and the Limits of European Experience*, Ithaca, NY: Cornell University Press.

Woodside, Alexander (2006) *Lost Modernities: China, Vietnam, Korea, and the Hazards of World History*, Cambridge, MA: Harvard University Press.

Wright, David (2002) "The Northern Frontier," in David A. Graff and Robin Higham (eds), *A Military History of China*, Boulder, CO: Westview Press, pp. 57–80.

Xin, Xu (2009) "The Power of Identity: China and East Asian Security Politics after the Cold War," unpublished manuscript, Cornell University, Government Department.

Yamada, Taiichi, and Kawamoto, Sanjurō (1995) "Aimai na fuan no jidai," *Sekai* (March): 24–35.

Yamauchi, Masayuki (2004) "Nihon no chūtō seisaku to sofuto pawā" [Soft Power and Japan's Middle East Policy], *Ronza* (January): 28–33.

Yang, Lien-sheng (1968) "Historical Notes on the Chinese World Order," in John K. Fairbank (ed.), *The Chinese World Order: Traditional China's Foreign Relations*, Cambridge, MA: Harvard University Press, pp. 20–33.

Yanow, Dvora (2006) "Thinking Interpretively: Philosophical Presuppositions and the Human Sciences," in Dvora Yanow and Peri Schwartz-Shea (eds), *Interpretation and Method: Empirical Research Methods and the Interpretive Turn*, Armonk, NY: M. E. Sharpe, pp. 5–26.

Ye'or, Bat (2005) *Eurabia: The Euro-Arab Axis*, Madison, NJ: Fairleigh Dickinson University Press.

Yoda, Tomiko (2006) "A Roadmap to Millennial Japan," in Tomiko Yoda and Harry Harootunian (eds), *Japan after Japan: Social and Cultural Life from the Recessionary 1990s to the Present*, Durham, NC: Duke University Press, pp. 16–53.

Yonetani, Masafumi (2006) *Ajia/Nihon* [*Asia/Japan*], Tokyo: Iwanami.

Yoo, Geun-ho (2004) *Chosŏnjo taeoe sasangui hurum* [*Flows of Ideologies on Foreign Relations during the Choson Period*], Seoul: Sungshin Women's University Press.

Yuasa, Hiroshi (2006) "Josefu nai no 'sofuto pawā' ron no mōten" [The Blind Spot in Joseph Nye's 'Soft Power' Argument], *Shokun* (August): 166–75.

Yun, Peter I. (1998) "Rethinking the Tribute System: Korean States and Northeast Asian Interstate Relations, 600–1600," PhD dissertation, University of California, Los Angeles.

Zaiotti, Ruben (2008) "Cultures of Border Control: Schengen and the Evolution of Europe's Frontiers," PhD dissertation, University of Toronto.

Zehfuss, Maja (2002) *Constructivism in International Relations: The Politics of Reality*, Cambridge and New York: Cambridge University Press.

Zielonka, Jan (2008) "How to Exercise Europe's Power," *International Spectator*, 43(2): 63–77.

Zürn, Michael (2007) "Global Governance oder American Empire: Über die Institutionalisierung der Ungleicheit," *Politische Vierteljahresschrift*, 48(4): 680–704.

Index